NOT BY
MIGHT

NOT BY MIGHT

——————oOo——————

A Journey in Faith and Politics

The authorised biography of
Jeffrey Donaldson M.P., M.L.A.

Noel Davidson

AMBASSADOR

Ambassador Publications
Providence House, Ardenlee Street,
Belfast BT6 8QJ, Northern Ireland

www.ambassador-productions.com

First published in 2004 by Ambassador International,
available in the United Kingdom and Republic of Ireland
from Ambassador Publications, from Ambassaor-Emerald
in the United States and Canada, from Ambassador/CLC in Australia
and New Zealand and from Ambassador/SKS in Singapore.

Copyright © 2004 Noel Davidson

ISBN 1-84030-160-0

Printed and bound in Northern Ireland

All quotations from Scripture, unless otherwise indicated, have been taken
from the New King James Version, Thomas Nelson Publishers.

DEDICATION

To the people of Northern Ireland who have
displayed remarkable courage and fortitude
in the face of many years of suffering and adversity.

To all who have 'kept the faith'
in the hope of a better future.

Noel Davidson   **Jeffrey Donaldson**

*'Not by might
nor by power,
but by My Spirit,'
says the Lord of hosts.*

Zechariah 4 : 6

When the righteous are in authority, the people have hope.

Jeffrey Donaldson MP is such a man. He brings the purity of his faith into the heart of his political career, and his integrity is a privilege to witness. This challenging story of his journey of love for his land and people, pursuing the call to 'stand among princes and offer up heaven's wisdom,' is a strong call to prayer. Jeffrey leads the Prayer for Parliament initiative with a vision to see many others stand in the gap for the nation, before God.

This book is a must!

Julie Anderson
Founder – Prayer for the Nations, London

A strong Christian influence in our national Parliament is so vital to the well-being of our nation. Jeffrey Donaldson, as a Christian and Parliamentarian, has shown that faith and politics can be brought together to good effect.

This book reveals the impact these two important influences have had upon his life in a compelling biography.

Nigel Dodds
Member of Parliament for North Belfast

As fire tempers steel, so Jeffrey Donaldson has been shaped by 'The Troubles' of Northern Ireland. The bold courage of his convictions, the depth of his dedication to peace, and his passion for public service are all undergirded by an authentic faith in God, a faith that was established and strengthened in the raging fire of conflict.

His life story, set against the backdrop of terrorism, is one that underscores the truth that strong moral character is not an accident. It is the result of a personal relationship with God, hammered out on the anvil of daily choices. It is the story of a faith that is beautifully, yet uncompromisingly, interwoven with politics.

This is the story of a life that counts.

It is the story of someone I am privileged to call my friend, Jeffrey Donaldson.

Anne Graham Lotz
President - AnGeL Ministries, Raleigh, North Carolina

CONTENTS

FOREWORD

BY THE RT. HON. LORD MOLYNEAUX OF KILLEAD KBE

For me, a possible conflict of conviction came in 1940. As a twenty-year-old Christian I had been moulded by Sunday School, Confirmation, Communion and sacred music. All of this in a rural farming community overlaid by an enquiring mind. Following enlistment in the Royal Air Force I was posted to what is now Aberdeen Airport. Intentional or not, I got no home-leave for eighteen months. During that period I was introduced to the reality of war – frequent bombing of Aberdeen port and city; air cover for Scapa Flow; the loss of aircraft in the Highlands in one of which the late Duke of Kent lost his life, out of reach of our mountain rescue team.

In 1941 I was launched on a form of 'tourism' in the shape of frequent postings down the east coast of Britain until in 1941 I arrived at bases in South East England – a convenient launching pad for the Normandy landings. D-Day brought me face to face with the heat of battle in France, the beginning of a gruelling journey across Europe, which included the horror of entering the German concentration camp at Belsen shortly after it had been liberated. Those early years of my life could be described as a slow-motion education for later life as a churchman, politician and public figure. That period was preparation leading to fulfilment.

I record these facts of life because they are of a pattern that reflects the notable career of my friend and colleague Jeffrey Donaldson as so ably portrayed in this book. Jeffrey was confronted with the tragedies of life at a much earlier stage than me. Only someone with sound moral convictions could have endured the murder of so many family and friends. Only a true Christian could recognise that the answer lies with God and not with the might of violence or revenge. As his career develops Jeffrey gives evidence of his strong Christian faith in the face of what has often been referred to as "apparent disbelief."

In politics it is sometimes tempting to manipulate the truth or take the popular line even though it can involve being dishonest to ones self and to the people that we have the privilege to represent. In this age of 'spin,' Jeffrey Donaldson has proven that there are politicians of conviction who will act with integrity and will 'tell it as it is.' It takes both courage and determination to stand for what is right and to maintain that stance. I have often repeated the words first learned as a child: 'Grant us to know that it is not the beginning but the continuing of the same, until it be thoroughly finished which yieldeth the True Glory.' From our respective experiences of public life Jeffrey and I both know that when others let us down, underneath are the everlasting arms of our Creator.

Jim Molyneaux

INTRODUCTION

"Does anyone ever remark on the little sign of the fish badge you always wear in your lapel, Jeffrey?" I was curious to know. Long before I had ever met Jeffrey Donaldson MP, I had admired him for wearing this sign, first used by the early Christian church, so openly on whatever suit he had on, wherever he was.

"Yes, very often," the Lagan Valley MP replied. "Nearly every week I have someone come up to me to say that they are Christians too. Many even go on to assure me that they are praying for me."

That was three years ago. On that occasion I had called at Jeffrey's home in Moira to interview him for a magazine article and I was impressed with him from the moment we met. He came across as a sincere Christian, an honest and hard-working politician and a very down-to-earth man.

Having been afforded the privilege of writing this biography on his busy and varied life has only served to strengthen that opinion.

As we have worked closely together now for months I have been amazed at the diversity of activity that Jeffrey can cope with, extremely efficiently, in any one day.

It has been fascinating to interview him in his constituency office, in the centre of the city of Lisburn, and observe casually the various aspects of his life. Perhaps this is best represented in the range of phone calls he receives. Although busy with me, these incoming calls are important to Jeffrey because they are important to the members of his family, the people from his constituency, or the Christian friends at the other end of the line, and so he attends to them. These calls have often momentarily interrupted the train of our research, but they have provided me with a deep appreciation of the life of a Christian Member of Parliament, that could not have been obtained through hours of talking.

One of the first phone messages I heard him take was from the Prayer for Parliament group at Westminster. They had been contacted by a similar group in Seoul, South Korea, anxious to know if Jeffrey would be free to come and address their annual Prayer Breakfast in May.

"I would love to go there, Noel," Jeffrey told me. "But I just can't fit it in."

Another call was from a fellow-politician, but not about politics. It was to enquire about Claire, Jeffrey's daughter, who was in hospital for treatment.

One other day Jeffrey smiled across at me, telephone in hand. "Affairs of state, Noel," he whispered. "The bonfire site in Moira."

The next call was from Gillian, Jeffrey's very efficient secretary, from the main office next door. "John Spellar's department is on the phone," she said. "Could you meet them at ten-thirty tomorrow morning?"

Jeffrey chuckled gently one other afternoon as he switched off his mobile. "That was Laura," he said. "She has lost a video-tape and just thought her daddy might know where it is!"

The range of calls represented the scope of activity of an MP who is not only an astute and single-minded politician, but also a dedicated Christian and a caring husband and father.

There were many more, too. Like the young woman whose mother had just passed away and she couldn't understand why God should allow this to happen, for 'Mummy was a good Christian woman and she was only sixty-three.' Jeffrey's response to this situation was to tell me that he would call and pray with her and leave her a copy of John Blanchard's 'Ultimate Questions.'

A senior DUP member rang to arrange an Executive meeting to prepare for the talks at Lancaster House.

Somebody phoned in to complain that their bin hadn't been collected for two weeks in a row.

Jeffrey's wife Eleanor called him for advice. The men who were fitting a replacement fireplace in their new home outside Dromore had come upon a problem. What should they do?

It has been both a privilege and a challenge to research this book and obtain an insight into the life and work of someone as highly respected as Jeffrey Donaldson MP, MLA.

On completing the magazine article three years ago I gave it the title, 'For God and Lagan Valley.' This summed up, for me, the content of Jeffrey's Maiden Speech, delivered in the House of Commons on Tuesday, May 20, 1997.

That title would still be appropriate. Jeffrey Donaldson is still for God and Lagan Valley. He works tirelessly for both. There is another element that I have discovered, however, in Jeffrey's life and it could be added to that title, to read, 'For God, Lagan Valley, and Eleanor, Claire and Laura.'

We have subtitled this book, 'A journey in faith and politics,' but it is more than that. Jeffrey Donaldson is a husband and father, a son and a brother, and the little fleeting glimpses of the joys and concerns of family life that I have been pleased to observe will give the book that human touch, I trust.

If you are reading this book because you admire Jeffrey Donaldson as a politician, (or even if you don't!) you will certainly find some interesting information on these pages. Drumcree, The Belfast Agreement, The Joint Declaration, the move to the DUP. They're all here.

If you are reading it because you admire Jeffrey Donaldson's practical faith and his work for evangelical Christian causes in Parliament and beyond we trust that you will find it inspiring.

The book is entitled, 'NOT BY MIGHT,' for Jeffrey recognises that anything he has ever done or achieved has not been by his own strength or wisdom but through the power, and under the guidance, of God.

His, and my desire, in sharing this story with you is that you may feel encouraged, or perhaps even challenged, as you read. And above all, may you be led into a closer relationship with God through it.

Noel Davidson
September 2004

1
THE KNOCK AT THE DOOR

"Annie, I've just heard some dreadful news," the father of five croaked.

He had pushed open the door into the living room where his wife was nursing their youngest son Andrew, who still demanded much of her time and attention. He stood clutching the door handle. It was obvious from his ashen face, his shaking free hand and his breaking voice that something horrific had happened.

Jeffrey Donaldson, who at seven-and-a-half was the oldest of the family, and his four-year-old brother James, looked up from the floor where they had been playing away quite happily. A few strategically placed mats had created a complex network of 'roads' and there were cars and lorries in various stages of their 'journeys' all around the room. The empty shoebox below the chair in the corner was the garage.

Both boys froze to the floor when their dad appeared at the door.

They had never seen him in a state like this before.

Jeffrey was leaning forward on all fours, grasping a suddenly stationary fire engine.

The preoccupied brothers had heard a knock at the door five minutes before and a subsequent period of solemn, muffled conversation in the hall. They had thought nothing of that, though. It was a regular occurrence. Their father had many friends from his various interests and responsibilities in life and these people used to call at all hours of the day to talk to him in serious grown-up tones about things they could never quite understand.

This, though, was different.

It was late morning on Wednesday, August 12, 1970. James and Jeffrey had been outside playing with their friends for nearly two hours after breakfast. Their sister Diane, who was six, had been out with them too. She had joined in their games from time to time but had always reserved the right to hive off with a few of the other girls occasionally to dress dolls or play 'school.' There were many children around their age where they lived in Donard View, Kilkeel, Co. Down, and they all usually enjoyed many carefree, play-filled hours together in the summer holidays.

The two boys had come back into the house about half-an-hour ago, however. Some of their friends had gone off for day trips with their parents so they decided that they would have some fun inside with their own toys before lunchtime. Diane was still outside as far as they knew, and Elaine, who was little more than a toddler, was toddling around. Her seeming fixation for picking up the particular car they were about to use and carrying it away somewhere else evoked spontaneous outbursts of frustration from her not always very patient brothers, every now and again.

Father's sombre figure in the doorway had imposed an instant involuntary silence on the cosy domestic scene. An unusual, unnatural unease descended on the room.

Annie Donaldson, wife and mother, closed her arms tenderly but more tightly around little Andrew who had begun to whimper, as though sensing that something was the matter. Then she stammered out the obvious question.

"What's wrong, Jim?" she enquired.

Her husband chose a car free spot to step into the middle of the floor allowing his brother William, who was undoubtedly the bearer of the terrible tidings, whatever it was, to follow in behind him.

"It's Samuel," Jim Donaldson went on to say, his voice trembling with shock and virtual disbelief. "He and another policeman were blown up when they went to investigate an abandoned car near Crossmaglen last night. We have just heard that he died in Daisy Hill Hospital in Newry this morning."

"Oh no!" Annie cried. She had been startled almost speechless by this staggering piece of news. Samuel Donaldson, who was Jeffrey's cousin, was twenty-three years of age. He had been four years in the RUC but had only been stationed in Crossmaglen in south Armagh for eleven months.

There was a big Donaldson family connection in and around south Down in the lee of the scenic Mourne Mountains. William only stayed a short time in his brother Jim's house that fateful morning. Not all the relatives had telephones so he was soon on his way to bring heartbreak to a few more homes.

As the dreadful news of Samuel's death spread amongst them their automatic reaction was exactly that of the appalled Annie. "Oh no!" they would exclaim immediately. "Who would want to kill Samuel? He was such a fine young Christian man!"

A period of grief and gloom settled over Jim Donaldson's home from the moment they heard the heart-rending news of Samuel's murder. Life in number three Donard View changed dramatically for the next few days, then significantly forever, in the wake of that horrendous event. And it wasn't their home alone that was affected. Samuel's parents, John and Isobel, were devastated and the entire community in and around the town went numb. People didn't know what to do, say, or even think. Minds struggled to comprehend it and any offer to help, however generous or well-intentioned, appeared paltry, possibly even pointless, in the light of it.

The sense of mourning that descended like a clinging mountain mist over that entire Mourne community affected even the children from the time the news smashed into the daily routine of their parents' homes.

Jeffrey and James didn't have to be told to tidy away their toys that morning. They knew intuitively that the time for play was over, although it was still only the middle of the day. The boys weren't quite sure what to do but they knew somehow what *not* to do and that was talk, fight or clutter up the floor with plastic cars.

The distressed Donaldsons began to come and go in one another's houses. This allowed them to vent their emotions by sharing snippets of information as they were received from various sources, and to weep silently together while trying to suppress a growing surge of anger at the sacrifice of such a promising young life.

No one ever missed a TV News bulletin if possible. Samuel and the other policeman who had been murdered in the same bomb blast, twenty-six year old Constable Robert Millar from Ahoghill, Co. Antrim, were the first policemen to be killed by the IRA in 'the Troubles' and their deaths had made the headlines both in the press and on local and national radio and television.

As one anguished day blurred its way into another Jeffrey and his younger brothers and sisters were occasionally taken out for a few hours by their aunts Harriet and Liz, in an attempt to shelter them from the sorrow surrounding the family. They had to come home to bed in the evenings, however, and it was then that Jeffrey began to savour something of the true horror of what had taken place.

From listening in to adult conversation when sitting quietly in the corner of the living room or by eavesdropping outside a door when he was supposed to be in bed, he built up in his boyish mind a picture of what had happened to his big cousin.

On piecing together the story as the adults recounted it, time and time again, he gathered that Constables Donaldson and Millar had gone to investigate a stolen red Ford Cortina parked outside Crossmaglen. They had tried to open a door with a piece of wire hooked around the lock button. When they eventually succeeded in opening the door the car exploded and both officers were blown over a hedge into the nearby field.

Young Jeffrey often found tears trickling down his own cheeks as he heard the distraught relatives sobbing inconsolably when describing Samuel's injuries.

"He must have taken the full force of it in the face," one would say.

"Aye, that's right," another would add. "Apparently his sergeant didn't even recognise him when he arrived on the scene at first."

As further distressing details such as these continued to filter through, the mind of the bewildered seven-and-a-half year old soaked them all up like a sponge.

He had also to cope with the unfolding ghastly circumstances of Samuel's death in the context of what was happening all around him day by day.

The murdered constable's parents were touched by the floral tributes arriving at their home, not only from the grief-laden community in Kilkeel but also from right across the province. Amongst these were a number of wreaths from shocked and sympathetic residents of the Crossmaglen area.

On the day of the funeral the trucks from the Outside Broadcast Units of the local television stations rolled into Kilkeel to cover the event for the national News. The Presbyterian Church, in which Samuel had sung in the choir, was packed for the service. Hundreds of mourners stood outside unable to gain admittance.

When Jim and Annie had considered their position they agreed that their children were too young to attend a funeral of any kind, not to mention one so tragic and traumatic, so their mum stayed at home with them.

No one could stop the older members of the family following the day's proceedings on television, however. Jeffrey sat silently watching every news bulletin. He saw his dad outside the church, his uncles, Samuel's broken-hearted parents and his grief-stricken girlfriend. A close-up of one of the wreaths would reveal her name. The inscription read simply, 'Hazel.'

The centrepiece of the day was a coffin with an RUC cap sitting on it.

The images of those trying times left a profound impression on young Jeffrey Donaldson. He felt dazed, confused and continually vexed by all that was going on.

Rev. Robert Johnston had just been installed as minister in Kilkeel Presbyterian Church at the end of July and had set about trying to get to know his new congregation. One of the first people he had met was Samuel Donaldson who had been a prominent figure in the youth programme in the church and had also sung in the choir. He had been impressed with Samuel's quiet, consistent Christian life and his vision for the work amongst the youth. They had already begun discussing the programme of activities for the approaching autumn and winter season when Samuel was killed.

The funeral of the promising young policeman who had died when it seemed that he had everything to live for, was to be the first Rev. Johnston would be called upon to conduct in Kilkeel. He chose as his text for the occasion the words of Jesus in the Bible when describing himself as the Good Shepherd. 'I give unto my sheep eternal life and they shall never perish,' He had declared. 'No one can pluck them out of my hand. My Father who gave them to me is greater than all and no one can pluck them out of my Father's hand.' These were reassuring thoughts for the sorrow-stricken family circle. It would be difficult to concentrate long enough or hard enough to contemplate them, though, so great was their grief.

The text of the sermon didn't make headline news in the media that day but another comment made during the service was beamed across Britain. It was an observation on Samuel's outlook on life and his view of the growing sense of unrest in Northern Ireland.

The words struck Jeffrey very forcibly when he heard them quoted on the News more than once. They seemed such a fitting tribute to the kind and caring cousin he remembered, the man who had always appeared so friendly and relaxed at family get-togethers.

"It is well worth putting on record that Sam Donaldson saw no future in the extreme policies of either side in Northern Ireland," Rev. Smylie Fullerton, the former minister of the church had declared, when asked to pay tribute to Samuel. "Those who offer extreme policies as a political expedient, either in word or action, are saying that to further their ends the Sam Donaldsons can be sacrificed to the bullet and the bomb."

Although not yet eight years of age, Jeffrey had already become vaguely aware that the population of Northern Ireland seemed to be divided into two 'sides.' If what the minister had called 'extreme policies' had killed his sadly-missed cousin Samuel, then he wanted nothing to do with them.

But what could he do?

When all the fuss of the funeral had passed, he determined, with a still childish but nonetheless single-minded resolve, that he would try to help the people of his divided country, in whatever way he could, when he grew up.

He didn't think it was 'very fair' what the Donaldson family circle had to pass through in August 1970. There was no way that he wanted them to have to experience that awful grief again, or any other family to have to experience that awful grief at all.

Would they have to, though, before he had the chance in life to do something about it?

2
THIS IS JUST THE START OF IT

The Donaldson family circle were never allowed to forget the tragic circumstances of Samuel's death in the months and years that followed. When it seemed that something like normality had returned to the beautiful Kingdom of Mourne the breaking news of another terrorist atrocity brought the nightmare of that awful August morning flooding back. It could have been a soldier shot in Londonderry, another policeman killed in a booby-trap device in Belfast or a number of innocent civilians caught up in a bomb explosion somewhere else. The location or the manner didn't really matter. It was the loss of life that came as the jarring reminder.

The Ulster Defence Regiment was inaugurated in April 1970 and Jim Donaldson joined it in the autumn of that same year, little more than a month after Samuel had lost his life. He saw this as his personal contribution to helping restore a sense of stability to an increasingly volatile situation in Northern Ireland. His involvement with this new regiment meant that he was often out overnight patrolling the roads of south Down with his unit. It also led to him taking a keen interest in what was happening in the political scene in the province and particularly the measures being proposed, or introduced, to curb the spread of paramilitary activity.

His life depended on them, to a certain degree.

Apart from the fact that their dad was often out of the house at odd and unpredictable hours and the inevitable anguish that the news of another death brought to their mum and dad, life continued as normal for Jeffrey and his brothers and sisters. Those who were old enough to go to school went to school and the under-fives stayed at home with mum. Their parents were anxious that they should enjoy a happy, uncomplicated childhood as far as possible, and they succeeded in achieving their aim.

There were occasions, though, when the children had passing, fleeting glimpses of what was taking place, and then returned to the routine of daily life. It was like spotting a tiny ship on a vast ocean through a break in the clouds from the window of an aeroplane. You saw it, became engrossed in it for a split second of time, and then it was gone for good, leaving you wondering if you had merely imagined it. You hadn't, though, for it had left an indelible mark on your memory.

Something like that happened to the Donaldson family one sunny summer Sunday afternoon. When they were clearing up after dinner Jim said to his wife and kids, "That's a lovely day. I think we should go down to Newcastle and have a walk around for an hour or two."

This suggestion caused great excitement amongst the children. They didn't often get away anywhere together as a family so an afternoon out to the seaside town of Newcastle, fourteen miles away along the County Down coast was a big event.

Within half-an-hour all five children had been 'spruced up' as their mum called it, and packed into their dad's Cortina. Mum nursed Andrew, her youngest, leaving Jeffrey who was by then ten years of age, and the other three, to squabble for the remaining space.

When they reached Newcastle Jim Donaldson parked on the Main Street. He had a reason for that. His favourite ice-cream parlour was less than a hundred yards from where they had pulled in and he had secretly planned to make this an extra special day out for his family. He was going to buy them all an ice-cream.

This was sheer bliss for the children. A sunny day. A trip out to Newcastle in daddy's car. And now an ice-cream for everyone. What could be better?

With all seven of them licking contentedly on their ice-cream cones dad had another idea. "Let's go down and have a walk along the Promenade," he suggested.

That was great. There would be lots to see on Newcastle Promenade on a summer afternoon and so the family started to thread its way along the crowded footpaths in that direction. It seemed as though they were either being carried along on a wave of, or battling against the outgoing tide of, a sea of carefree people dressed in summer clothes, out for the day.

They had to stop a couple of times to allow mum to help Andrew, who is disabled with cerebral palsy, with his ice-cream. Mother Annie was attempting a balancing act with two dripping cones, her own and that of her little son. It was a race to see if she could organise to have them eaten before either or both of them melted into a sticky mess in her hands, There was another enforced stop when mum noticed that Elaine had dropped a blob of ice-cream tinged red with raspberry topping down the front of her best Sunday dress. That called for an energetic rub with dad's clean handkerchief to make her 'respectable' again. Jeffrey, Diane and James kept trying to push ahead of the others and were persistently, and for them, frustratingly, being called back.

They could hardly wait to reach the Promenade. What would be happening along there? Maybe mum and dad would even allow them down for a run across the beach...

Then suddenly the atmosphere changed.

11

Jeffrey became aware that a number of policemen were walking down either side of the street, at the outer edge of the footpath. There didn't seem to be any moving traffic about now. When they had arrived less than an hour before it had been bumper to bumper around the town.

"Keep in! Keep back! Stay on the pavements!" the policemen were advising the once happy-go-lucky day-trippers. An imperceptible sense of concern soon began to silence the chattering crowd. There was an unnerving air of urgency about the policemen's attitude and orders. Parents began to carry out instinctive checks on the whereabouts of their children and make contingency plans for their safety. The three older daring Donaldsons didn't have to be called back now. They were keeping as close to their parents as possible.

"We'd better make for the car!" their dad announced loudly enough for all of them to hear. Having made an instant appraisal of the state of affairs around him it was clear that he didn't like what he saw. He had developed a sixth sense for the security implications of any situation and that day it smelt trouble.

Jim Donaldson grabbed James and Elaine by the hand, his wife manoeuvred Andrew around in his pushchair and Jeffrey and Diane were commanded emphatically to 'stay near us.' That was a pointless instruction in the circumstances for they had become so scared that they wouldn't have contemplated doing anything else.

As they started to retrace their steps towards the car the Donaldson family noticed two things. The first was that everybody seemed to be moving more resolutely now, wherever they were going. All the laughing and light-hearted loitering had evaporated into the warm air. Their second observation was that a moving mass of people was bearing down upon them. They were filling the entire roadway, and surging forward.

It was a civil rights march of some kind.

The marchers were carrying placards and shouting slogans.

Recognising that they weren't going to reach the parked car before the oncoming march enveloped them, Jim Donaldson told his family to move to the inside of the pavement and stand against the wall.

When they found a spot where they could all be together, backs to the wall, they stood huddled close to one another.

It took about five minutes for the march to pass, but those five minutes seemed like five hours to Jeffrey Donaldson. There was so much noise and confusion. This was by no means a silent, peaceful protest. A number of participants were shouting insults at the accompanying police. The ten year-old couldn't quite make out what they were saying in the melee with so many yelling at once, but he was certain that it wasn't, "We love you!"

He was coming face to face with a sense of hatred he had never experienced before. And it was frightening.

The march had attracted a very pronounced security presence. There were police officers walking alongside it and a number of soldiers were fanned out across the road behind it. A solitary police Landrover brought up the rear.

Within seconds the scene turned ugly. The protestors began to vent their anger on the police who were endeavouring to restrain them. Bottles, sticks and stones started to fly.

In an effort to contain what threatened to escalate into a full-scale riot the soldiers fired a number of CS gas canisters towards the protestors. The sea breeze quickly carried the gas towards the milling mob. All of a sudden choking people were struggling to tie handkerchiefs around their faces.

Jim turned to Annie and made his second dramatic announcement of the afternoon. "We had better get out of here! And fast! " he said.

He didn't have to repeat himself. It was an urgent expression of the patently obvious. His wife and children were all terrified by then.

It was only a short distance to the reassuring familiarity of the car and its promise of a means of escape from the upsetting episode unfolding around them, when they found enough space on the pavement and strength in their legs to be on the move again.

As soon as everyone had been reinstalled in his or her appropriate place in the car the worried mother voiced what all the rest of them felt. "Can we go home now, Jim?" she asked. Her question was more a plea than an enquiry.

"Yes, we can Annie, and we will," her husband replied emphatically before adding, "That is if we can make it out of here."

He had seen that the cars, which had now started coming down the one-way street again, were only shunting forward at less than walking pace. And they were lined up behind him as far back as he could see in the mirror.

The car had been sitting closed up in the scorching sun and had become unbearably hot. All four windows had been opened as far as possible to try and cool it down. With the heat, the disturbing effect of the march which had just passed, and the fact that they weren't going anywhere fast, the four children in the back began to become fractious. They weren't quite sure what was wrong with them. All they knew was that their big day out had been spoiled by something that had left them feeling shaky and scared.

They sat there, with Jim trying to find a space to allow him to join the stream of traffic, for fifteen minutes. An eventual break in the flow allowed him to pull out before another half-cooked family drew in behind them.

Progress was slow, but at last they came to the cause of all the hold-up. Two policemen were stationed at the end of the Bryansford Road and were diverting all the traffic in that direction. The main route to Kilkeel had been closed for the marching mob had stopped at the police station on that road and were attacking it with an assortment of missiles.

As they set out on the more scenic route home through the heart of the Mourne Mountains Jeffrey noticed that they had started to meet a number of police and army vehicles hurrying towards Newcastle. Reinforcements were on their way to try and defuse what was obviously developing into a very volatile situation.

"Oh Jim, this is awful," Annie Donaldson remarked with bated breath when yet another Landrover came speeding along to meet them.

"Aye, you're right, Annie, it is," her husband replied sagaciously. He paused for a moment and then went on to make his own personal prediction. "And this is just the start of it," he prophesied. "Things will probably get worse before they get any better."

'Just the start of it,' were the words that came drifting into Jeffrey's hot seat in the back, and they shot his rather befuddled brain back into sharp and instant focus.

Just the start of *what*? he wondered.

What on earth was **IT**?

3
I WOULD GLADLY GIVE MY LIFE

By the time he had entered his teenage years Jeffrey Donaldson had become an ardent supporter of Chelsea Football Club. It was the fashionable thing amongst schoolboys of his age with even the slightest sporting interest or inclination to align themselves with a prominent English or Scottish League Club. For Jeffrey there was only one team worth mentioning and that was Chelsea.

His friend Jackie Orr was a Leeds supporter and there had always been periods of light-hearted banter between them as to the relative strengths and weaknesses of their respective clubs. Sunday morning in Senior Sunday School had become a favourite venue in which to conduct an in depth analysis of the fluctuating fortunes of their teams and the performances of individual players. This could be quite detached and objective when they had encountered 'neutral' opposition the previous afternoon.

When Leeds and Chelsea clashed, however, whether in League or Cup competition, that was an entirely different matter. Discussions could become intense, even passionate, then.

That scenario occurred on a weekend early in 1976. Chelsea had beaten Leeds and Jeffrey was cock-a-hoop. He was determined to have a good laugh at Jackie's expense that Sunday morning.

It mattered little to either of them that June Glanville, their Sunday School teacher, had come prepared to read the Bible with them and talk about God and Jesus or miracles and parables. All they were concerned with were goals and bookings, points and performances.

Jackie had come well prepared with his list of excuses. "The referee was diabolical," he said. "We should have been awarded a penalty for that blatant hand ball in the box."

"We won, Jackie. That's all that really matters," Jeffrey would respond with a sly smile.

"It would have been different if our two best players hadn't been on the injured list," was another reason advanced for Jackie's team's under-par performance.

"But they were, Jackie, that's the thing. And if Leeds had any sort of a decent squad that shouldn't make a big lot of difference anyway," Jeffrey smirked. "And as I said before, winning matches is all that counts in the long..."

He could see that Jackie was becoming more and more needled with his constant repetition of the result. The triumphant Chelsea supporter was therefore rather annoyed to have his opportunity to press home his advantage thwarted by the intervention of the Sunday School teacher.

June had paused before continuing with the lesson and was gazing intently at the inattentive football fans. She had just finished reading the story of the Prodigal Son from the Bible and considered it important to bring the two wandering minds in her class back on track before continuing.

The remaining seven members of the class, who had been listening to Miss Glanville, followed her gaze. Jackie and Jeffrey had suddenly become the centre of attention.

There was a short, awkward silence.

Having waited until all eyes were fixed on the pair of talkative teenagers June spoke. "You know boys I was once just like you," she began with no hint of anger or even annoyance. "I used to enjoy coming to Sunday School and the Youth Fellowship here in the church but it was for all the wrong reasons. I didn't come because I wanted to hear Bible stories or learn about the love of God. The part I liked best was meeting my friends, having a chat and generally larking about. There was nothing very strange about that. That's what we all did, I suppose."

Everybody was listening carefully to what she was saying now. They knew the feeling about Sunday School. Some of them had even begun to think that they were too old to come. After all they were mostly thirteen years of age. Indeed one or two of their more mature members had already turned fourteen.

Jeffrey didn't mind going, though, as long as Jackie, his buddy, went too.

And he liked Miss Glanville. She had been an officer in the Junior Boys Brigade and understood about games for eight-year-olds but displayed what for the boys in the Senior Sunday School was an appalling ignorance of the English First Division. Jeffrey had loved the Junior B.B. and the care June had taken of him and the kindness she had shown to him back in those days had contributed greatly to his enjoyment. He had learnt a lot from her.

"Then something happened one night in the Youth Fellowship that changed my whole outlook on life," the teacher went on to explain. "It had just been another Sunday night at the Fellowship after church and two or three of us were paying little attention to what was being said. Samuel Donaldson had been doing his best to speak but we were talking away to each other, and not paying one blind bit of heed to what he was trying to tell us."

June thought that the mention of Samuel's name would strike a chord in Jeffrey's heart. She was right. It did. The door to the vault in his memory bank had been opened and a series of haunting

18

images came spilling out.

"I will never forget it," Miss Glanville declared. She and her pupil had both indelible memories of the same person, but for different reasons. The silence of expectancy that had replaced the hubbub of heedlessness was remarkable as she continued, "Samuel had been talking about Jesus and His death on the cross. He was so full of it and so sincere about it that he was nearly in tears and we weren't even showing the slightest iota of either interest or respect."

She paused a moment before going on. Her young listeners realised that she was finding the memory of the moment upsetting.

"Samuel stopped in the middle of his little talk and looked right down at us where we were nudging each other and carrying on. 'You young people all know,' he said, 'that Jesus Christ, the Son of God, died on the cross so that you could be saved. And I want to tell you that I would gladly give up my own life if just one of you would come to know Jesus as your Saviour.' That thought stopped us in our tracks that night," June told her now mesmerised audience.

Jeffrey felt embarrassed now. Samuel had said that, and he knew only too well what had happened to him. So did June. So did Jackie. So did all the rest of the class.

The story wasn't over yet, though. There was more.

"Those words never left me," the teacher confessed, "and it was just a matter of months after Samuel had told us that he would gladly give his own life if one of us would come to Jesus as our Saviour that he was killed. When I heard of his death it was like a sermon to my heart and I did what Samuel had begged us to do. I gave my life to Jesus. I trusted him as my Saviour. In fact by May of the following year ten of us from the Youth Fellowship had become Christians and were taking part in our first Communion Service."

Before returning to her prepared lesson with a mightily subdued group of young people June took the opportunity to make an appeal to them, "And what I would love more than anything would be to hear that one of you had given your life to Christ."

When he arrived home that morning Jeffrey Donaldson had a lot to ponder. And it all seemed to be about people giving their lives.

Jesus Christ had given His life so that we could have our sins forgiven and become His children.

Cousin Samuel had said that he would gladly give his life if one of the young people in the Youth Fellowship would trust in Him as Saviour.

Then June had told them that as a result of all this she had given her life to Christ.

Where, he wondered, did he fit into the picture? To who, or to what, was he going to give his life?

4
THERE IS A GREEN HILL

Jeffrey promised himself that he would give these matters due consideration sometime in the future. It would be time enough when he was older, or working, or married. There was no need to become all worked up about them just yet. It was important, he reckoned, that he didn't let these 'religious' thoughts clog up the channels of his mind. These were reserved for football, friendship and fun.

He was determined to enjoy every hour of every day with his mate, Jackie. The pair of pals were lively, enthusiastic, and at times mischievous, teenagers. They were pupils at Kilkeel High School and members of 2nd Kilkeel Boys Brigade Company.

Gordon Mc Cullough, who was a craft teacher in the school, and was also an officer in the B.B., provided a connecting link between these two vital elements in the education and character development of Jackie and Jeffrey. The two high-spirited youngsters benefited from a series of most exhilarating experiences under Gordon's supervision.

They attended the weekly Boys Brigade session in Kilkeel Presbyterian Church Hall every Tuesday evening. The Bible Class at the beginning of each session was something they tolerated knowing that an interesting programme of events, including the opportunity for a game of football, was the reward to follow.

The big bonus for the lads, and the times they looked forward to with eager anticipation, however, came at the weekends during the B.B. season, which stretched through from the autumn of one year until the late spring of the next. On a Friday afternoon they would rendezvous with four or five other lads from the B.B. in Mr. Mc Cullough's room where they would arrange for their Saturday hike in the Mourne Mountains. Gordon was a keen, and experienced, mountaineer and he took a group of the older boys climbing amongst the higher peaks of the Mournes once a month.

To be up high in the mountains was an emancipating experience for all of them. It was great to spend a day away from school, homework and the routine of family life. The lads felt invigorated by the cool mountain air. They revelled in the freedom of the wide-open spaces and the reverberating echo of shouted voices. Days out on the mountains came with their challenges, too. One always encountered the fast-flowing streams to be crossed and the steep rock faces to be scaled. The biggest test of all came on the cold winter days when the swirling mist came down. This drenched the intrepid adventurers to the skin and reduced visibility to almost zero forcing them to navigate solely by map and compass.

Jeffrey seldom ever missed a mountain walk and he launched himself into all the activities with such vigour that he was amongst a number of boys chosen to represent the B.B. in showcase events.

During the celebrations to mark the Queen's Silver Jubilee in 1977 he was part of a team chosen to climb a steep rock face on Hen Mountain. Then again, when BBC Bristol were filming a series of TV documentaries on Outdoor Pursuits in Schools Jeffrey and a number of other senior students from Kilkeel High were featured climbing in the Mournes as part of the programme on mountaineering.

The call of the hills was strong. It was both stimulating and satisfying to scramble up a stiff slope, survey the scene from a summit and then descend into the world of men again. That was

O.K. but it only lasted a day. It was far too short for some of the boys. They felt that they could have stayed up there for days on end.

Appreciating their appetite for adventure and as a special treat, often at the end of the season's climbing, Gordon would take the boys up into the mountains to camp out overnight. This was a particular pleasure. To help carry the camping gear up into the hills, choose a suitable site and then pitch the tents made them think that they were graduating into fully-fledged mountaineers.

On one of these outings in late April the group had camped overnight on the shoulder between Little Bignian and Big Bignian, two adjacent mountains. On the Saturday morning after a breakfast cooked and eaten outdoors they struck camp and began climbing to the top of Big Bignian, the higher of the two peaks.

When they had reached the summit they all sat down on the short stiff grass or a convenient boulder for a rest and a welcome drink.

As Jeffrey sat there gazing down on the panorama stretching away off into the distance below him he found his eyes drawn inexorably towards Leitrim Hill. This was a rolling grass-topped hill at the outer edge of the Mourne Mountain range. Jeffrey knew it well for his grandparents, Jimmy and Ivy Donaldson lived in its shadow on their small farm. He and brother James had spent many fun-filled summers there.

Leitrim Hill stood out in a distinctive green, highlighted in the early Saturday morning sun. Sheep grazed undisturbed and little lambs frolicked beside them in the postage-stamp like fields, bounded by dry stone walls, at its foot.

Suddenly, inexplicably, the words of a hymn came into his mind. It was one that he had sung with all the others in church on Easter

Sunday. He had no idea the words had embedded themselves in his memory, but as he sat there looking down at Leitrim Hill, bathed in spring sunshine, they came drifting back.

'There is a green hill far away,
Outside a city wall,
Where the dear Lord was crucified,
Who died to save us all,' they reminded him.

This was strange.

Why had he begun to think about a hymn, sitting on top of a mountain, looking down on a little green hill?

Then he remembered another verse of it. Involuntarily, almost subconsciously, he began to repeat, moving only his lips,

'He died that we might be forgiven,
He died to make us good,
That we might go at last to heaven,
Saved by His precious blood.'

Although he had said that he would leave any further consideration of 'religious matters' until he was much older, he couldn't seem to escape them. Even on a weekend camping trip he was being reminded of Christ's death and his responsibility.

Jeffrey was glad to hear Gordon's voice transporting him back into the real world of mountain walking and teenage talking. "Right lads," he was announcing, "it's time we were on the move again. Let's go!"

Those were happy times at School, at the B.B. and up over the mountains. Jeffrey often wondered why Mr. Mc Cullough took the trouble to devote his leisure time to taking a group of lads, who often liked to mess about and have their own way, off at the weekends. He concluded that he must be genuinely concerned, not only for their physical, but also for their spiritual welfare.

When Jeffrey became sixteen he left school and was accepted for a three-year practical study in electrical engineering with the firm of Hugh J. Scott in Belfast. Adam Barber, who had been in the same year as Jeffrey at Kilkeel High School was chosen to begin the same course and so the two young lads began their first permanent employment together.

As Kilkeel was too far from Belfast for daily commuting by sixteen year olds the young apprentices were forced to find accommodation in the city. After making a few enquires, Mrs. Irvine of Delaware Street, off the Ravenhill Road, was recommended to them. The commendation proved justified, as Mrs. Irvine soon became a kind of mother figure to the 'two boys from the Mournes.'

As there was no suitable bus from their home town on a Monday morning Jeffrey and Adam's week in Belfast began on a Sunday evening. The bus stop where they dismounted in the city was at the top of the Ravenhill Road some distance from their lodgings. They didn't mind the walk down that road, however, for the timing was such that they always seemed to be passing the front of the Martyrs Memorial Free Presbyterian Church when the people who had been at the evening service were beginning to spill out onto the opposite footpath. They often slowed their pace past the church to see if they could spot the church's dynamic minister, Rev. Ian Paisley, saying goodbye to his capacity congregation at the door. If they did manage to catch a glimpse of 'The Big Man' as they called him they carried on down the road, satisfied.

After an initial settling in period Jeffrey began to enjoy the work in Hugh J. Scott's, and learnt quickly. He was assigned to various departments within the company to observe and experience different processes in his first months there, and it was then that he met Tommy Latimer. This older man was always friendly, cheerful and helpful, but that wasn't all. Tommy spoke very openly and unashamedly about his Christian faith to all he worked with whenever the opportunity arose. Jeffrey often heard the other employees describe Tommy as 'good-livin" but it was clear that they held him in high regard nonetheless.

As Jeffrey was coming towards the end of his training programme he was to be given a pleasant surprise one morning. It was from Tommy who came up beside him where he was working and said, "Jeffrey, I have something for you. Would you accept a little gift from me?"

Although somewhat taken aback Jeffrey indicated that he would be pleased to accept 'anything that was going.' On opening the brown envelope that Tommy presented to him he discovered that the 'gift' was a shiny black New Testament. When Jeffrey opened it he found that Tommy had written a simple inscription on the flyleaf. It said, 'Jeffrey Donaldson. With best wishes and a cordial invitation to attend Scott's Thursday Fellowship. Proverbs 3 v. 6.'

Here was somebody else who seemed deeply interested in him for some reason or another. Why were all these people so keen to spend time and money in an effort to direct him towards God, and the Bible and the Christian gospel, he wondered? What fired them up and kept them going? What was their hidden source of inspiration?

Whatever it was he secretly hoped that one day, some way, he would find it out for himself.

It must surely be worth having.

5

WHO WILL TAKE HIS PLACE?

On February 23, 1981, little more than two months after his eighteenth birthday, Jeffrey Donaldson joined the Ulster Defence Regiment. This was not surprising. He had attained the legal status of an adult and he was descended from a family background of involvement in the security forces

Frank Charleton senior, his maternal grandfather, had served for a number of years with the 'A' Specials, the full-time equivalent of the Ulster Special Constabulary and his other grandfather, Jimmy Donaldson, had risen to the rank of Sub District Commandant in the U.S.C., otherwise known as the 'B' Specials. Jeffrey's father, who had joined the Ulster Defence Regiment shortly after its inauguration was by then a Colour Sergeant and Platoon Commander.

When he enlisted in the U.D.R. at Ballykinler Army Camp Jeffrey felt proud to be following in the family tradition. As soon as he joined he was sent on a two-week training course as a part-time soldier before being posted to B. Company Co. Down Battalion based in Mourne Abbey in his native Kilkeel. There were now two men leaving the Donaldson home to engage in routine patrols on the roads in and around their town and district.

It was a dangerous, unpredictable year in which to have joined the Ulster Defence Regiment. The death of Bobby Sands and nine of his comrades on the republican hunger strike in the Maze Prison served to increase the tension in the province to an all-time high. Sixty-one people, twenty-six of whom were members of the security forces, and the remaining thirty-five of them civilians, were killed in paramilitary activity during the seven turbulent months between April and October.

The end of the hunger strike did not bring an end to the continual spiral of death and destruction, however, and one particular event had a profound effect on Jeffrey Donaldson.

He was sitting at the tea table just after five o'clock in the afternoon on Saturday, November 14. The T.V. was providing a backdrop of sound and colour in the corner of the room. Jeffrey had been paying little more than half-hearted attention to the sports results but the opening headline on the National News which followed them had him riveted to the set.

The Westminster MP Rev. Robert Bradford had been shot dead by IRA gunmen as he held an advice centre at a community hall in Finaghy, in his constituency. He had been Ulster Unionist Party MP for South Belfast for seven years.

A sadly familiar sense of shock descended on that living room again. Other members of the family who had finished their meal and dispersed to different parts of the house returned to assemble in awestruck silence in front of the television.

The local news that came on immediately after the national bulletin gave more of the gruesome details. Two gunmen who had arrived dressed as workmen in paint-splattered boiler suits had killed Kenneth Campbell, a caretaker at the centre as well. They had shouted, 'Freeze!' as they burst into the centre and one fired a single shot at the caretaker. A third gunman, armed with a machine-gun had guarded the door while his accomplices had fired several shots at Rev. Bradford as he sat behind his desk. He had been hit in the eye, ear, chest and neck and died instantly.

As news of the death of the first Northern Ireland MP to be

assassinated in the troubles spread across the province a sense of outrage gripped the Protestant community. On the day of his funeral there was a widespread stoppage of work amongst them and tax and rent strikes were later threatened as part of a protest campaign.

During all the unrest and tit-for-tat killings that took place in the wake of Robert Bradford's death Jeffrey Donaldson began to contemplate the long-term implications of his murder. Who, he wondered, would take his place? Would peace and stability ever return to the province or would it just continue on the apparently inevitable slide into mayhem and mass murder? What was the answer?

When such questions refused to go away Jeffrey decided to make his personal contribution to helping resolve the situation in the only way he could. Vaguely conscious of his childhood commitment after the death of his cousin Samuel, to become positively involved somehow, he considered his options. He was already taking risks with his life with the U.D.R. in helping mount security patrols throughout south Down. Now he determined to enter the political arena which Robert Bradford had been forced to vacate in such an untimely manner.

In late November 1981, just two weeks after the MP was shot, Jeffrey attended a meeting in Kilkeel Orange Hall and joined the Young Unionist movement. Robert Bradford had been Member of Parliament for South Belfast. Just before his nineteenth birthday Jeffrey Donaldson had signed up as a Young Unionist in Kilkeel. The locations and positions seemed poles apart, but the single-minded young man had been propelled into the enactment of his boyhood pledge by the cold-blooded killing.

Having placed his foot on the first rung of the ladder Jeffrey began to climb it steadily. In January 1982 he was elected chairman of the Mourne Young Unionist Branch. Having thrown himself into the cause with such passion and vigour he soon began to be invited as a guest speaker to Young Unionist meetings all across County Down and beyond.

His three-year term of employment with Hugh J. Scott in Belfast came to an end in the summer of that year, and having obtained his Diploma in Electrical Engineering Jeffrey returned home to live in his native Kilkeel.

When it was announced that elections were to be held on October 20 for the setting up of a new Northern Ireland Assembly at Stormont he began to campaign in a voluntary capacity in support of the four Ulster Unionist candidates in the South Down constituency. There was a keen public interest in this election, as it would see devolved government return to Northern Ireland for the first time since the dissolution of the previous local Assembly eight years before. Out every evening in a different town, on a different platform, but with the same political message, gave Jeffrey his first taste of election fever, and he liked it. The sense of commitment to a political ideology made him feel that he had begun to scratch at the surface of doing something worthwhile for his country.

When two of the Ulster Unionist candidates from South Down were elected to the new Northern Ireland Assembly Jeffrey became even more involved in the political scene. He made occasional visits to Stormont in his role as chairman of Mourne Young Unionists and it was there that he first met another man who was to leave a lasting impression on him.

His name was Edgar Graham.

Edgar was a lecturer in Law at Queen's University but it was in his role as Chairman of the Young Unionist Council that Jeffrey came to meet him. There was something about Edgar that appealed to the man from Mourne from the moment of their initial meeting. There could be no doubting his allegiance to unionism, but what appealed to Jeffrey was deeper than mere political affiliation. It was his absolute honesty and integrity. Edgar Graham was a Christian, and his spiritual belief was obviously an integral part of his life.

When Jeffrey was elected Treasurer of the Young Unionist Council in January 1983 he began to have more regular contact with Edgar Graham. The barrister and lecturer had been one of three from the Ulster Unionist Party to be elected to represent South Belfast in the Stormont Assembly in October.

Jeffrey thought this significant. Robert Bradford had represented South Belfast at Westminster. Edgar Graham would probably never do that for Rev. Martin Smyth had won that seat at the by-election in March 1982. He was, though, following in his footsteps to a certain extent in that he was representing South Belfast in the Stormont Assembly.

As the friendship between the two men developed Jeffrey Donaldson found Edgar Graham to be a discerning and understanding mentor. If in doubt about anything he often sought Edgar's advice.

He admired the man. Although recognising that he would probably never have his intellectual ability there was something about Edgar that Jeffrey constantly coveted.

It was the supreme sense of peace and divine destiny that seemed to hang like a delicate curtain over all that he said and did.

6
SWITCH ON THE RADIO

Bill Martin had been a Lieutenant Commander in the Royal Navy and was a Recruiting Captain in the U.D.R. He had been involved with Jeffrey in his early days in the Regiment and it was also Bill who encouraged the part-time soldier to become involved in the Young Unionist movement.

Having watched the young man, whom he perceived to be showing unusual political promise, make the transition from his teens into his twenties, Bill learnt of another position for which he reckoned Jeffrey Donaldson would be ideally equipped.

Enoch Powell, the sitting Westminster MP for South Down was anxious to employ an election agent to help him contest the next General Election which was expected to be in the late spring or early summer of 1983. Bill reckoned that Jeffrey, with his growing interest in the workings of the Ulster Unionist Party, would be well qualified for the job. The experience he had gained travelling around the constituency in support of the candidates in the Assembly elections the previous autumn must surely be regarded as strongly in his favour.

Bill encouraged him to apply for the position.

Jeffrey talked it over with his family, including his uncle, Frank Charleton, who was a leading member of the Mourne Unionist Association. Frank was highly respected in the local party, and in the wider community as a member of the Select Vestry of Christ Church in Kilkeel, the Charleton family having had a long connection with the Church of Ireland.

He listened very carefully as Jeffrey argued that there would be no chance of the renowned seventy-year old MP ever considering engaging a relatively unknown twenty-year old from Kilkeel as his election agent. Nonetheless, with his uncle's blessing he took Bill Martin's advice and sent in an application. He had nothing to lose, he reckoned. The prospect of an interview with the brilliant, and often outspoken orator would be an experience in itself, even if nothing more were to come of it.

The prospective election agent was interviewed by the MP and his Constituency Association Officers in Newcastle Orange Hall in January 1983. This proved to be a much more pleasant and much less intimidating encounter than Jeffrey had anticipated. He discovered that the formal, almost forbidding exterior concealed an element of warmth and friendliness that kept manifesting itself during the series of carefully chosen, probing questions.

As he drove home to Kilkeel later that evening Jeffrey felt that he would have no difficulty working with Enoch Powell, regardless of his international reputation. He felt he had acquitted himself as well as possible at the interview and all that remained was to await the outcome.

He didn't have long to wait.

Three days later he received a letter from the sitting South Down MP offering him the position of Constituency Agent, and arranging an initial meeting to discuss the terms of employment.

Jeffrey Donaldson was thrilled. He had pledged to do what he could to work for the peace of his country within the union with Britain, and how better could he serve that cause than by working alongside one of the most eloquent defenders of unionism, Enoch Powell?

Having been appointed in late January, Jeffrey's first task was to prepare the South Down Constituency Unionist Association for the General Election.

It was a daunting challenge.

Although in his seventy-first year, Enoch Powell was a tireless Member of Parliament, whose advice was sought by many in his own party and beyond. He was a respected figure at Westminster where he spent most weekdays, leaving his newly appointed agent to either arrange meetings for him every weekend or conduct them himself. The situation was further complicated by the redrawing of the constituency boundaries for the election. The Boundary Commission's recommendation that the number of seats in Northern Ireland be increased from twelve to seventeen meant a realignment of the boundaries. In the subsequent redistribution, Banbridge, Donacloney, Moira and a number of other, smaller, traditional Unionist strongholds on the fringes of South Down were allocated into other constituencies. South Down had suddenly become a marginal seat.

This was to make the enthusiastic twenty-year-old's task all the more difficult and the election result all the more unpredictable.

When the election date was fixed for June 9 the pressure began to mount in earnest. The sitting MP and his agent knew that they were in a do-or-die situation. Political analysts had already begun to comment that 'with the boundary changes the vote in South Down will be too close to call.'

From early March until after the election in June, Jeffrey Donaldson was barely ever at home. There were meetings every evening to organise the campaign and canvass support. Enoch Powell travelled back to South Down as often as possible, and for the duration of the campaign he based himself at his constituency home in Loughbrickland.

The count in Dromore High School was a very tense affair. The candidates and their agents shuffled about anxiously, unable to predict the outcome. It became clear that the final result would not be known until after the very last box was counted.

When a recount was requested the suspense was extended and the pressure prolonged. With that complete the Presiding Officer was in a position to make his announcement. Enoch Powell had been re-elected to serve as Member of Parliament for South Down with a majority of 548 votes.

The MP was pleased, and relieved.

Jeffrey was jubilant. He had coordinated a vigorous campaign that had seen his MP re-elected to a seat many pundits had suggested he could lose. The return of Enoch Powell to Westminster after that well-organised canvass operation had the knock-on effect of bringing the masterminding agent to the attention of the local media. The delighted, determined and dapper twenty-year old was interviewed both on radio and television on his interpretation of the implication of the election result.

When election fever had melted away, in the heat of summer, life returned to a less hectic routine. Jeffrey Donaldson, constituency agent to Enoch Powell, derived great pleasure in doubling up as his tour guide. The MP spent much of the summer at his Loughbrickland home and he and his wife, Pam, often invited their English friends over to spend a short holiday with them.

It was then that Jeffrey was often asked to take the party on a 'tour of the Mournes.' There were many happy picnics in such scenic locations as the Forest Parks at Tollymore and Castlewellan, and the Silent Valley. A favourite view of Enoch's, and one to which he often returned was the vista from the Ballymageough

Road, when travelling out from Kilkeel. On this narrow road on a clear day one comes over the top of a hill and the entire expanse of the Mourne Mountains explodes into view in breathtaking beauty, with the village of Attical almost smothered in yellow gorse bloom in the valley below.

As they relaxed together in scenic locations on sunny summer afternoons, occasionally just the three of them, Enoch, Pam and Jeffrey, but more often with appreciative company, the MP would reflect on his 'good fortune to have one of the most beautiful constituencies in the kingdom.'

On these leisurely day trips Jeffrey gleaned a wealth of information on the background of the famous parliamentarian who had selected him as his agent. Enoch Powell, he discovered, was the only man to enlist in the British Army as a Private at the start of the Second World War and emerge at the end of it having risen to the rank of Brigadier. He was a University Professor of Greek and a respected classical scholar. It was in 1950 that he first entered politics, having been elected as Conservative MP for Wolverhampton S.W. and he later served in the Cabinet as Minister of Health for three years.

As Enoch Powell recounted many anecdotes from the past Jeffrey began to appreciate more fully what he had recognised on the first night he had come face to face with him in Newcastle Orange Hall. Beneath a rather tough exterior there lay a soft and feeling centre. It was only those who came close enough to him to see that serious shell cracked open who realised that he had a tremendous sense of humour. He had a razor-sharp wit and an endless repertoire of jokes, some of them even against himself, at which he would laugh heartily even if the punch line was beyond everybody else.

Jeffrey Donaldson learnt a lot from working with, and often just listening to, the South Down MP. When exposed to the breadth and depth of Enoch Powell's intelligence and knowledge he felt strangely privileged. It was like being a young student who had been accorded a prized place at the feet of an eminent philosopher or theologian. This was particularly so on Monday mornings.

It was part of Jeffrey's job to collect Enoch from his home in Loughbrickland and drive him to Belfast International Airport to catch a flight to London at the beginning of another busy week at Westminster. On that journey, which normally lasted about an hour, the MP lectured his agent on just whatever subject he happened to have been contemplating at the time. These thoughts for the day, or reflections from the weekend, or whatever they were, could be on any topic of Enoch's choice. They ranged across themes as diverse as the battles of the Second World War, the fortunes and failures of the Conservative Party, the influence of ancient Greece on the civilisation of the world, and the importance of Winston Churchill's speeches to, and their impact on, the population of wartime Britain.

There were occasions when they were caught up in slow-moving traffic, with Jeffrey worried in case they wouldn't make the airport on time, and Enoch in full flow on the colonisation of Australia, that he found his attention slipping. What is the point of all these lectures? he often thought at such moments. Why is my mentor so keen to impart his knowledge, particularly on the history and function of government in Britain, to me? Is he schooling me for something? Surely he could never consider me as his successor.

Later in that eventful year Jeffrey Donaldson was brought face to face with the realities, and the uncertainties, of progression and succession within the Ulster Unionist Party, once more.

It was December 7, 1983, and his twenty-first birthday. He was attending to constituency business in Enoch's study in Loughbrickland and musing at odd moments, as people are apt to do on birthdays, on the events of the years that are past, and the challenges of those to come.

As noon approached a voice in his head seemed to say, 'Switch on the radio.'

Leaning forward, he turned the knob. The pips were going. He was just in time for the midday news bulletin.

The opening headline was startling. 'News is coming in of a gun attack in South Belfast,' the announcer began. 'A man has been shot dead outside Queen's University.'

"Oh no!" he said out loud, involuntarily. "Not Edgar!"

No name was given but a few phone calls eventually confirmed his dread premonition.

Yes. It was Edgar.

Jeffrey felt weak and sick with shock and disgust. Here was a man whom he had admired. Edgar Graham had been honest and upright, friendly and talented, an Enoch Powell in the pipeline. Then another thought came to him, and it was reinforced in his mind when he attended his friend's funeral a few days later.

If anybody had been ready to die, it was Edgar. The peace of God that seemed to surround him in life surely meant that he was prepared for death.

The funeral service was held in Randalstown Presbyterian Church and the minister began by giving a glowing testimony to the quality of Edgar Graham's Christian life. He went on to remark that Edgar's hadn't been the first, nor he felt, would it be the last, tragic death of someone who was prepared to stand up and make his mark on society in Northern Ireland.

Having followed the coffin, which was carried by grieving relatives up a long country lane to a remote rural cemetery, Jeffrey stood with hundreds of mute mourners at the graveside.

As the coffin was lowered into the grave he thought back to the death of Robert Bradford. He had wondered at the time who was going to take his place. Could it have been Edgar Graham?

Not now, it couldn't.

Edgar, too, was gone.

Jeffrey became lost in a distant world of earnest contemplation in that country graveyard that winter afternoon. Although one of a huge crowd he felt curiously alone. He began to reflect seriously on the brevity of life, and the verse from the Bible that the minister had quoted more than once in the service, earlier.

'Don't boast about what's going to happen tomorrow,' he had reminded them, 'for you don't know what this day will bring.'

It was a sobering thought.

7
ON THE UP AND UP

In an attempt to see Jeffrey Donaldson realize the potential which he claimed to see in him, Enoch Powell encouraged his diligent agent to undertake a course of part-time study with a view to meeting University entrance requirements and eventually obtaining a degree.

In the autumn of 1984 Enoch arranged for him to be interviewed by Trinity College, Cambridge, and following that interview Jeffrey was offered a three-year course in History, commencing the following academic year. That was something to prepare for and he looked forward to the prospect of University life. There could be no doubt that a degree from Cambridge would be a boost to the prospect of a life in politics.

Late in the year, and in the early months of 1985, however, a relationship began and he was offered a new job. Jeffrey was left with a difficult decision to make.

On Thursday, December 21 he attended a Band Aid Concert in the Slieve Donard Hotel, Newcastle. Bob Geldof's 'Feed The World' was the chart-topping record at that time and a large crowd of young people had gathered in the hotel for the event.

As the evening progressed Jeffrey became aware of the presence of a group of girls from his home town of Kilkeel. He knew most of them from High School days although they had been in the lower forms when he was in his last year there. They seemed quite happy to chat to him and he asked one or two of them for a dance. There was one of them, though, whom he found particularly attractive.

She had shoulder-length fair hair, and sharp, lively eyes.

When the concert was over and the revellers were pouring out on to the streets and into the car parks Jeffrey ventured to split up the party of girls. He asked Eleanor Cousins if she would like to return to Kilkeel with him. Eleanor was quite happy to accept and as they set off together Jeffrey realised that he really liked this girl, and determined to get to know her better, if at all possible.

Before he left her off that evening Jeffrey asked Eleanor if he could see her again. He could, and he did. On the Saturday evening, on Sunday night after church, and on the Monday night, which was Christmas Eve.

Life took on a new perspective for Jeffrey as the relationship with Eleanor developed. He often found himself rushing home in the evening to change before setting out to meet her. There were two ways in which Jeffrey was different from many of the young men in his circle of friends.

The first of these was in his attention to dress. Where other young lads he knew were happy to go out for an evening with their girl-friends casually dressed, Jeffrey usually turned up to meet Eleanor in shirt, collar and tie as though he were keeping a very important appointment. His second distinctive quality was his ability to talk. Whatever the subject, whether Northern Ireland politics or international affairs, hill-walking in the Mournes or the fluctuating fortunes of Chelsea Football Club, Jeffrey Donaldson could be trusted to give a good account of himself in any discussion. Having spent years as an Enoch Powell apprentice Jeffrey was beginning to assume the mantle of his master, almost unwittingly, wherever he was.

When their friendship lasted, and strengthened, over the Christmas and New Year holiday socialising season, Jeffrey and

Eleanor became what was described by the teens and twenties as, 'an item.'

In January 1985 Jeffrey was elected Chairman of the Ulster Young Unionist Council. His efforts with and for the South Down MP, and this most recent appointment to a senior executive position led to an offer of an even more responsible post. He was approached and asked if he would consider acting as personal assistant to the party leader, James Molyneaux, in Unionist Headquarters, Glengall Street, Belfast.

This unique opportunity further complicated the crisis of choice already facing Jeffrey Donaldson. Should he refuse the offer and take up his place at Cambridge later in the year? The prospect of a degree was very appealing but the chance to serve as personal assistant to the leader of the Ulster Unionist Party could prove more advantageous in the long term. And if he went to University would he have to resign from the Chairmanship of the Young Unionists so soon after his election? What, too, would become of the developing relationship with Eleanor, if he went off to Cambridge? He was beginning to appreciate this more and more with every 'date', but could it survive a three year absence?

It was a dilemma.

Jeffrey weighed up all the pros and cons of the situation seriously for a few days before opting to accept the position at Unionist Headquarters, and forgo the place at Trinity College.

In the busy life that followed he was never forced to regret his decision. He settled into the routine of a new job during the day while still maintaining a full programme of speaking engagements, both with the Ulster Unionist Party and the Orange Order, in the evenings.

On February 28, 1985, he had just arrived outside Spa Orange

Hall near Ballynahinch, County Down, where he was due to address a meeting, when the programme he had been listening to on the car radio was interrupted by yet another news headline to send shivers racing down his spine and anger welling up in his soul. 'Early reports are coming in,' the newscaster announced, 'of an explosion at the Police Station in Newry. There are no details yet of any casualties or the extent of the damage.'

Attacks on police stations and army bases had become all too commonplace in the ongoing Troubles, and so Jeffrey put the matter to the back of his mind and continued his meeting. Later that evening, still unaware of the full extent of what had happened in Newry, he returned to his lodgings in Belfast.

A telephone call from his mother in Kilkeel early the next morning brought heart-rending news. Nine members of the RUC had been killed in the bomb attack on Newry Police Station and the most senior of them had been Chief Inspector Alexander Donaldson. Alex, as he was known to the family, was another of Jeffrey's cousins. He had been Samuel's brother.

It was devastating for the entire family circle.

At the funeral a few days later Jeffrey heard the minister speak of Alex's Christian commitment. He had accepted Christ into his life as Lord and Saviour as a young man of nineteen. While rising through the ranks in the R.U.C. he had witnessed consistently to his faith and was an active member of the Christian Police Association.

All these funerals were beginning to tell on the young political activist. And it wasn't just the tragic, needless loss of life that was getting to him, either. Cousin Samuel, after whom his church had named its new hall the Samuel Donaldson Hall, Edgar Graham and now Alex. These men had all been practising, practical, genuine Christians. A common theme, running through all three funeral services, was the declaration at some stage by the officiating minister of the love of the deceased for the Lord, and the assurance that they were now with Him in heaven.

Jeffrey had known each of the murder victims well, and wholeheartedly agreed that everything that had been said about them was true. He knew, though, deep in his heart, that such things could not have been said of him.

It was painful to stand at the graveside in the church cemetery. Alex was to be buried beside his brother Samuel. His heartbroken widow Ida, and his three now-fatherless children, Samuel, Joanne and Andrew, looked forlorn figures as the coffin was lowered into its final resting-place.

What could be done to stop all this?

Every death of someone he knew and every distressing funeral he attended, all set against a background of attack and counterattack, made Jeffrey Donaldson all the more determined to help bring a just and lasting peace to the longsuffering people of Northern Ireland if at all possible.

His chance was to come sooner than he had ever expected.

He was selected by the South Down Unionist Association to stand as their candidate in a constituency by-election to the Northern Ireland Assembly at Stormont on October 17, 1985. This was to take place following the death through illness, in June that year, of Raymond Mc Cullough, one of the men for whom Jeffrey had canvassed in the election campaign, three years earlier.

Having obtained 17258 first preference votes, Jeffrey Donaldson was elected to represent South Down in the Northern Ireland Assembly. As he took his seat he was conscious of a mixed sense of pride and privilege. He was pleased that the people of his constituency had given him such a resounding mandate. His sense of personal achievement was boosted by the fact that at twenty two years and ten months he was the youngest ever member to sit in the Assembly.

Now he had been afforded the privilege of representing the people of South Down he was determined to do what he could to put their case before the locally elected body. He had also been granted a platform on which to air his opinions on the state of affairs in the Province.

Jeffrey Donaldson thought that he had 'arrived.' He was on the up and up. Things would be different now.

Would they, though?

This recently elected Assemblyman had strongly held views, unavoidably coloured by bitter personal experience, and lots of questions for political parties, especially those with links to terrorism.

But did he have any answers?

8
THE SOLUTION ON THE
SCRAP OF PAPER

Although pleased to have been elected to the Northern Ireland Assembly Jeffrey Donaldson was only privileged to represent South Down in that forum for eight months. This was not due to any lack of interest or commitment on his part but to the fact that the Assembly at Stormont was dissolved on June 23, 1986.

This caused him considerable frustration as he had felt at home in the debating chamber and was a tireless advocate of the Ulster Unionist position. It also meant, more practically, that he needed to seek permanent daily employment, and he began working for a firm of financial consultants in Belfast but continued to speak at meetings across the province in his capacity as chairman of the Young Unionist movement. One aspect of his election to the Stormont assembly that he regretted was that he had to resign his position as agent to Enoch Powell MP as they were then representing the same constituency in different elected bodies. An effectual working relationship, and more than that, a warm friendship, had developed between the two men, however, and Jeffrey maintained close links with the masterly Member of Parliament, often seeking his valued advice.

In mid-November 1986 he was invited to preside over the election of office-bearers in two Ulster Unionist branches in the heart of County Armagh. The meeting was held in Tullyhappy Orange Hall near the village of Bessbrook and Jeffrey was introduced, and then welcomed by his friend Danny Kennedy, a local unionist councillor.

With the formalities of the meeting completed the chairman invited Jeffrey to address the expectant crowd. At a personal level, there were two entirely different factors which led to this being a particularly poignant, and politically rather emotive, evening for the young speaker. One was to do with location, the other with tradition.

As he had been driving along the country roads to Tullyhappy Orange Hall for that meeting he had been reflecting on its setting. Where he would be standing to speak was just a matter of miles across the country as the crow flies from the spot where Samuel had lost his life in 1970 and three miles from Newry where Alex had been killed in the mortar attack eight months earlier.

The Anglo-Irish Agreement between the British Prime Minister Margaret Thatcher and the Irish leader Garret Fitzgerald had been signed on November 15, 1985, a year previously that very week. It was the first anniversary of an Agreement which had sparked little but disagreement. The Unionist MPs at Westminster had all resigned their seats in protest in January 1986, forcing by-elections in fifteen constituencies, and there had been countless demonstrations and protests amongst the unionist community all through the year. Their main objection to the Anglo-Irish Agreement was that they saw it as affording the Irish Government a consultative role in the internal affairs of Northern Ireland, and their unrelenting and vociferous opposition to it had contributed to the downfall of the Assembly in June.

With his personal and political sensitivities both cut to the quick Jeffrey Donaldson delivered a very forthright and impassioned speech that evening. He began by highlighting the unionist opposition to the Anglo-Irish Agreement using arguments with which his audience were completely familiar but which they had no objections to hearing repeated time and again. With speaker and listeners well warmed up to the subject Jeffrey then turned his attention to the solution to the problem. One could knock the Anglo-Irish Agreement forever but that wasn't going to bring peace and stability to the province. What then could be done in the current circumstances?

According to the fired-up guest speaker the solution was in security. Increased patrols, more intensive searches and a more aggressive approach to the defeating of terrorism, from whatever quarter, would eventually lead to a reduction in violence and the return of peace. The Government's problem was not that it lacked the resources, but the resolve, to take corrective measures, he suggested.

Such sentiments, dynamically delivered, were enthusiastically endorsed by the audience, many of whom had nodded their agreement at various points and with varying degrees of vigour throughout.

As Jeffrey mingled with the members of both local branches during the supper that followed he was pleased with the overwhelming support they voiced for the policies he had proposed.

When the supper was over people began leaving the hall in small groups, still engaged in earnest conversation. Jeffrey started singling out a number of the senior figures present, to say goodbye to them. Everyone agreed that it had been a 'good night' and the man who had acted as chairman throughout the proceedings accompanied Jeffrey to the door.

Just as he was about to step out into the winter night the man handed him a scrap of paper. It looked like half a page from a notebook or diary, hastily torn out but neatly folded for ease of transfer.

"Have a read at that when you go home," the chairman whispered as he slipped it into the hand of the speaker whose rousing message had been heartily approved by all present. "I believe that it is the answer to the problem in Northern Ireland."

As he crossed to where he had parked the car Jeffrey was bemused. He wondered how anyone could write the answer to the problem of the province on the scrap of paper he was holding tightly between his fingers. Earlier in the evening he had been outlining a security solution to the situation, but it had taken him the most of an hour to do it. How then could this man condense his explanation into few enough words to fit on to half a page of his pocket diary?

Having settled himself into the car Jeffrey switched on the courtesy light before starting the engine. It would be interesting to discover a definitive answer to a problem on which there were such strongly held and diametrically opposed shades of opinion.

He unfolded the little note.

To his great surprise it did not contain any words of political wisdom. There was no quote from some famous statesman, no condemnation of paramilitary violence or no recommendation of an alternative form of government.

There was nothing on the piece of paper except a few figures and letters.

2 CHRONICLES 7 V 14. That was all it said.

Jeffrey Donaldson's earlier experience of Sunday School classes, Boys Brigade epilogues and church services helped him recognise that peculiar type of combination of words and letters. They were a reference from the Bible.

Not having a Bible in the car, Jeffrey decided to look it up later, tossed the scrap of paper across on to the passenger seat beside him, and set off for home.

He felt rather pleased with himself motoring back to Kilkeel. The evening had been a resounding success. Lots of people had told him that they supported him in every word he had said. If the Government would just act on his recommendations things would soon improve.

Everybody at the meeting had been agreed on that.

Well, almost everybody.

What about the chairman's Bible reference solution?

Would it be in keeping with the 'toughen up on terrorism' policy he had been advocating?

His curiosity had been aroused.

As soon as he reached home Jeffrey began searching the house for a Bible. He hadn't one in his bedroom but after a period of rummaging through all the likely, and a few unlikely, places, he discovered a copy in a drawer in the living room. Some of the younger members of the family had been carrying it back and forward to Bible Class every Sunday and it rested in peace in the drawer the rest of the week.

Having procured a Bible at length, Jeffrey's next problem was finding 2 CHRONICLES 7 V 14. He leafed through the Bible idly for about half-a-minute, but he hadn't the faintest idea where to look in it to locate the promised all-embracive solution, whatever it was.

Realising that he wasn't well enough up in the books of the Bible to find his reference unaided he turned to the index at the front and found a page number for 2 CHRONICLES. Although not a Bible scholar he knew how to crack the next code. 7 V 14 meant chapter seven verse fourteen. After flicking through quickly to the seventh chapter he ran his finger down the page until he came to verse fourteen.

He began to feel a strange thrill of excitement. It was like a boy he had read about in a book once. He had found a map on a dirty, discoloured scrap of paper, and when he had decoded the instructions and followed them he had found buried treasure.

Jeffrey had arrived at the moment of truth. The lid of the casket was about to be opened. The treasure was soon to be revealed in all its sparkling glory. The answer to Northern Ireland's problems, all in one Bible verse. That was, at least, according to the chairman of the meeting in Tullyhappy Orange Hall.

An initial reading of the verse brought a sense of bewilderment.

So he read it again.

The second reading didn't help.

So he read it again.

This brought a sense of anticlimax.

So he read it again...

'If my people, which are called by my name, shall humble themselves, and pray, and seek my face, and turn from their wicked ways; then will I hear from heaven, and forgive their sin, and will heal their land.'

Jeffrey closed the Bible in his hand, keeping a protecting finger in the page he had worked so hard to find, as he cast his mind back to what the chairman had said. Could he possibly have taken him up wrongly?

No. Definitely not.

What he had said was, 'I believe that it is the answer to the problem in Northern Ireland.'

How could it be?

What did it all mean anyway?

And if it was so great, why had nobody, who understood it, ever tried it?

9
ENOCH'S FAREWELL

Those were busy days. Jeffrey continued his work with the financial consultancy based in Belfast, although his job took him to many parts of Northern Ireland to meet clients. He was not now involved in full-time politics but he did so much voluntary work in various capacities that serving the interests of the Ulster Unionist Party, particularly in South Down and with the leader, James Molyneaux in Party Headquarters, had become his consuming passion. It occupied every moment of his spare time that he was not spending in the other pleasurable pursuit of his life.

That was seeing Eleanor. The young couple had become engaged and there were wedding plans to be made.

Although not formally employed as Enoch Powell's election agent, Jeffrey continued to maintain close links with the veteran politician. He addressed a number of campaign rallies in support of the South Down MP in the run up to the General Election on June 11, 1987.

As an Ulster Unionist Party officer and former agent for the sitting MP Jeffrey was admitted to the count in Dromore High School. As the first boxes were opened and the counting of votes began, Jeffrey noticed that the man whom he had come to respect, not only as an able MP but also as a counsellor and friend, appeared unusually edgy. It was clear that the result was going to be very close, just as it had been in the previous General Election, four years before.

This time, though, when Jeffrey spoke to Enoch he found him much more pessimistic than he had been on that occasion.

"I think we may have lost this one," he remarked with a deep sigh. The normally relaxed and confident Enoch Powell seemed to have been overcome by an impending sense of doom.

His fears were well founded. When the result was declared an increase in his personal vote was still not enough to hold off the challenge of Eddie Mc Grady from the SDLP. Enoch Powell had been beaten into second place by a margin of 731 votes.

The elderly politician was devastated by this defeat. Jeffrey Donaldson, who had worked so closely with him, and come to know him so well over a four-year period, could see that he was deeply hurt. He was just a few days short of his seventy-fifth birthday and probably recognised that his parliamentary career was over. Apart for a short six-month break in 1974 when he switched from representing Wolverhampton SW as a Conservative to representing South Down as an Ulster Unionist, he had never left the political arena. He had been a dominant figure in the House of Commons for thirty-seven years.

Now all that had come to a sudden stop.

It was a bitter pill to swallow.

As he left the counting centre later that evening Enoch Powell was surrounded by media reporters all anxious to gauge the former MP's reaction to the election result. This defeat would make headline news on television and in the papers next morning. What would Enoch Powell, the accomplished orator, have to say for himself?

One jostling reporter asked the question to which all in the media melee were anxious to know the answer.

"Why do you think you lost the election, Mr. Powell?" he called out.

"I think it was because the other candidate got more votes than I did," the outgoing MP replied curtly and precisely, before pushing through the wall of reporters to his waiting car.

It was hurtful to have lost his seat and Enoch seemed so despondent that Jeffrey wondered if the enthusiasm he once had for Northern Ireland and its people would have gone with it. Would he ever have any heart in returning to the province? Or would he retire in England and consign his thirteen years in South Down to history? Put it behind him like a bad dream, pretending it hadn't even happened?

No. His erstwhile election agent was convinced that he wouldn't do that.

He couldn't, for he had only gone fifteen days when he had another important engagement in South Down, to which he and his wife had been invited, and which they had promised to attend.

It was Jeffrey and Eleanor's wedding on Friday, June 26, in Mourne Presbyterian Church, Kilkeel.

The marriage ceremony was conducted by Rev. Dr. David Mc Gaughey, the church minister, assisted by Rev. Ian Mc Nie, from the church which Jeffrey's family attended, Kilkeel Presbyterian. Friends and family members from both churches joined many other invited guests from the town and beyond for the happy occasion.

James was his older brother's best man and Eleanor's sister Lynda was matron-of-honour and her little daughter Emma-Jayne was the charming flower girl. It was a beautifully warm summer day and both families enjoyed meeting friends and relations they hadn't been in contact with for years. 'We only seem to meet at weddings and funerals now,' they confessed to each other with slightly embarrassed laughs.

After the wedding the newly married couple were driven off to Castlewellan Forest Park, a picturesque setting for those treasured wedding photographs. By the time they had returned to the Slieve Donard Hotel for the reception all the other guests had arrived there and were either sitting inside in the shade or strolling around in the grounds appreciating every aspect of the idyllic location, 'where the Mountains of Mourne sweep down to the sea.' The bridegroom of the day was by then the oldest of eight, and Kingsley, Julie-Anne and Glen, the three youngest of the Donaldson family, had a great time, going from one group of relatives to another, laughing and joking.

It was a nostalgic return to the Slieve Donard for Jeffrey and Eleanor. As they sat at the meal they reflected on the mid-winter evening when they had met in that same Hotel, two and a half years before.

A number of speakers extolled the qualities of the radiant young couple during the course of the reception and spoke for everyone present when wishing them every blessing for the years to come. Both MPs with whom Jeffrey had been associated during the hurly-burly of the previous four years, James Molyneaux and Enoch Powell, paid tribute to his dedication to unionist principles and his capacity for hard work.

The former South Down MP, who had been so put out to witness his political career hit the buffers with a bump a fortnight earlier, raised a laugh when he disclosed a secret. "I have given this young man lots of good advice since he came to serve as my election agent back in 1983," he quipped, "and most of it he seems to have taken on board. There is one small crumb of my counsel, though, which he has chosen to ignore. I told him once, 'Don't ever consider getting married until you are forty. Sort your career out first and then look around for someone with whom you can happily share it.'"

He paused to look across at where the new Mr. and Mrs. Donaldson were sitting before continuing, "On this occasion, however, I have to admit that he was wiser than me. When I see Eleanor and he together today I think Jeffrey has proved me wrong!"

10
AWESTRUCK

With Jeffrey now working mostly in Belfast it may have been more convenient for the newly-weds to live in or near the city. However, their ties with Kilkeel were so strong that they didn't feel inclined to leave it, and so they set up home in Kilmorey Court on the Newcastle Road out of their home town.

As they began to become familiar with their new neighbours Jeffrey often found himself in contact with a young man who lived in Carginagh Road just around the corner from him, and whose interests were much the same as his own. Alan Johnston was a few years younger than his friend and neighbour but they were both active members of the local Young Unionist Branch and when Jeffrey had been in the Ulster Defence Regiment they had been stationed together in Mourne Abbey. Although Jeffrey had left the UDR when he had been elected to Stormont as an Assembly member Alan was still serving as a part-time Lance Corporal with the Regiment. There had been close links between the two families and when the two men met, whether at a church or political function or on a summer evening in the lee of the purple-heather-covered mountains, they enjoyed sharing their views on life around them in the Kingdom of Mourne.

That friendship was to be brought to a dramatic end on Monday, February 15, 1988.

Jeffrey was just preparing to leave the house to drive to Belfast for a business appointment when a neighbour came to the door to tell him some startling news he had just heard. Alan Johnston had been murdered. All the details of the incident hadn't been confirmed but the story the neighbour had been told was that Alan had just arrived to start his shift at the Kilkeel Joinery Works when a gunman came up behind him and shot him at close range.

This was a sickening blow. Having known Alan and his family so well Jeffrey knew that he couldn't concentrate on business in the city that morning so he cancelled his appointment and went round to the Johnston home.

It was a heart-rending, but to Jeffrey Donaldson becoming an all too familiar sight. He found a set of parents whose lives had been shattered by a gunman's bullet. Their son had called goodbye to them quite cheerily two hours before. Now he was dead.

As news of Alan's murder spread, other members of the family began to arrive at his home, red-eyed, pale-faced, tight-lipped, sombre in grief, and sullen in anger.

Later that morning the Outside Broadcast Units from the local television stations rolled up into Carginagh Road. They were anxious to interview someone about Alan's death. The family were, understandably, devastated with grief and declared themselves in no fit state to speak to anyone. In deference to their wishes the rapidly increasing number of reporters moving around with microphones, mini tape-recorders and notebooks referred to the Johnston family very sensitively as being 'unavailable for comment.' Having driven all the way from Belfast to Kilkeel, though, they weren't going to go back to base without 'a story' and so hastily set off in search of someone else.

That someone else was Jeffrey Donaldson. He had gained a little experience in media interview procedures in his various political roles and so was asked to speak to the waiting journalists.

When asked to recall his memories of Alan, Jeffrey described him as 'an ordinary, honest young man.' Feeling aggrieved, no doubt, at the reason for his friend's death he went on to refer to him in a different interview as being 'one of the many young men in Ulster whose only desire is to serve their community and provide protection for us all.'

The next few days were very tense for the community around Kilkeel. The police believed that Alan's killers were still in the area and threw a tight security cordon around the town. That indescribable emotional mix of anguish and indignation had taken the town by the throat again. People only spoke to their friends in feverish whispers when out on the street. And they didn't speak to strangers at all.

When the day of the funeral came the town closed down, united in grief for its murdered son. Shops put up their shutters. Streets stood empty and silent. Fishing-boats lay tied up, row upon respectful row in the harbour.

More than fifteen hundred people crammed into Mourne Presbyterian Church for the service. Every seat was taken and every spare square foot of standing space was occupied as well. A tangible sense of sorrow and loss hung in the funereal atmosphere.

Rev. Dr. David Mc Gaughey began by paying tribute to Alan Johnston. He spoke of him as 'a promising, pleasant young man from a highly-respected family. He had come up through the Sunday School and Boys Brigade and was someone who had been regular in his attendance at church.'

The minister then went on to echo the feelings of many of the vast company of mourners when he expressed dissatisfaction with the Government's security policy which was, he claimed, 'standing by while young men were gunned down and blown to pieces.' He also roundly condemned those who had carried out the killing, voicing the sense of revulsion felt by all at assassins who could 'shoot a man in the back on his way to work, with his lunch box in one hand and a set of tools in the other and no means whatsoever of defending himself.'

Jeffrey Donaldson had been able to push into the end of a pew towards the back of the church. Looking up towards the front from that position he had a clear view of his former colleague's coffin. It was draped in the Union Jack, and crowned in solitary state with the victim's UDR beret. Having attended so many funerals of friends and relatives without ever having become reconciled to the experience, Jeffrey agreed entirely with the sentiments expressed on the security situation.

When the speaker moved on in his address from personal tributes and political comment to the wider implications of the possibility of untimely death, Jeffrey became inwardly agitated. Funerals always seemed to affect him that way. Rev. Mc Gaughey urged the capacity crowd to think of the future while still in the present, and to prepare to meet God in eternity by trusting in Christ for salvation while they had the opportunity.

Although stirred into a contemplation of the uncertainty of his present life and the ultimate importance of his future by the minister's address it was the hymn sung during the service that had an unexpectedly arresting effect on the man in the pew.

He had sung 'Abide With Me' hundreds of times before. The tune was familiar and the words had tripped easily off his tongue, remembered and recognised but invariably unconsidered.

That day, though, it was different.

In the context of the death of someone whom he had spoken to so often and served with so happily, and while now gazing numbly up at his flag-draped coffin, that hymn seemed to assume a much deeper meaning for him than ever before.

When the congregation began to sing the fourth verse every word seemed to cut right into the core of his being.

'I fear no foe with Thee at hand to bless,
Ills have no weight, and tears no bitterness,'

they were singing.

What could that mean? he thought.

Nearly everybody he had been speaking to over the past few days had been reflecting on the apparent injustice of Alan's death. It had even been commented upon during the service. Could a situation ever arise where 'ills have no weight?' And what was this about tears without bitterness? He had seen more tears in the past few days than he had witnessed for years, and was surrounded by people weeping at that very moment. What kind of people could weep tears of anguish without resulting bitterness?

'Where is death's sting? Where grave thy victory?
I triumph still if Thou abide with me!"

The congregation finished the hymn and were rustling as they resumed their seats, but Jeffrey Donaldson had been transposed into a world of awestruck wonder. It was as though he had been struck, and paralysed by an unexpected bolt of lightning. He sat down again, deep in thought.

Could he triumph over the prospect of the grave? Had the sting been drawn from death for him? What if it were him in that coffin? Whose victory would it be?

A succession of pointed questions had begun to tumble over

each other, and jumble through each other, in his troubled mind. They were crying out for instant answers.

Jeffrey knew, from having listened to what Rev. Mc Gaughey had said that day, and from other speakers at previous funerals, that the only way to triumph over death was to have everlasting life within him. And that, he had also learnt, only came through trusting in Jesus Christ as his Saviour.

As Alan's coffin was being carried out of Mourne Presbyterian Church in solemn, tearful reverence, and as he followed it in the company of hundreds of others around to the church graveyard for burial, Jeffrey Donaldson resolved to sort this matter out.

He was going to come to Jesus. Definitely.

Procuring inner peace in the present and eternal life for the future had to be accorded top priority.

Regardless of how much it cost, either in terms of material prosperity or political prospects, he was determined to prepare to meet his God.

What was more, he was going to do it soon.

11
CAN I COME IN?

That was the plan.

Between the drawing up and the carrying out of any plan, however, between the formation and the implementation, there is often an interval. This interval, if permitted to become prolonged, provides an opening for something apparently more pressing to creep in or crop up, and divert the attention.

So it was with Jeffrey.

The image of the coffin at the front of the church lived with him for days. The words of the hymn that had so perturbed him kept recurring in his consciousness, often at most unexpected times, for weeks. He could be shaving in the morning, facing a client across a desk or driving home in the evening when his mind would suddenly freeze. Whatever he had been thinking about would instantly disappear to be replaced by the words that he seemed totally powerless to delete from his subconscious soul,

'Where is death's sting? Where grave thy victory?
I triumph still if Thou abide with me.'

With the passage of time, though, the recollections, which had once proved disturbing, became little more than distracting, and much less frequent. Other matters had begun to take precedence in his life.

One of these was his election, in March 1988, just a month after Alan's funeral, to the post of Honorary Secretary of the Ulster

Unionist Party.

He had become a senior Party Officer.

With renewed political responsibilities it was now tempting to try and relegate spiritual concerns to his mental deep-freeze. It was irritating to have to keep contemplating matters like God, and death, and the grave, and heaven or hell in the hereafter.

Although Jeffrey had endeavoured to carry on with his life and disregard all such considerations, they refused to go away. It was as though God had determined that He wasn't going to give up on him. The problem was that he was forced to confront these issues every day he went to work, for Stephen, one of the men in his office was a Christian. Stephen lived in Annalong, just five miles from Kilkeel and Jeffrey and he had been in the same class in High School.

As he watched Stephen live his life and go about his work in the office Jeffrey was often stirred to reflect yet again on the importance of being right with God. There was a calm confidence about Stephen's attitude and approach to life that he knew was missing from his own. He could deliver a feisty speech in a country Orange Hall or appear ever so efficient as he organised the programme for a political meeting. Underneath, though, deep inside his innermost being, he realised that there was something vital missing. He seemed to have become possessed of a sixth sense that was forcing him to recognise, with increasing regularity, that all was not right between God and himself. The lines of communication were not open. There was some kind of a block, a barrier, between them.

Stephen made use of every possible opportunity to speak to Jeffrey about his Christian faith. He was never aggressive or offensive in his approach, but if asked on a Monday morning, for example, if he had done 'anything interesting or exciting over the weekend,' he would take the chance to describe a meeting or service that he had found particularly encouraging or challenging. If he considered it appropriate, and Jeffrey appeared sufficiently attentive, he would on occasions go a step further by recounting the impactive points of the address.

As they continued to share the same office Jeffrey began to feel more at ease sharing his misgivings about his own spiritual condition with Stephen. He described the thunderbolt of conviction that he had experienced at his friend Alan's funeral to him more than once, telling also how that he had been recalling the hymn 'Abide with Me' at all sorts of strange times of the day and night ever since.

Stephen's immediate reaction to such confessions was to tell Jeffrey that he had no doubt that God was 'speaking to' him, or 'calling' him.

More than a year had passed from Alan's funeral when Jeffrey decided to share the thoughts he was having about his longing for peace with God and lasting satisfaction, with Eleanor. They hadn't been going to church regularly but one Sunday afternoon, after one of their hit-and-miss morning attendances, he broached the subject.

"You know, Eleanor," he began, "I have been thinking for quite a while now that I would like to become a true Christian. Going to church is all right but it doesn't mean anything to me for I feel that I am not in touch with God in the way I need to be. I want to have peace with Him and know also that I will go to heaven when I die."

The unexpectedness of this declaration took Eleanor by surprise. The content of it didn't though. She had noticed how quiet and thoughtful her husband had been after Alan's funeral and different things he had said over the year in between helped her to recognise that he was thinking seriously about the claims of God on his life. He had obviously more on his mind than merely offering financial advice to clients or arranging political programmes for the Ulster Unionist Party.

It was Jeffrey's turn to be surprised at Eleanor's reaction to his expressed desire to get right with God. She confessed to having had similar thoughts for some time also. Eleanor's sister Joan and her husband Mervyn were Christians and they had made a similar impression on her as Stephen had made on Jeffrey. They were saved, and it showed. Their faith in God was demonstrated in their compassion and concern for others.

She told Jeffrey that if he ever decided to talk to anybody, at any time, about what it meant to become a Christian to count her in on it. She was anxious to know the joy in her life that many others, who had a living vibrant faith in Christ, seemed to possess.

This request from Eleanor served to put further pressure on Jeffrey. If the persistent thoughts he had been having were, as Stephen had maintained, 'God speaking to him,' it had now become perfectly clear that He had been 'speaking to' his wife as well!

He determined, if that were the case, that it was time they did something about it. What, though, should they do? Having discussed it with Eleanor a number of times, the couple decided that since they both knew Stephen they should ask him to come to their home some evening and talk to them about becoming a Christian.

The opportunity to issue such an invitation came one Wednesday evening in late July 1989. Jeffrey and Stephen had been talking over events in relation to their work and the situation in Northern Ireland, a continual topic of conversation for all those living in the province at the time, when Jeffrey felt he should change the subject.

"You know that we have talked many times about Christianity and things like that," he said. "Eleanor and I were wondering if you would be free to come around to our place sometime and tell us more about it. We feel that there is something sadly lacking in our lives. We are convinced that we need to come into a deeper relationship with God."

That request was music to Stephen's ears. Here was someone actually coming to him, wanting to find peace with God. He willingly agreed to call with them two evenings later, on Friday, July 28.

Stephen turned up as arranged at Jeffrey and Eleanor's home in Kilmorey Court. He sat down on one of the couple's two armchairs and they sat side by side on the small settee. The room wasn't very big and with three people sharing it with the furniture it was almost full. It was an intimate setting for a spiritual discussion.

After the polite preliminaries Stephen opened the little Bible he had carried in with him. He explained that it was important that Jeffrey and Eleanor understood that what he had come to talk to them about wasn't some hare-brained scheme thought up by a clever philosopher or ardent religious group somewhere. It was God's rescue plan for the world and was described in detail in this divinely inspired book, the Bible.

He began by showing them why men and women needed to be saved in the first place. It was because of something called sin. Stephen read from his Bible a verse which stated that 'all have sinned and come short of the glory of God.' Having established both the universal and personal nature of sin he went on to show, again from the Bible, that the sin of mankind had created a barrier between a holy God in heaven and the people He had created on earth.

This made sense to Jeffrey. He had long since recognised that for some reason there always seemed to be an insurmountable obstacle between himself and God.

How then could that gap be bridged?

Stephen was coming to that.

The answer, he said, lay in the love of God and in the death of His Son, Jesus Christ. There would have to be a mediator, or a go-between, found, who would have the capacity to operate both in heaven and on earth. That person was God's one and only Son, Jesus, who was, is, and ever will be God, but whom God sent into the world to deal with the matter of sin and the separation it brought with it.

Having flicked through his Bible again Stephen read out another verse which he described as 'the Gospel in a nutshell.' It was one both husband and wife could remember having been taught in Sunday School and as they heard John chapter three and verse sixteen read they were able to quote it under their breath.

It said,

'For God so loved the world, that he gave his only begotten Son, that whosoever believeth in him should not perish, but have everlasting life.'

Stephen summarised the verse he had just read by pointing out that it consisted of three elements. Firstly there was the love of God for the men and women who were estranged from Him because of sin. This led Him to send his Son Jesus, who was

69

absolutely sinless, into the world to die on the cross to bear the punishment for those sins. Jesus had died, was buried and had risen again and returned to heaven.

When it came to explaining the last section of the verse Stephen made it clear that what Jeffrey and Eleanor had to do to have their sins forgiven, the communication channels with God restored and everlasting life assured was accept that Jesus had died for them, and accept Him, individually, into their lives.

He illustrated this by reading a verse from the last book of the Bible. It pictured Jesus standing outside people's hearts, knocking to be admitted, and making a genuine offer of lasting peace and endless communion, he told them.

'Behold, I stand at the door, and knock:' it said, *' if any man hear my voice, and open the door, I will come in to him, and will sup with him, and he with me.'*

The situation was that the Saviour who had died on the cross was now standing, figuratively speaking, outside their hearts, with a single, simple request.

It was, "Can I come in?"

Stephen went on to emphasise that Jesus was anxious to enter their lives and become their Lord, but He would never force Himself upon anyone. It was up to them to open their hearts and lives to Him.

Before asking the young couple for any response he went on to say that although having Christ in one's life brought a wonderful sense of joy and satisfaction God didn't guarantee that it would always be 'plain sailing.' The temptation to sin wouldn't suddenly disappear. The Lord Jesus called his followers to 'deny themselves, take up the cross and follow Him.' He spent His life on earth 'going about doing good' but was despised and rejected by men nonetheless. People who trusted in Him and who were determined to live for Him shouldn't expect an easy ride either. The Christian life wasn't a soft option.

Summing up all he had said, Stephen assured them that having the peace of God in their lives while on earth and the prospect of a home in heaven forever, would make any sacrifice made, or slight sustained, in this life seem totally inconsequential. The choice was theirs. Jesus was outside each of their lives, waiting to come in. And the fact that they had invited him along to their home to discuss these matters would seem to indicate that they were at least considering opening the door to Him.

There was a short silence after Stephen had finished. It was up to Jeffrey and his wife to respond, not merely to Stephen's presentation of the Christian gospel but to the particular challenge it represented.

Deeply conscious of how he felt, but unsure of what Eleanor's reaction to it would be, Jeffrey turned to her and asked, "Do you feel that you are ready to open your heart to Jesus? As far as I'm concerned, I want to become a Christian tonight."

"So do I," was his wife's short, but utterly sincere, reply.

Recognising that both people before him were ready to invite Christ into their hearts and lives, Stephen offered to lead them in a simple prayer of repentance and acceptance. He made it clear that each of them must pray it from his or her own heart as an individual. Salvation was a personal matter, an issue of a one-to-one relationship with God.

All three of them bowed their heads, and Stephen began, 'Lord Jesus, I know that I have sinned and I confess my sin before You.'

Jeffrey had Eleanor repeated these words, recognising the truth of them.

'I also want to thank You for dying on the cross so that my sins could be forgiven, and I ask You to take away my sin and come into my life and be my Lord. Please lead me and guide me as I would seek to live for You for the rest of my days. Amen.'

It was obvious to Stephen as both Jeffrey and Eleanor prayed together as a couple, but as separate souls before God, that the words they were using were coming not merely from their lips, or their minds, but from their hearts. There could be no doubt that they each recognised the importance of the spiritual step they were taking and the implications of it for their lifetimes and beyond.

When he opened his eyes and raised his head to look across at Stephen who seemed to be still praying away silently, Jeffrey felt that a huge burden had been lifted from his shoulders.

All the uncertainty was gone. All the doubts about God, and life, and death, and the hereafter had vanished in a matter of seconds.

He was suddenly at peace with God. An inexplicable tranquillity that could only have originated in heaven flooded his soul.

Jeffrey and Eleanor Donaldson's lives had been changed, for the better, forever.

And it had all happened with a simple commitment, made from sincere hearts, in a moment of time.

12
NEW LIFE

It was late in the evening before Stephen left Jeffrey and Eleanor's home that day. He was thrilled to have had the privilege of leading them into living contact with God through His Son, Jesus Christ, but there was so much that he felt he needed to tell the newly converted couple. Having been suddenly transformed from being citizens of an earth-based kingdom to that of a heavenly one there was so much they would have to learn about the lifestyle in this spiritual realm.

Stephen knew from the Bible what Jeffrey and Eleanor were beginning to recognise within themselves. Jesus had come into their lives and they were now children of God. He had received them into His family. They had been afforded a new identity. It was as though life had begun on a different and higher plane.

One of the many pieces of advice Stephen gave them was that they should tell other people that they had become Christians. 'Witnessing' was what he called it. He told them that there were hundreds of others in the local churches and the wider community who had also been born into the family of God through salvation. They would be delighted to meet new Christian friends. By contrast, there were also hundreds of others whom they met in the course of their daily living who were not Christians, and Jeffrey and Eleanor's experience of conversion might cause such people to consider their own position. Apart from all of that, they would find that actually speaking about their faith in Christ would afford them a tremendous sense of joy and peace. This would come from a growing awareness of being involved in a relationship with God that was universal and eternal but which remained at the same time local, practical and intensely personal.

Even after Stephen left it was a long time before Jeffrey and Eleanor felt like retiring to bed. There was so much to talk about. The question of telling others, as their counsellor had advised, was one they had to consider seriously. The issue was not *if* they should tell somebody, or everybody. They felt so full of the new life within that they would have no problem with that. It was where should they start? **Who** should they speak to first?

The best person, they decided, would be Rev. Mc Nie, their church minister. He would know what they were talking about. When they had 'broken the ice' with him they could then concentrate on letting others know as well.

For the first time in their married lives they went to church that Sunday morning because they really wanted to rather than out of some vague sense of religious obligation. They met the minister Rev. Ian Mc Nie on the way into church and arranged to speak to him when the service was over. Later, when the church was almost empty, they met in the minister's room and Jeffrey and Eleanor told their minister that they had invited Jesus into their lives two nights before.

Ian Mc Nie was thrilled at the news. He had been preaching in the church for years and it was always a delight to learn of a member of his congregation coming to faith in Christ and in this instance he was hearing of two at once! Here he was seeing not only the lives of two individuals touched for God but the potential for the establishment of a Christian home. Rev. Mc Nie prayed with them, asking God to bless them in their lives together, before arranging to call at their home a few evenings later to see them.

On Sunday afternoon they set out to tell their parents and their first call was out in the country. Jeffrey's mum and dad had moved from Kilkeel out to Ballinran, a rural district two miles from the town. When their son and daughter-in-law told them that they had become Christians they were pleased. Jeffrey was the first in the family to commit his life to Christ and they said that they knew it was 'the right thing to do' and were 'very happy' for the both of them.

Since Eleanor's sister was already a Christian there was no difficulty in telling her mother their news when they moved on to visit her former home later that afternoon. Eleanor told her mum that she had 'accepted Jesus into her heart' and she appeared very pleased.

When Jeffrey and Eleanor began to contact the wider family circle Joan and Mervyn were overjoyed. They had been praying for Eleanor, and then for her husband, for years. Now they could return to thank God for answering their prayers and drawing the young couple to Himself.

On Tuesday evening, about an hour after Jeffrey had returned from work, Rev. Mc Nie called to visit at the home. He had some sound advice to give the new Christians and a couple of little books to leave with them.

He emphasised the need for regular prayer and Bible study in the life of the Christian. It was important that they should keep in daily contact with God, who was now their Heavenly Father, using the communication facilities He had provided. These were through prayer and the reading of the Bible.

Christians can use the opportunity to pray to God at any time, or under any circumstance, Rev. Mc Nie explained. He never misses a call and will always answer, in His own way and time, and in the best interests of His children.

If we can talk to God through prayer, he went on to say, then we can hear what He is saying to us through reading His Word, the Bible. It is the essential handbook for the Christian, as it outlines the basis of his or her faith, as well as affording essential instruction for living.

Recognising that knowing where to read in the Bible to obtain maximum spiritual benefit can be difficult at first for those not completely familiar with its layout, Rev. Mc Nie had brought a small book with him for the couple to give them some initial help. It was called 'Read Mark Learn,' by John Blanchard, and contained a series of simple notes on selected short sections of the Gospel according to St. Mark.

The minister recommended that Jeffrey and Eleanor begin a systematic study of the Bible starting in Mark's Gospel, using the book as a study aid. He also left another booklet entitled 'The Way Ahead,' by Norman Warren, with them. It summarised, he said, all the advice both he and Stephen before him had been giving them as to how to proceed through life as Christians.

As he was leaving, later, he also encouraged them to attend church regularly. If they did that they would meet others with similar beliefs as themselves and discover that church had now become an inspiring, rather than boring, place to be.

Jeffrey and Eleanor took his advice and began to go to the services in Kilkeel Presbyterian Church every week. They went gladly twice every Sunday. Rising for church wasn't a chore any more. As they began to appreciate the change that had taken place in their lives they were soon anxious to become involved, in any way possible with the ongoing activities of the church. The God who had given them such a deep settled peace in their hearts could give it to others also. It would be up to them to live out their joy, share their experiences and tell what Jesus meant to them.

With the autumn and winter programme of activities being planned Jeffrey approached Rev. Mc Nie and enquired if Eleanor and he could assist with the work.

Church ministers are usually glad of eager volunteers to help with any branch of their activities and Ian Mc Nie was no exception. He realised that Jeffrey and his wife were keen new Christians with tremendous potential and he immediately suggested that they could help with the flourishing Youth Fellowship.

This appealed to Jeffrey particularly for sentimental, as well as spiritual reasons.

His cousin Samuel had been a leading figure in the Youth Fellowship up until his death nearly twenty years before. The Fellowship was held in the new church hall which had been named the Samuel Donaldson Memorial Hall, in his memory. And now Samuel and Alex's brother Edmund was still a leader in that work.

Counting it a privilege to be able to do something, however small, for God, and the teenagers of the church who had meant, and still meant so much to his cousins, Jeffrey offered his and Eleanor's willing assistance.

It was a pleasure to be involved with those lively young people.

Having gained years of experience in the organisation of political events Jeffrey was soon able to put his acquired skills to good use in arranging speakers and activities for the Youth Fellowship. Just before Christmas he took his first turn at sharing the message of the Gospel with the young people during the talk at the start of the evening. Again years of political oratory helped him with his confidence in standing before a crowd but the content of his address was entirely different.

This time it wasn't an analysis of the security situation in Northern Ireland and its mounting toll of death and injury. It was a declaration of a solution to the sin of the world through the death of Jesus Christ.

As the winter programme of activity progressed into 1990 the Youth Fellowship Choir made a tape of modern praise. The two new leaders had found some of the more modern hymns and choruses unfamiliar at the start of the season but they soon learnt them and by the time the choir came to make their tape they were singing along enthusiastically.

One of the pieces that was popular at the time was, 'As the deer pants for the water,' and it became a favourite not only at the Youth Fellowship but also with the young couple who had come along to help. Jeffrey and Eleanor felt that it expressed exactly how that they now craved the continual closeness and calm of the presence of God in their new life as Christians.

That wasn't the only experience of new life that Jeffrey and Eleanor were to encounter that year either, for before it ended God was to bless them with the joy and privilege of parenthood.

Their first little daughter, Claire, was born on November 21, 1990. They had been born into the family of God some sixteen months before and now their own little family had arrived. What a thrill to be both God's children and new parents!

Jeffrey and Eleanor continued to enjoy their work with the Youth Fellowship and found it so rewarding. In particular, they enjoyed the occasional weekend or summer trips away when they had the opportunity to get to know the young people even better. Something especially memorable occurred on one such long weekend outside Enniskillen, County Fermanagh.

Jeffrey was to be responsible for speaking to the young people at the evening talks and at that weekend, not long after he had become a Christian himself, he experienced another spiritual thrill. Before the weekend was over two teenage girls had come to him on different occasions, but each with the same particular request. They wanted to accept Christ into their lives, just as he had done some time before. His wife accompanied him as he counselled them and both of the girls opened their hearts to allow the Lord Jesus to come in.

Now Jeffrey and Eleanor had savoured another source of soul satisfaction. Not only had they been saved themselves but they had now become soul-winners as well, leading others to the Lord. It was a delight to see two young girls accept Jesus as their Saviour and experience new life in Christ.

What a thrilling period this had been. They had become children of God through faith in Jesus Christ. They had a lovely little baby girl to love and care for. Now, to crown it all they had been used to lead others to the Lord.

God had been so good to them.

How could they best record their appreciation?

What could they do for Him?

13

THE KIND OF MAN
THIS COUNTRY NEEDS

There was just one cloud on the horizon.

Sometimes it seemed white, fluffy and far away and thus hardly likely to bring a storm crashing in around Jeffrey Donaldson, Christian, church worker and proud father. At such times he could ignore it and carry on with the busy round of life. There were other occasions, though, and they seemed to become more frequent as time went on, when it appeared to darken and demand his attention.

It was the question that he had been asking himself ever since that night back in July 1989 when he had given his life to Christ. And the difficulty with this question was that he didn't seem to be able to come up with any easy, immediate, or definitive answer to it.

Jeffrey recognised that since he had become a Christian his pattern of life had changed. The Bible taught that he was now a 'new creation in Christ Jesus,' and he was increasingly grateful to God as he began to discover the truth of that statement in various aspects of his own experience. The man who had been born again by the Spirit of God had a new goal in life, a new Master to serve, and a new Heavenly Father to please.

When he had become the youngest member in the Northern Ireland Assembly at Stormont, five years before, Jeffrey felt that he was in control of his own life. He was on the up and up, set to soar higher and higher like a lark on the wing. His election success had helped kindle a personal, political aspiration. Wouldn't it be marvellous, he thought, to go right to the top in politics and become a Member of Parliament like his mentors Enoch Powell and Jim Molyneaux?

Remarks made to him as he travelled back and forward across the province addressing political meetings only served to fan this latent ambition into flame.

It had become a common occurrence, after Jeffrey had addressed an Ulster Unionist Party Branch meeting, for earnest countrymen with V-necked pullovers, hardened hands and iron grips to shake his hand until he thought they were about to break his wrist.

"Keep at it Jeffrey!" they would declare enthusiastically. "You are the kind of man this country needs. You will go far in politics."

The difficulty with these well-meant observations of sincere men was that they had the effect of causing the cloud of doubt and indecision to close in on the Honorary Secretary of the Ulster Unionist Party.

The question which his conscience kept throwing up to him at such times was, 'Is it right for a Christian to be involved in politics?' This issue often took over his thinking for days on end and it was usually accompanied by a second, equally significant consideration. It was the idea that perhaps God had an alternative, more spiritually productive, plan for his life.

It was a struggle.

There were times when Jeffrey felt unusually close to God. As these periods often coincided with the hours he spent preparing for, and then leading the Youth Fellowship, perhaps he should abandon the political arena for good and become more involved in

Christian work. Should he consider training for full-time outreach amongst young people or perhaps even the Christian ministry?

Having contemplated those options carefully and in prayer before God for a few days he would then find himself addressing a unionist rally in a packed-out venue and the natural appeal of the alternative career would come flooding back.

"You are the kind of man this country needs," would echo in his ears from many members of an appreciative audience after the meeting.

Then Jeffrey Donaldson was ushered back into the will-I? won't-I? world of wavering once more.

Many considered themselves qualified to offer him advice as to his future career. The problem with their counsel, however, was that it was ultimately unhelpful, for it was irreconcilably conflicting.

One school of thought maintained that since Christ had informed Pilate one day that His kingdom was not of this world, His followers should not become mixed up with this world's systems of government. They should be pursuing, and promoting, the interests of their heavenly calling and citizenship. And what was more, politics was a dirty, messy business. Why should a Christian even want to waste his or her life and talents on it? Would they not be more profitably employed in spreading the Gospel?

Others disagreed. Totally. They would argue that since Christ had also commanded his disciples to 'occupy until I come,' this meant that they should live meaningful lives in every aspect of society where they were not called upon to compromise their Christian principles. And what of the 'Great Commission' to go into all the world and preach the Gospel? Were the seats of government, like Stormont and Westminster excluded from that? Should there not be someone responsible for maintaining a Christian witness and testimony in those institutions? Furthermore, there was the matter of the shaping of the laws by which we are governed. Was it right, or even logical, to leave the lawmaking solely to non-Christians and then complain that the country was becoming increasing godless? What too, of the influence of Christian MPs of a bygone age, like William Wilberforce or Lord Shaftesbury for example? Had they not campaigned tirelessly to bring about social changes which had affected the lives of thousands of underprivileged people?

It soon became clear to Jeffrey that he would have to make up his own mind on the matter in the end, for the more he listened to others, the more confused he became. Nothing remained but to read more widely on the subject, both in the Bible and other relevant works and pray about it daily and seriously. Meantime he would carry on with his Christian work and also continue to monitor the world of politics to see if he could somehow come to a conclusion on God's will and purpose for his life.

As he did this, his personal observations and contemplations presented him with widely differing results, and even these were not entirely conclusive. They could fluctuate with his current level of spiritual commitment or the political climate of the month.

Back in the busy days of the mid-1980's when all Jeffrey could envisage ahead of him was a budding, and eventually blossoming, career in politics, he had been given a book which had made a profound impression on him. It was Norah Bradford's biography of her husband Robert, the MP who had been murdered in November 1981. She had called it 'A Sword Bathed In Heaven,' from her husband's vision of his responsibility as a politician. 'My role is to say harsh things oft times, but to bathe the sharp sword of my words in heaven, to temper what I say with love, and to lead people from their folly to a life of fuller service with the King,' he had declared.

Although not yet a Christian, Jeffrey read the book with relish. He had admired Robert Bradford as an outspoken champion of the unionist cause in Ulster, and noted, almost casually, while reading the book, that his life had been greatly influenced by his deep Christian convictions. At that time, though, he had been more concerned with the MP's political stance, which corresponded very closely to his own, on a number of crucial issues, than he had been on his 'religious beliefs.'

As he considered the matter of his future life as a child of God, Jeffrey thought about the book and went hunting for it to read it again. He remembered that Robert Bradford had been a Christian and a Member of Parliament. How did he reconcile those two separate callings in life?

Jeffrey was rather disappointed initially to find that he couldn't locate his original copy of the book, having lent it to someone who had heard him recommend it and was anxious to read it straightaway. The only solution was to procure a copy by the same method as he had managed to lose his own. He simply borrowed it from someone else!

He reread that book avidly. This time, though, it was from a different perspective. Jeffrey could now envisage Robert Bradford as a Christian who just happened to be a politician, and not the other way round.

The early chapters described how Robert had invited Jesus into his heart at a Methodist Mission conducted by the famous preacher W.E. Sangster in the Grosvenor Hall, Belfast, when a boy of eleven. The book traced his life as a Methodist minister and his mental and spiritual struggle before consenting to put his name forward for Westminster as a UUUC candidate, and his subsequent election in February 1974. It then went on to outline Robert Bradford's life and influence as a Christian Member of Parliament.

Jeffrey Donaldson identified with so many aspects in the life of Robert Bradford. And the big question was, if the murdered MP had been able to accomplish so much for God, and his constituents, why shouldn't he try to emulate him, and do the same?

Well, why shouldn't he?

One valid reason was that his continued study of the political scene tended to confirm the viewpoint held by those who contended that a diet of political involvement could severely damage one's spiritual health.

During those days there was constant bickering amongst the main political parties in Northern Ireland about the Anglo-Irish Agreement and the future of the Ulster Defence Regiment.

Over in Westminster it was no better.

In the period between his conversion and Claire's birth, those sixteen months when Jeffrey had experienced such peace in his soul, and such satisfaction in Christian activity, he had also witnessed many changes in the parliamentary picture.

Nigel Lawson, Chancellor of the Exchequer had resigned in October 1989, after disagreeing with Prime Minister Margaret Thatcher, on the European Exchange Rate Mechanism. The Prime Minister had to face two leadership challenges, amidst continual backstabbing, and allegations of 'cash for questions.' The word 'sleaze', a relative newcomer to the English language, became extremely popular with journalists for it engendered a graphic image of the sickening, sordid, slithery slime in which the current administration was considered to be wallowing to the neck.

Nick Ridley and Sir Geoffrey Howe, both Government Ministers, resigned in a flurry of accusation and speculation during 1990. Margaret Thatcher found herself increasingly alone and she eventually resigned as Prime Minister after Michael Heseltine's damaging challenge to her leadership in November 1990.

Could it be true what they had been asserting all along? Was politics the 'dirty, messy business,' they had professed it to be? 'Definitely not the place for a Christian?'

With such contrasting points of view to consider Jeffrey discussed it often with the church minister, Rev. Ian Mc Nie, who had been so pleased to note his spiritual progress but understood his career dilemma. Although Jeffrey was still working in Belfast in a finance company, Rev. Mc Nie soon realised that he didn't intend to stay there forever. He had higher aspirations, but the minister found it difficult to give him clear-cut advice. It was like standing with a traveller at a fork in a path leading up a mountain. Both tracks would ultimately lead to the summit, but which one should the guide recommend that the traveller choose?

Aware of Jeffrey's keen interest in matters both spiritual and political Rev. Mc Nie bought him a copy of 'Kingdoms in Conflict,' Charles Colson's book which was sub-titled 'an insider's view of politics, power and the pulpit.'

This was fascinating reading as it examined, through the example of many political figures and situations and a number of the author's experiences with Prison Fellowship, the relationship between the Kingdom of God and world government systems. The chapter to which the prospective politician found himself returning almost daily, until he had practically memorised parts of it, was entitled 'Christians in Politics.'

That was where Colson advanced his 'three compelling reasons why Christians must be involved in politics and government.

First, as citizens of the nation or state, Christians have the same civic duties all citizens have; to serve on juries, to pay taxes, to vote, to support candidates they think are best qualified. They are commanded to pray for, and respect authorities...

Second, as citizens of the Kingdom of God they are to bring God's standards of righteousness and judgement to bear on the kingdoms of this world...

Third, Christians have an obligation to bring transcendent moral values into the public debate. All law implicitly involves morality; the popular idea that 'you can't legislate morality' is a myth...'

This was the other side of the argument.

Jeffrey and his minister spoke often of the issue, but the most suitable situation in which to hold a prolonged conversation came during a long weekend away with the Youth Fellowship.

It was in early May 1991. Rev. Mc Nie was due to leave Kilkeel to take over as minister in Trinity Presbyterian Church in Ballymoney, Co. Antrim, in June so he recognised that the long weekend away in The Warren, Donaghadee, would probably be his last with the young people he had come to know so well in Kilkeel.

Since both Jeffrey and he were attending the weekend alone they shared the same bedroom. That provided the ideal opportunity for them to discuss the question of the role of the Christian in politics in general, and the future career of Jeffrey Donaldson in particular, in depth. Conversations lasted until almost three o'clock in the morning on two consecutive nights.

Rev. Mc Nie's original attitude was to encourage Jeffrey to consider the possibility of training for the Presbyterian ministry. With his eager Christian faith and his undoubted capacity for presenting a cause with absolute sincerity, Ian Mc Nie could recognise that his friend would make a most effective ambassador for the Christian gospel.

Jeffrey had given this possibility serious consideration many times in the last two years, at the suggestion of Rev. Mc Nie. Many of his Christian friends who saw it as an infinitely more worthwhile occupation than politics had urged him to think of it both carefully and prayerfully, also.

Such people were always assured by Jeffrey, who was more anxious than anybody to ensure that he was in accordance with the purpose of God for his life in whatever it was he decided to do, "Don't worry. Believe me, I'm doing that."

Now the minister had adequate time to make his case. And Jeffrey had adequate time to reply. He listened to what his roommate had to say, and then he gave the alternative argument, quoting liberally from Norah Bradford, Charles Colson, and the Bible, to support his stance.

By the end of the second night Ian McNie had begun to recognise that Jeffrey had a vision for, and perhaps a leaning towards, the political scene. The ardent young man affirmed that his idea was not to use it as a vehicle for personal advancement, but as an avenue for upholding, and demonstrating, in a public and practical way, Christian values and beliefs. It was evident to the minister that Jeffrey Donaldson had all the qualities required to be a successful politician, and his desire and ability to witness unashamedly to his faith could only be seen as a bonus.

As they were parting in Kilkeel at the end of the weekend away, Ian Mc Nie encouraged Jeffrey to continue 'searching the scriptures' for guidance.

Like the prayerful consideration, delving into the Word of God in search of a solution to his situation, would be nothing new for him. He had been doing that conscientiously for nearly two years.

Other than various references to the Christian's duty as a good citizen to 'be subject' to the government of the day, 'for the powers that be are ordained of God,' Jeffrey could find little to enlighten him in the New Testament.

So he turned to the Old.

And there he found stories of men whom God had raised to senior government posts for His glory and for the blessing of His people.

Joseph, who had been despised and rejected by his brothers and thrust into prison in Egypt, eventually rose to become Prime Minister in the country to which he had been exiled.

Daniel, who had been carried away captive into Babylon, became a trusted policy advisor in the royal court of the country, rising to the rank of third in the kingdom.

It was the story of David, though, that Jeffrey found most fascinating. When Saul was deposed God sent Samuel to Jesse's home to appoint his successor. As the sons of the family, all sturdy men of war, were brought in one by one, they were rejected. God had not chosen any of them to be the King of Israel. When, eventually, David was sent for, and brought in, all glowing and fresh-faced, from the fields where he had been looking after the family's flock of sheep, God instructed Samuel to anoint him straight away.

He was God's chosen man.

The brother who looked least likely to be appointed to the honour had been crowned King, and he was to rule God's people for forty years. This was an encouragement to Jeffrey Donaldson. When God had been giving Samuel his instructions for selecting a suitable candidate for the throne of Israel He had warned him not to be taken in by outward appearance. It is only man that 'looks on the outward appearance,' He had cautioned. 'God looks on the heart.'

Since this was the case, Jeffrey concluded that as long as his heart was right and open before God, with an honest desire to serve Him, and put Him first in all things, then there was nothing to hinder him continuing in political life.

A defining moment for him was when he discovered a particularly arresting New Testament reference to the life and work of King David. It came in the course of an address by St. Paul to a synagogue full of Jews in Antioch during one of his missionary journeys. While outlining the history of the nation of Israel he referred to King David by saying, amongst other things, 'For David, after he had served his own generation by the will of God, fell asleep, and was buried with his fathers...'

Two thoughts in that verse stood out for Jeffrey. The first was what David, ruler of Israel had done. 'He had served his own generation.' There could be no escaping it. David had been 'the kind of man his country needed.' He had been in the right place at the right time.

The second point that Jeffrey found important to note in addition to **what** David had done, was **how** he had done it. It was 'by the will of God.'

At last, Jeffrey had come to a conclusion.

He would serve God first, and his country second, in whatever way the political arena would open up for him.

His simple aim was to be 'the kind of man' God wanted and his country needed, whatever that entailed, and whatever it would cost.

14
MASTER PLAN

By the autumn of 1991 the decision had been made.

It hadn't come suddenly like a mushroom springing up in the night, but had rather matured, through seasons of storm and sunshine like an apple on a tree, until at last it hung ripe and ready to be relished. Jeffrey was convinced that he should continue to pursue his political interests insofar as they were aligned with 'the will of God.'

The combination, and the contrast, of the political and spiritual issues which were the overriding concerns in Jeffrey Donaldson's life, and the perceived value of his counsel, was best illustrated by his inclusion in two distinctly different committees towards the end of 1991.

Since Rev. Mc Nie had been called to Ballymoney in June, Kilkeel Presbyterian Church had been left without a minister, and this was not a satisfactory situation for any congregation. They were anxious that a successor should be appointed as soon as possible, and this should be someone who would continue the pattern which had already been established, of presenting the claims of the Christian gospel in the community.

Jeffrey was one of those chosen to make up a Hearing Committee, with the appointed task of listening to particular ministers preach in their current churches and select from them one, or even more, for consideration by their home congregation. Amongst those whom the committee chose to 'hear' was Rev. Eddie Kirk, from 3rd Portglenone Presbyterian Church, and they visited the Co. Antrim village in mid-November. The committee were impressed with Rev. Kirk's zeal in the Gospel, and they conveyed their recommendations to the congregation back in the Kingdom of Mourne. These were accepted and Rev. Kirk was installed as minister of Kilkeel Presbyterian Church in February 1992, with Jeffrey continuing as leader of the Youth Fellowship.

While the deliberations aimed at filling 'the vacancy' in Kilkeel Presbyterian Church were taking place a new political initiative had begun. A round of discussions on the constitutional future of Northern Ireland had commenced at Stormont, chaired by Secretary of State, Peter Brooke. Having worked closely with James Molyneaux, MP, leader of the Ulster Unionist Party, on previous occasions, and as a Party Officer in his role as Honorary Secretary, Jeffrey was invited to become a member of the Ulster Unionist delegation at the talks.

Jeffrey Donaldson and his party leader shared very much the same political outlook and confided often in one another during the course of those negotiations. The announcement that a General Election was to be held in the spring of 1992 led the two men to contemplate their future career in politics with a certain immediacy, and to discuss the matter together often.

When it came to the selection of candidates to represent the various parties in the constituencies across the province in the Election to be held on April 9, Jeffrey was approached and asked if he would consider allowing his name to be put forward for selection as Ulster Unionist Party candidate in his home constituency, South Down. He was an obvious choice, they argued, since he lived in the constituency, had worked as election agent for Enoch Powell when he was its MP, and had also represented the constituency himself in the Assembly at Stormont for a time.

Although many were all for it, James Molyneaux advised against it. "South Down will always be a marginal seat for the unionists, Jeffrey," he would counsel. "I believe that you have a promising future in politics, but I don't think it will be there. I would strongly advise you not to stand for South Down in this election." He would then go on to outline what he considered to be a more appropriate course of action for the young man whom he envisaged as an eventual senior figure in the party.

"Just keep your powder dry, Jeffrey. Hang fire in the meantime," was what he recommended on more than one occasion.

That was sound practical advice from an experienced politician and it was in line with Jeffrey Donaldson's own personal intuition. It was strange for someone planning to spend a lifetime in politics to turn down the opportunity to be nominated as a candidate in a General Election, but that's how Jeffrey felt. As he prayed about the matter an unusual, spiritual sixth sense seemed to tell him that South Down wasn't the seat for him. This led to him refusing to allow his name to be put forward for selection to the bewilderment of many in the local branches of the Ulster Unionist Party who saw him as 'the natural choice.'

He had no regrets, however.

The election came and went, and just four days after it he became a father again. The birth of Laura, Jeffrey and Eleanor's second daughter, on April 13, doubled their family, their joy, and their parental responsibility, all at once.

A few weeks after Laura's birth one of the older girls from the Youth Fellowship wrote to Jeffrey expressing her best wishes to the husband and father. She, too, had recognised that Jeffrey had abilities and aspirations beyond travelling from Kilkeel to Belfast every day to work in a financial consultancy.

Having assured the popular Youth Fellowship leader of her continued prayers in the days ahead the well-wisher concluded her letter with a quote from the Bible. It was a modern rendering of Jeremiah chapter twenty-nine, verses eleven to thirteen. Jeffrey was pleased to receive the letter and both reassured and challenged by the words as he read,

'For I know the plans I have for you, declares the Lord, plans to prosper you and not to harm you, plans to give you hope and a future. Then you will call upon me and come and pray to me, and I will listen to you. You will seek me and find me when you seek me with all your heart.'

Jeffrey read those words over so many times that he had soon committed them to memory. The concept was thrilling. The Lord had a plan for his life. It was his Master's plan, and hence a master plan in more ways than one. And every aspect of the plan was positive. It promised prosperity, hope and a future.

An indicator that the plan had been fully activated would be that it would generate a desire to act within the will of God, and a conscious craving of God with all his heart.

It was while perusing this idea that Jeffrey realised that God was assuring him that he had acted wisely in declining the offer to put his name forward for South Down. He had never felt, 'with all his heart,' that it was the proper thing to do.

What then should he do?

If God had a master plan for his life, where, or what was it?

All he could do was wait and see.

The talks at Stormont on the possibility of returning devolved government to Northern Ireland continued after the General Election with a change of chairman. Sir Patrick Mayhew replaced Peter Brooke as Secretary of State for Northern Ireland, but Jeffrey continued to work very closely with the party leader, James Molyneaux, as they attended the various meetings as part of the Ulster Unionist Party delegation.

As the talks continued on into the summer of 1992 the two men had frequent private discussions about the future of the negotiations and internal party matters.

On one such occasion Mr. Molyneaux said to Jeffrey as they chatted after a meeting at Stormont, "I am beginning to feel increasingly that I may not stand at the next General Election, Jeffrey. You might want to consider putting your name forward for Lagan Valley."

It was an interesting, and as far as Jeffrey was concerned, intriguing, suggestion. He noted that the party leader had been careful not to promise him anything. That would be ill advised, for anything could happen in the lives of either of them in the coming four years that could change the perspective completely. What he had done, though, was sow the seeds of possibility, which, if carefully considered sprout up into the plant of possibility, which, in turn, if painstakingly tended, will eventually bear the sweet-scented flower of fulfilment.

This suggestion from the party leader came at a time when Jeffrey was already considering restructuring his life pattern. It was another ingredient to toss into the mix in the melting-pot.

He now had a wife and two children to support, and was finding it difficult to maintain the balance between parental and church responsibilities in Kilkeel, his daily work in Belfast and his still continuing participation in the political process. Although Jeffrey's employers were most accommodating he had a conscience about constantly having to ask for time off to attend talks.

After a period of serious heart-searching Jeffrey resolved the employment situation by setting up his own business in Bridge Street, Banbridge, Co. Down. It was an estate agency and financial services consultancy, working closely with some local firms of solicitors. The advantage of this arrangement was that he was now able to attend political appointments when he needed to, leaving the business in the care of a competent staff.

As he travelled out of Kilkeel every day, either to work in Banbridge or attend a round of meetings in Belfast, Jeffrey began to consider his party leader's suggestion more seriously. Kilkeel was his home town, and he loved it, and all the people in it, but it wasn't exactly central. It had a unique beauty, sandwiched between the purple mountains and the blue sea, but he had passed up the opportunity to stand for election as its Member of Parliament and he was never likely to return to permanent employment there.

Should he consider moving house? The prospect of relocation into the Lagan Valley area began to appeal to him, for a number of reasons.

Virtually anywhere in that constituency would be more central to both Belfast and Banbridge than Kilkeel, thus cutting down on travelling time and expense. Secondly, it could be advantageous from a political point of view also, if he ever decided to pursue the idea of 'putting his name forward for Lagan Valley.' If he were known in and to the local Unionist Party branches it could be a help when it came to the selection of a candidate to represent the constituency in a few years time. Besides, he had already represented part of the area in the Assembly when Dromore and Moira had formed part of the old South Down constituency.

There was a third, more personal and sentimental rather than practical or political, reason that led Jeffrey Donaldson to contemplate moving into the Lagan Valley area. He felt an affinity with the constituency for, as he had grown from boyhood through teenage into manhood, his parents had often told him stories of when they had lived in that area for two years. It was in the period from Jeffrey was just over a year old until he was three-and-a–half. His father had worked on a large farm at Ballymacbrennan, between Lisburn and Saintfield at that time, and they had lived there. It was fascinating to discover that his sister Diane had been born in the Lagan Valley Hospital in Lisburn during those days.

Thus the notion of returning to the part of the country where he had learnt to walk held a faint but friendly, nostalgic appeal for Jeffrey.

There was also the other side of the question to consider. If he and Eleanor did ever decide to leave Kilkeel it would be a big wrench for them. It would come as a bigger break for Eleanor for she hadn't been travelling out of the town every day to meetings or on business all across the province. She had always been in Kilkeel along with most of her immediate family connections. Her mother, Kathleen Cousins, and her two sisters Joan and Lynda would certainly miss her if she moved out of the Mourne district.

Then there was the church affiliation and commitment to think about as well. Jeffrey and Eleanor both enjoyed Rev. Kirk's preaching and Jeffrey was still heavily involved in the Youth Fellowship. Their ties with Kilkeel Presbyterian Church would be hard to sever.

Jeffrey's conviction that they should leave the town of their birth, and settle somewhere between Banbridge and Belfast grew as the months passed, despite these church and family considerations.

If they did decide to move at some stage, though, what part of the region should they settle in? That was the next important point to consider.

The answer to this question was revealed to Jeffrey in a most unusual way.

In the spring of 1993 he had been across in County Fermanagh, in the west of Northern Ireland, visiting some clients and on his way back decided to pull off the M1 motorway at the village of Moira for a break. He parked in the Moira Demense and decided to go for a walk around the park before resuming his journey.

As he strolled along past the houses in Castle Avenue, which backed on to the park, a voice seemed to speak to him. It was strange, but it could only have been the Lord, for the message was most definite.

'This is where I am bringing you to live,' it said.

Jeffrey slowed down, and the voice seemed to come again.

'This is where I am bringing you to live,' it said.

The stroller stopped.

'Lord,' he whispered, in a kind of a thinking-out-loud prayer in response to this strange revelation,' I know that You have a master plan for my life. I understand that. If coming to live in Moira is part of that plan, I will be happy with it. But please show me Your way.'

When he returned to Kilkeel and shared his experience with Eleanor she was just ever so slightly sceptical. She knew that her husband was thinking seriously of making a move to be more convenient to his work, and she also recognised that he had been praying constantly for God's guidance about the matter. Was breaking your journey in Moira Demense and then having a divine revelation that you are going to live in one of the houses nearby, not stretching it a bit, though?

"That's interesting, Jeffrey," was her rather non-committal response. "Time will tell. Let's just wait and see what happens."

They hadn't long to wait to see what happened, either, despite Eleanor's doubts. Time wasn't long until it told.

Two weeks later Jeffrey received an updated copy of the Property Magazine and discovered that there was a house just newly on the market in Castle Avenue, Moira. Could this be a further part of the Master's master plan?

All Jeffrey and Eleanor knew about Castle Avenue, Moira, up until that point was that Adrian Hanna, who had been a school friend of Jeffrey's, and his wife Ruth, lived there. Jeffrey made an appointment to go and view the property on a Saturday morning and he was impressed. If he were ever to move out of Kilkeel, he would be quite happy to live there. The house seemed to have everything that anyone could want and the location was just perfect.

Would all the factors about the house that he rated as plus points mean as much to his wife as they did to him, however? That remained to be seen. He arranged to bring her to view the property with him one afternoon the following week and when Eleanor saw it she was taken with it straightaway.

If her husband was sure that moving away from her beloved Kilkeel was the right thing to do then she would happily go along with him, and she couldn't think of anywhere more suitable to which to move than that particular house in the award-winning village of Moira.

Jeffrey Donaldson believed that God had shown him very clearly over the previous two years that He had a specific plan for his life, and when the family moved to live in Moira on July 3, 1993, he saw that as the implementation of a very definite element in it.

15
THAT'S ALL BEEN SORTED

Moving house can be a traumatic experience.

The upset of it, in human terms, can be even more acute when a family is moving out of an area where they have spent all their days up until the time of the move, as Jeffrey, Eleanor and their two infant daughters had done. Knowing that the relocation is an integral part of a divine master plan helps relieve the stress, but it can be a trying time nonetheless.

It was good then for Jeffrey and Eleanor to have Adrian and Ruth, who had strong Kilkeel connections, as neighbours while they were making the break from the County Down fishing port and settling into Moira. Jeffrey knew Adrian from schooldays and their wives struck up a friendship when Ruth asked Eleanor if she would like to bring the girls along to the Mums and Toddlers Group in the local Baptist Church.

When Eleanor had told Jeffrey about the warm welcome she had been given and how 'at home' she felt among the woman she had met there, the couple began to attend the Church on Sunday mornings. It was important for people with a vibrant Christian faith like theirs to find somewhere to worship that practised the kind of evangelism and fellowship to which they had become accustomed. Having discovered that kind of atmosphere in Moira Baptist they soon came to regard it as their new spiritual home.

The Donaldson family soon settled happily into life in the picturesque village of Moira. Jeffrey found, as he had expected, that it was a lot more convenient to Banbridge for his work, and a lot more central for travelling to Ulster Unionist and Orange Order meetings across Northern Ireland, than Kilkeel had been. He spent the summer settling in to his new situation, and then joined the Young Unionist Branch in Lagan Valley in September 1993. His main interest, next only to his Christian faith and his wife and family, was in politics, and he was anxious to become acquainted with the local party members as soon as possible.

When he had been some time in the Branch the other members recognised that he was infinitely more experienced in local politics than any of them and appointed him as their Chairman. As holder of this post he was then entitled to attend the management committee meetings of the Lagan Valley Ulster Unionist Association.

It had always been Jeffrey Donaldson's style to approach every job he was given to do, or any post he was appointed to fill, with absolute commitment, and so he began to attend every management committee meeting he could, with a view to sharing opinions and discussing policy with the other members. He soon made friends with, and was accepted and appreciated by, the 'grass-roots' members of the party. These were people who agreed with his position on policy and welcomed his contribution to the senior management team.

There were others, though, leading figures in the Lagan Valley Unionist Association, who were not so openly welcoming. They soon came to recognise that this 'young upstart,' with his apparent ability to discuss or debate any policy matter off-the-cuff, could eventually pose a threat to their jealously guarded positions. They had begun to feel, no matter how much they tried to deny it, like King Saul in the Bible. He had been unable to control a sullen, smouldering envy when the people of Israel switched their allegiance from him to a stone-slinging giant-killing shepherd lad called David.

Forward-looking mainstream members of the party would make the situation even worse by remarking, unwittingly, to some of them in the course of an occasional casual conversation, "That young man Donaldson is going to go far. It's great that he decided to come and live in Moira."

The gruff reply or occasional outright rebuff that such comments evoked could only be regarded as firm evidence that some on the senior management committee of the Lagan Valley Ulster Unionist Association would have been much happier if Jeffrey Donaldson had never left Kilkeel. Now that he had, though, they saw it as their mission in life to stop this 'blow-in,' as they called him, dead in his tracks.

The monthly committee meetings became very acrimonious affairs. Every single suggestion the newcomer made, however sensible it seemed to some, was vehemently opposed by others. He had adversaries, who were determined to prevent him rising any higher in the Association, whatever the cost to the Association or indeed the Ulster Unionist Party.

Jeffrey came home one evening after a particularly rancorous meeting and threw himself down in a chair exhausted, discouraged and confused. As he thought back over some of the bitter, hurtful remarks that had been made to him he began to question the advisability of ever having moved in the first place. And he directed his enquiry to God, who, he was convinced, had guided him to Lagan Valley.

"Could I have got it all wrong, Lord?" he cried out, thoroughly vexed. "Surely there must be some mistake. I'm quite sure You didn't bring me here to have to put up with all this. Should I really be somewhere else?"

Half an hour later he had settled himself sufficiently to concentrate on his daily Bible reading. He would normally have begun the day by reading the Scriptures but on that particular morning he had an early appointment and rushed out not having allowed God to speak to him through His Word.

The reading for that day was Psalm 37 and Jeffrey flicked over the pages of his Bible rather disconsolately until he found it.

As he read the first words of the Psalm he sat bolt upright, jolted unexpectedly out of his cycle of uncertainty.

'Do not fret because of evildoers...,' it began. 'For they shall soon be cut down like the grass, and wither like the green herb.'

Jeffrey was hooked. A few minutes before, his mind had been floundering around in frustration. Now it had suddenly become focussed on the book in his hand.

He read on.

'Trust in the Lord, and do good; dwell in the land, and feed on His faithfulness.

Delight yourself also in the Lord, and He shall give you the desires of your heart.

Commit your way to the Lord; trust also in Him, and He shall bring it to pass.

He shall bring forth your righteousness as the light, and your justice as the noonday.'

This was astounding stuff! It sounded as though David had written that Psalm just for him!

'Rest in the Lord, and wait patiently for Him,' it went on.

'Do not fret because of him who prospers in his way. Because of the man who brings wicked schemes to pass.

Cease from anger, and forsake wrath;

Do not fret. It only causes harm.

For evildoers shall be cut off; but those who wait for the Lord, they shall inherit the earth.'

Jeffrey sat, Bible in hand, stunned. Totally mesmerised.

He could barely believe what he was reading. How could David have summed up his current situation so succinctly?

That wasn't it all, either. There was more.

Farther down he discovered the striking prediction,

'The wicked have drawn the sword and have bent their bow, to cast down the poor and needy, to slay those who are of upright conduct.

Their sword shall enter their own heart, and their bows shall be broken.'

Then, as he read on, entranced, he came upon an astonishing promise.

'Wait on the Lord, and keep His way,' it counselled, *'and He shall exalt you to inherit the land.*

When the wicked are cut off, you shall see it.'

When he had continued down to the end of the Psalm, Jeffrey paused, thrilled to have come across the verses he had just read. Then he began to go down it all again, just to make sure he hadn't imagined any of it.

No. It was true. It was all there.

As he read back over Psalm 37 once more a number of thoughts seemed to jump out at him. The first was the Psalmist's emphasis on having one's actions controlled by 'the Lord.' *'Trust in the Lord,'* it commanded. *'Delight yourself in the Lord...Commit your way to the Lord...Rest in the Lord...Wait on the Lord.'*

It was so reassuring to note as well that almost every exhortation was followed by a promise. What was going to happen if Jeffrey, a child of the Lord, obeyed these simple instructions?

The Lord would allow him to *'dwell in the land, and feed on His faithfulness,'* give him *'the desires of his heart,'* and bring things *'to pass'* for him. He would also *'bring forth* his *righteousness as the light, exalt* him *to inherit the land,'* and permit him, eventually, to witness the wicked being *'cut off.'*

Finally, there was the explicit command that was to come as both a challenge and a comfort to the confused Christian. It was contained in three words, used three times.

It said quite simply, *'Do not fret.'*

Jeffrey sat silently as the lessons of the Psalm sank in.

He began to realize that he had, in his eager impatience, been running ahead of God. Now he recognised that the Lord was telling him to slow down. All that he was asked to do was wait, trust, commit, delight and rest, then leave the action to Him.

There would be no point in worrying himself sick about it either. His future was in the Lord's hands. The omnipotent God was perfectly equipped to deal with any opposition, whatever the motive for it or the venom of it.

One day had slipped silently into the next and the house had become still and cold, and still Jeffrey sat, revelling in the lessons he had learnt, praising God for His impeccable timing. If he had read Psalm 37 in the morning it wouldn't have meant nearly as much to him as it did in the evening.

It were as though the Lord had addressed him directly through the words of the Psalm and said, "Don't you worry about a thing, My child. Be still. Settle yourself and leave everything else to Me. And wait for Me. Don't fret about your future. That's all been sorted. And by the way, don't trouble yourself about the timing of it, either. I will get that right, too. Just trust Me."

What wonderful reassurance!

Jeffrey lived through the next few weeks, and then months, with a tremendous peace, and yet sense of purpose, in his heart. God was in control of his life, and everything would work out according to His plan. In His time.

The spiteful attacks by some at the Lagan Valley Unionist Association didn't stop, though. If anything, they seemed to become more vicious and vitriolic.

Jeffrey's attitude to them now was different, however. Before going out to the committee meetings he prayed along the lines, 'Lord, I acknowledge that You are my Master and that my life and all men are in Your hand. Please help me to remain calm here tonight, for Your sake, and for Your glory. Amen.'

In difficult days he also found it helpful to recall a sermon he had heard once. It had been about 'gold tried in the fire.' The speaker had explained that gold was refined in fierce furnaces to remove any impurities, and the hotter the furnace, the purer the resulting gold. Could it be that God was trying him in the fire of bitter opposition and jealous rejection to make him a more perfect instrument to do His will?

If it were, it was certainly an encouraging and comforting concept.

Having continued to attend various Ulster Unionist Party meetings across the Lagan Valley constituency, Jeffrey Donaldson began to consider the suggestion Jim Molyneaux had made to him, with growing interest. Some other members of the management committee, including the chairman, never ceased to make life difficult for him, but he recognised that he was becoming more and more appreciated by the rank-and-file members of the Association.

Could it be that God was working out His purposes in their attitudes?

At home in Castle Avenue, life had settled into a normal routine. The family were happy in Moira Baptist Church and Eleanor continued to take the girls to the Mums and Toddlers Group. As Claire and Laura grew older their mum took them along to the Busy Bees Playgroup in Hillsborough Elim Church. Jeffrey was encouraged to see that his wife and daughters seemed to be adjusting well to their new environment, building up a network of friends and becoming involved in a range of activities.

When circumstances were starting to look at least slightly more promising the next wave of doubt came rolling in. In 1994 the Boundary Commission announced that it was conducting a Review and that some of the Northern Ireland constituency boundaries may have to be revised before the next General Election. One possibility being considered, apparently, was moving Moira, which was on the outer fringes of Lagan Valley, out of that constituency and into neighbouring Upper Bann.

There was much speculation and endless talk about population growth and redrawn lines of demarcation.

What would happen if Jeffrey suddenly found himself outside Lagan Valley altogether? Could there be a big mistake after all? Or had the bellows just been applied to the fire to make it even hotter to purify the gold even further?

Despite the lessons Jeffrey thought he had learnt, he began to worry about it.

Yes, he had been happy enough to leave it all to God. But what plans had He for this one?

Again the answer came from God, and from His Word, and from the Psalms.

Jeffrey was reading one morning in the sixteenth Psalm and paused momentarily at verse six. Then he read it over again,

'The lines have fallen to me in pleasant places; yes, I have a good inheritance.'

That was it! The lines! He had been thinking, and talking, about lines for weeks.

Now, God was telling him that they would fall to him, 'in pleasant places.'

It was revision time. Jeffrey had forgotten the basic facts from the former lesson in Psalm 37. His patient heavenly Teacher was just reminding him of what he was supposed to have learnt.

'Don't worry about a thing, My child. Leave it all to Me.

'Do not fret' about the redrawing of the boundaries of Lagan Valley.

That's all been sorted, too.'

And it had!

When the Boundary Commission had completed its Review, and made its recommendations, the village of Moira remained in Lagan Valley!

16
A VICTORY FOR COMMON SENSE

Jeffrey was enjoying a relaxing weekend at home in early January 1995 when he had a telephone call from Rev. Martin Smyth, Grand Master of the Orange Order. This wasn't an uncommon occurrence for Jeffrey still continued to be a much sought-after speaker at Orange Order functions and the Grand Master often arranged for him to attend a wide range of venues and events.

The purpose for this call was different, however.

Having made a few general introductory remarks Rev. Smyth lost no time before introducing the main reason for phoning that evening.

"The time has come round again for me to appoint two new Assistant Grand Masters to the Order, Jeffrey," he began, without further preamble, "and I was wondering if you would be willing to serve as one of them for the next three year term?"

What a shock, and what an honour! Jeffrey was flabbergasted at the proposal at first. Surely it must be quite unusual for such a senior post to be offered to someone in his early thirties! He accepted the position, recognising the privilege of being considered for such a prominent office and adding that he hoped he would prove worthy of the confidence that the Grand Master was obviously prepared to place in him.

After discussing the varied responsibilities of his new post with Rev. Smyth, Jeffrey put the phone down, sat down, and began to reflect on his rise through the ranks in the Orange Order.

The Donaldson family had been members of their local Lodge in Mourne for more than a century. When Jeffrey first started playing the triangle in Orangefield Part-Flute Band as a boy at Primary School, his grandfather, father, and uncles were all active members of the Institution, 'walking with the men' in the Twelfth of July demonstration every year. Upon his progression, in early teenage, from tapping the triangle to playing the flute, he became a founder member of The Pride of Ballinran Melody Flute Band. The practising, the playing and the marching in local and county parades had been part of a proud tradition for many young boys and girls down the years and Jeffrey Donaldson had considered himself 'extremely lucky' to be a member of the recently assembled Band in their smart new uniforms.

When he turned sixteen years of age Jeffrey joined Orangefield L.O.L (Loyal Orange Lodge) 564, Ballinran, and became a fully-fledged member of the Order. As a boy he had often heard his father and other family relatives quote and discuss the aims and ideals of the Institution but these never really became meaningful to him until he had to undertake to accept them himself.

These were a mixture of religious and moral issues and included the conditions that 'an Orangeman should have a sincere love and veneration for his Heavenly Father and a steadfast faith in Jesus Christ, the Saviour of mankind, believing in Him as the only Mediator between God and man. He should cultivate truth and justice, brotherly kindness and charity, devotion and piety, concord and unity, and obedience to the laws...His conduct should be guided by wisdom and prudence, and marked by honesty, temperance and sobriety. The glory of God and the welfare of man, the honour of his Sovereign, and the good of his country, should be the motives of his actions.' The religious beliefs and social expectations of the Orange Order were often summarised in the maxim, 'Civil and religious liberty for all.'

These principles had meant much to Jeffrey as he endeavoured to endorse them, and his ardour for the values and ethics of the Order soon led to his promotion to leadership posts within it.

He began by being appointed as Secretary to Orangefield L.O.L. 564, Ballinran, his home Lodge, and after a number of years he was elected as Deputy District Master of Mourne District, which had almost a thousand members. Having served in that position for some time he had been appointed to an even more senior post, that of Assistant Secretary to the Grand Orange Lodge of County Down.

The phone call twenty minutes before had set him off on the upward spiral again. He had now become an Assistant Grand Master of the Orange Order in Ireland.

This appointment meant that he was expected to attend another series of executive meetings and Jeffrey enjoyed it. He was still familiarizing himself with the diverse demands of this responsible position when his negotiating skills and faith in God were both put to the test over a tense two-day period.

It was Sunday, July 9, 1995, and the traditional march organised by the Portadown, County Armagh, Orange Lodges to commemorate the Battle of the Somme had been refused permission to proceed from Drumcree Parish Church, where a service had been held, back into the centre of the town.

About nine o'clock that evening Jeffrey had a phone call from Jim Molyneaux, leader of the Ulster Unionist Party. He had been monitoring events as the day had gone on and recognised that there was an ugly set of circumstances developing in Portadown. Tempers were being lost, patience was wearing thin, anything could happen.

His message was urgent. He wanted to know if Jeffrey could meet him early the next morning at Carleton Street Orange Hall in Portadown to see if there was any way they could help defuse an increasingly volatile situation.

They agreed a time and when Jeffrey met James Molyneaux they began, as leader of the Ulster Unionist Party, and the most senior member of the Orange Institution present, to talk to the different people and groups concerned. It was important to hear their slant on the story and suggestions for a solution. They had separate meetings with the officers of the Portadown District Orange Lodge, the local Police Commanders and David Trimble, the MP for the Upper Bann constituency.

Mr. Molyneaux had to leave Portadown at lunchtime to fly to London and he asked Jeffrey to remain and continue the negotiations, liasing with Rev. Martin Smyth and himself when necessary and possible.

During the afternoon Jeffrey and David Trimble had a series of discussions with the Police Commanders on the ground at Drumcree and the leaders of the Portadown Orange District, to see if an accommodation could be reached.

It appeared, however, that it couldn't.

It was a hot day, and by late afternoon crowds of Orangemen from all over Northern Ireland began to converge on the site. All the approach roads to Drumcree Parish Church were blocked solid for miles. An almost carnival atmosphere existed for a while. Sunburnt men in shirtsleeves sat around and chatted, declaring that they weren't going anywhere until they walked down the Garvaghy Road. That was not looking as though it were going to happen in the immediate future, however, and Jeffrey Donaldson and the other members of the Orange Order negotiating team realised that the longer this stand-off continued the more difficult it would be to contain.

Hundreds more men were arriving on the site every hour, determined to support their 'brethren' from Portadown. As evening approached with a line of police Landrovers still blocking any access to the route of the proposed march for a second night, the would-be marchers became even more frustrated. 'Brotherly kindness and charity' were becoming less apparent and it was obvious that all the 'wisdom and prudence' that could be mustered would be required.

Some of the more recently arrived younger men, many of whom were not members of the Orange Order, began to hurl abuse and then occasional missiles at the police lines. Jeffrey Donaldson found himself in a buffer zone between the two groups, trying to make the more militant young men see that their only answer was to negotiate with the authorities. Bottles, bricks and batons flew through the air as he tried to persuade them that attacking the police, who were only there to do their job, wasn't going to advance their cause in any way.

In the midst of the melee Jeffrey was conscious of a real sense of God's presence and an assurance that no harm would come to him. It was an extraordinary feeling to experience such inner peace in the eye of the storm that was gathering all around him.

David Trimble, Rev. Ian Paisley and Harold Gracey, District Master of Portadown Orange Lodge, also took turns at attempting to convince the increasingly hostile crowd that they could broker a settlement.

This was going to take time, and Jeffrey was well aware that time was not on their side. Some who saw it as the right of the

Orangemen to 'walk the public highway,' as they had done without objection for so many years, were threatening to force the issue into all out confrontation.

Later on that evening Jeffrey joined Rev. Ian Paisley and David Trimble in Edward Street Police Station in Portadown and there they met with the Police Commanders to put forward their suggestions for solving the current impasse. These proposals were considered by the police and passed on by them to the Mediation Network. This hastily convened group had begun shuttling between the representatives of the residents of the Garvaghy Road and the Police Commanders.

It seemed hopeless.

No accommodation could be reached.

It was late, and dark, when Jeffrey returned to Drumcree Parish Church to spend the night, with hundreds of others, in the Church Hall. No one slept. An air of uncertainty, of uneasy anticipation, filled the air. Jeffrey moved around chatting to various groups of resolute insomniacs. They were going to stay there, they told him, until they were allowed to 'walk' their traditional route. He sensed their determination and yet if the stance of the Garvaghy Road residents, as reported by the Mediation Network, remained the same, it was doubtful if they would ever achieve that objective.

Talks began early next morning. There was a meeting with the police team in Rev. Pickering's house shortly after dawn, to assess what progress had been made during the night.

It would seem that there had been very little, but the senior police officers present held out some hope of the impasse being broken.

There were crowds of people around when he came out of that

meeting even though it was still only seven o'clock in the morning. Many had stayed the night, either in the hall or outside. Those who hadn't been resident overnight had already begun to arrive for another day. The media were there in force. The deadlock at Drumcree had become national news.

A solution to the situation would have to be found. And soon.

Recognising that all human efforts seemed to be making little headway, Jeffrey Donaldson decided to speak to God about it. The Parish Church was open and he slipped into it quietly and sat down on one of the pews near the back. He then bowed his head and asked God, 'with whom all things are possible,' to intervene in the minds of all involved, and show them a way out so that further confrontation could be avoided. He was deeply concerned that if the situation continued to deteriorate, and yet more clashes occurred, then people could end up being seriously hurt.

After a few minutes spent in prayer and quiet reflection Jeffrey returned to the bustle of the Church Hall for breakfast. This was being served in relays and he chatted to others who were also patiently waiting their turn. The sole topic of conversation was the ongoing stalemate and the prospect of escalating unrest. It was now the eleventh of July, and if this wasn't settled soon there could be more than bonfires burning tonight. There was every possibility that some of the more militant factions in the community would decide to take the law into their own hands.

With breakfast over Jeffrey moved out of the hall and down towards the police lines for, as he had expected, another day of anxious arbitration. He quickly became conscious, however, of an unusual busyness. All the aimless hanging around and waiting seemed to be over. And it was!

News had just come through that the members of Portadown

Orange Lodge were to be permitted to complete the march back into the town.

When the parade had formed up and then eventually moved off in the direction of Portadown Jeffrey Donaldson remained at Drumcree with the thousands of others who were preparing to make their own way home.

Before he was ready to return to his own car he was interviewed by a reporter from Ulster Television News.

He asked Jeffrey the question to which he thought so many people would want to know the answer. "Do you see this as a victory for the Orange Order?"

"This is a victory for common sense," came the Assistant Grand Master's instant reply.

It was true. It was. But Jeffrey also knew that it was much more than that.

It was an answer to prayer.

He had prayed that God would intervene to prevent the situation spiralling out of control. And he hadn't been alone in that either.

Thousands of other concerned Christians all across the province had been praying the very same thing.

17
THE LIGHT AT THE END
OF THE TUNNEL

The peaceful resolution of the standoff at Drumcree came at a significant period in the recent turbulent history of Northern Ireland. The IRA had called a ceasefire in 1994 after twenty-five years of devastating violence in which both republican and loyalist attack and counter attack had seen over three thousand people killed and thousands more critically injured and maimed for life.

The political impasse continued, however, despite the reduced level of violence and a gradual return to something resembling normality on the streets of the towns and cities. With this encouraging progress having been made the Government recognised that it was imperative that they initiate dialogue between the various political groupings with a view to finding a viable way forward in the province.

As a first step towards this goal, the Prime Minister, John Major, decided to hold elections to a Forum which would provide the basis for the negotiations. All parties elected to this body would be represented at further talks to help resolve the deadlock.

The Forum elections were called for May 30, 1996, and they were to be conducted, for the first time in any Northern Ireland poll, using a complicated voting procedure known as the List System. This involved all interested political parties submitting a 'slate' of candidates in each constituency. The slate, or list, was to be submitted in order of preference, thus the higher up any candidate was on the party list, the greater his or her chances of becoming elected. When it came to polling day the electorate were then asked to cast their vote for a party rather than an individual candidate. Consequently the higher the vote the party received in any constituency the more candidates from their list would be accorded places in the proposed Forum.

The Ulster Unionist Party meeting to draw up the list for Lagan Valley was held in Lisburn Orange Hall in late April 1996.

Jeffrey Donaldson spent any spare minute he had on the day of the meeting planning his approach for that evening. Not only did he make out the main points of a speech on the political issues of most concern to his party at that time but he also spent occasional moments in prayer. He asked God to guide him throughout the evening's proceedings and to show him very clearly if this was to be the first rung on the ladder of a political career.

This would be the first time that Jeffrey had allowed his name to go forward for political office since becoming a Christian and it would also prove the litmus test for the move to Lagan Valley. Had it been, as he had been forced to imagine on a number of unhappy occasions since, a mistake based on a selfish ambition, or was it, as he had been thoroughly convinced at the time, a strategic move in God's great overall plan for his life?

He should have a definitive answer to that question by ten or eleven o'clock that night. And Jeffrey knew that the selection meeting was set to be an unpleasant affair. Taking into account the ongoing, and indeed intensifying, acrimony and bitterness on the local Management Committee, a number of the members would be actively opposed to his selection as one of their representatives.

With the level of animosity he was expecting to encounter Jeffrey thought that he might find it difficult to make it on to the final 'slate' of five candidates. He was well aware, too, though, that if he were to stand any realistic chance of being elected to the Forum he would not only have to make it on to the list, but end up amongst the top three in the order of names submitted.

More than two hundred delegates from the constituency crowded into the Orange Hall for the selection meeting. Each of the candidates was expected to address the assembled gathering and then answer a number of questions from the floor.

Much to Jeffrey's relief he was chosen to speak last. As he began to address the meeting he could sense that he had the sympathetic ear of many of the constituency representatives, but certainly not all. This was borne out by the nature of some of the questions put to him 'from the floor' after he had delivered his speech. Jeffrey suspected that a number of the delegates had been primed and then 'planted' in various locations in the Hall to ask controversial questions in an attempt to trick him into saying something that would prove unacceptable.

It was amazing but that was when Jeffrey felt most calm. God had answered his prayer for help and guidance. He seemed to perform better under pressure.

With all the questions satisfactorily answered it was time for the first vote. This was to determine the final five on the selection 'slate.' When the results were declared Jeffrey was happy to have been chosen as one of the five.

That was only the start. It was like progressing through the qualifying rounds of a sporting tournament. The real contest was still to come.

The next vote was the crucial one. This second ballot was to place the candidates in order on the selection list, with the possibility that only the first two, or at the most, three, would go forward to the Forum.

There was loud applause from Jeffrey's supporters and glum faces amongst his antagonists when the result of this important vote was announced,

Jeffrey Donaldson had received two-thirds of all the votes cast, with the other four candidates sharing the remaining third among them. He was delighted, relieved, and reassured.

The doubts that had plagued him on his 'down days' for nearly three years had been finally and conclusively put to rest. He took this overwhelming vote in the selection procedure as a sure sign from God that he was to continue to pursue his career as a politician. And that he was to continue it in Lagan Valley.

Although Jeffrey was now totally persuaded that the move to Moira had been in God's plan, and the decision to stand for Lagan Valley was a progression in that programme, it was obvious that others were going to prove more difficult to convince. This group, now shown to be in the minority in the constituency, were nonetheless amongst the number one candidate's most vociferous opponents, and they were not going to succumb and accept the decision of that meeting as a final verdict. The 'blow-in' had effectively dealt their personal ambitions for ultimate advancement within the party a staggering, if not a knockout blow. They would have 'to get their own back' somehow.

The election campaign, which took place through the month of May, was a fairly uneventful affair as the electorate were being asked to compare the policy of parties rather than the personalities of the participants. It did, however, allow Jeffrey to get out on the hustings for the first time in years, and he was encouraged by the response of the people he met 'on the doors' in the towns and villages of the constituency.

When the election was held at the end of the month the Ulster Unionist Party was given enough votes to have three seats from Lagan Valley in the new Forum.

Jeffrey Donaldson was on his way back to Stormont as his constituency's first choice candidate.

There had been occasional glimpses of light at the end of the dark tunnel of frustration and opposition he had battled through since leaving Kilkeel. More recently he had been able to actually distinguish the shape of the end of the tunnel framed in daylight.

Now Jeffrey had emerged from that tunnel completely. He wasn't driven by a sense of his own importance this time, however, as he had been when first taking his seat in Stormont more than a decade before.

He was now travelling on a track that he believed had been laid, and was being maintained, by God, and he was acutely conscious that he had burst forth into the full glare of public responsibility, accountability and scrutiny once more.

It was an exacting load to have to carry, but the signals had all turned green ahead.

The question was, would they stay that way?

18
IS PEACE POSSIBLE?

The delegates to the newly elected Forum at Stormont set to work within weeks to try and fulfil the brief they had been given. With so many shades of opinion represented, no one ever imagined that it would be easy to find a way forward for the province, but the Forum was at least a base from which to set the wheels of negotiation turning.

Sinn Fein were excluded from the talks process as the IRA had broken their ceasefire in February of that year, 1996. The bomb which they planted at Canary Wharf in London killed two people, injured many more and caused widespread damage to property.

All of the remaining political parties were asked to select negotiating teams, from those members elected to the Forum, to operate at different levels within the framework of the discussions. It would be the responsibility of the most senior team from each party to represent that party's position before the three Government-appointed independent arbiters, General John de Chastelain from Canada, Harri Holkeri, a former Prime Minister of Finland and Senator George Mitchell from the USA.

David Trimble, who had been elected leader of the Ulster Unionist Party following the retirement of James Molyneaux in September 1995, headed up the UUP delegation. The other four members of his team were Reg Empey, Ken Maginnis, John Taylor and Jeffrey Donaldson, who was the youngest member.

Before negotiations commenced all parties engaging in the talks were asked to sign up to a set of principles which had been drawn up by the three convenors. These were later to become widely referred to as the Mitchell Principles of democracy and non-violence.

They were presented to the parties as follows: -

'To reach an agreed political settlement and to take the gun out of Irish politics, there must be commitment and adherence to fundamental principles of democracy and non-violence. Participants in all-party negotiations should affirm their commitment to such principles.

Accordingly, we recommend that the parties to such negotiations affirm their total and absolute commitment:

a.   To democratic and exclusively peaceful means of resolving political issues;

b.   To the total disarmament of all paramilitary organizations;

c.   To agree that such disarmament must be verifiable to the satisfaction of an independent commission;

d.   To renounce for themselves, and to oppose any effort by others, to use force, or to threaten to use force, to influence the course or the outcome of all-party negotiations;

e.   To agree to abide by the terms of any agreement reached in all-party negotiations and to resort to democratic and exclusively peaceful methods in trying to alter any aspect of that outcome with which they may disagree; and,

f.   To urge that "punishment" killings and beatings stop and to take effective steps to prevent such actions.'

One of the first tasks of the senior negotiating groups, after their parties had all signed up to the Mitchell Principles, was to appoint a Chairman to conduct future proceedings. A number of names were considered, one of which was President Clinton's special envoy to Northern Ireland, the former Majority Leader of the U.S. Senate, George Mitchell.

Jeffrey reckoned that he was more qualified than some to pass judgement in this regard since he already knew the Senator, having met him on a number of previous occasions. This came about because Jim Molyneaux had appointed him, as a Party Officer, to develop the Ulster Unionist Party's links with the U.S. capital. It was obvious that this assignment could only be effectively fulfilled by undertaking a few trans-Atlantic crossings and so Jeffrey made a number of trips to Washington. These included visits to both The White House and Capitol Hill. He had been present at the first meeting between the Ulster Unionist leader and an incumbent American President when Jim Molyneaux met Bill Clinton in a room off the Oval Office. George Mitchell had been a member of the American deputation they had met that day, and Jeffrey had been impressed by his thorough appreciation of the situation in Northern Ireland and his apparently robust opposition to terrorism. After all it was he who had drafted the Principles of democracy and non-violence.

Thus, having considered all the positive pointers the leadership of the UUP concluded that his appointment as Chairman of the talks should not be a matter of undue concern for unionists.

There were other unionists, though, who were strongly opposed to the involvement of the Clinton administration in the affairs of Northern Ireland.

The talks were scheduled to take place in Castle Buildings, which despite its somewhat distinguished sounding name is nothing more than a rather nondescript office block of little architectural significance in the Stormont estate. One of the first meetings of the senior negotiating teams to be held at this unimpressive venue had one single item on the agenda, the Appointment of a Chairman.

A lively discussion took place on the issue and a vote was called. It was then that the first sign of unionist division emerged with the Ulster Unionist Party supporting the appointment of Senator Mitchell and the Democratic Unionist Party vigorously opposing it. When the votes were counted, George Mitchell had been accorded the required quota for appointment and he was consequently installed as Chairman of the talks process.

The DUP team were incensed at this development and there were angry exchanges between them and their UUP counterparts as they left the room.

Jeffrey was unhappy to see this occur for he firmly believed that more could be achieved for the good of his country at the talks if all shades of opinion within unionism were to present a broadly united front. On the other hand, with his growing understanding of the U.S. administration in Washington and their apparently more balanced approach to Northern Ireland, he also felt that the appointment of Senator George Mitchell as Chairman was the proper decision in the circumstances. He reasoned that if unionists rejected George Mitchell it would result in Washington becoming more hostile to their position, and reverting to a deeply unbalanced view of the Northern Ireland situation.

The negotiations began during the summer and progress was slow. Having appointed a Chairman the delegates then began attempting to agree an agenda for further talks. This proved difficult to finalise as different parties had different priorities.

IS PEACE POSSIBLE?

While the politicians were actively disagreeing about what should be on their agenda, however, the IRA was actively pursuing its single-minded agenda of armed aggression, in total disregard of the stuttering start at Stormont.

On Monday, October 7, 1996, Jeffrey learnt with dismay that two car bombs had gone off in Thiepval Army Barracks in Lisburn, in the heart of the Lagan Valley constituency he had been elected to represent at the talks. He rushed to the Barracks to discover a scene of devastation. Thirty-two people had been injured and one of these, a Warrant Officer, was later to die from the injuries he sustained. He had only been ten yards from the first car when it exploded.

A Television News team interviewed Jeffrey, seeking his reaction to the bombing. He gave it, contending that it was pointless for a number of elected representatives to sit up at Stormont, trying to agree a way forward towards peace in Northern Ireland while the men of violence insisted on continuing their reign of terror.

When the interview was over Jeffrey began reflecting on the words he had just used. 'A way forward towards peace in Northern Ireland.'

Was there such a thing as 'a way forward towards peace in Northern Ireland?' he wondered.

When he was a mere schoolboy his dad had remarked after a civil disturbance in Newcastle, that this was 'just the start of it.'

He had been right.

Where, though, or when, was it going to end?

In peace?

19
SELECTION FOR ELECTION

Having stepped down from the leadership of the Ulster Unionist Party, Jim Molyneaux, who was still the MP for Lagan Valley, was knighted by Her Majesty The Queen and became Sir James. With a different round of engagements to fulfil and responsibilities to undertake following this honour, the new knight advised the UUP Lagan Valley Constituency Association in the autumn of 1996 that he did not intend to seek re-election to Parliament in the next General Election, due to be held the following year.

Was this the moment Jeffrey Donaldson had been waiting for?

With his high profile within the Ulster Unionist Party and his involvement as a member of the senior negotiating team in the continuing talks process in the Forum, he was in a strong position to seek the nomination as the party's candidate to succeed his mentor and friend.

There were others, however, who did not see it that way. They were the malevolent minority on the Senior Management Committee who had campaigned so actively to have Jeffrey sidelined in the election to the Forum and who had lost face so dramatically when he had come top of the poll with a huge majority. This fresh-faced, clean-cut, smooth-talking, johnny-come-lately would not be given the opportunity to represent their constituency in the national Parliament if they had anything to do with it. Having seen their plans thwarted in the previous selection for election procedure less than a year before they were determined to learn by their mistakes. They would mount a 'stop

Donaldson at all costs campaign.' It was pay-back time.

In late 1996 the date of the meeting of constituency representatives to choose a candidate to contest the Lagan Valley seat in Westminster on behalf of the Ulster Unionist Party was announced. It was to be held on Friday, January 17, 1997.

Those anxious to forestall Jeffrey's selection urged two candidates, David Campbell and Ivan Davis, to put their names forward in opposition to him. David Campbell, who had finished second in the Forum election, had been a Lisburn councillor before marrying and going to reside in East Antrim. Ivan Davis was the third of Lagan Valley's representatives in the Forum and he was also a prominent Lisburn councillor.

It seemed a strange decision to force both these men to the forefront of the fray. Would the scheming strategists not have stood a better chance of seeing their closest rival beaten into second place by throwing their weight behind one single candidate, rather than fielding two?

Despite those apparently plotting his downfall there were many of his colleagues in the party who urged him strongly to seek the nomination as UUP candidate for Lagan Valley. Jeffrey was well aware that he had been supported by two thirds of the delegates at the Forum selection meeting and he had no reason to believe that anything had changed as far as they were concerned. The insistence of those supporting him and telling him that he was 'the only man for the job' was only one of a number of factors which led him to put his name forward for selection.

Another was his personal interest in the political scene and his desire to have the privilege of representing Lagan Valley at Westminster. Jeffrey had developed a great love for this constituency, and a genuine admiration for its people, since coming to live in Moira three years before. He had learnt much about what was required of a Member of Parliament when working for Enoch Powell and Jim Molyneaux, and had enjoyed his time in Stormont as Assembly member for South Down. Although still only in his mid-thirties he felt that he had adequate personal experience to qualify him for the position.

Perhaps the most important consideration, though, was the conclusion he had come to after a period of profound heart-searching, that God was leading him into a career in politics. Jeffrey had never forgotten the letter he had received from the girl in the Youth Fellowship when still in Kilkeel. It had contained a quotation from the Bible about 'the plans' God had for him. These were 'plans to prosper him, not to harm him, plans to give him hope and a future.'

He reasoned that if God's plans for his future included representing the people of Lagan Valley in the House of Commons, then he had better put himself in the running to secure the seat. Then God would undoubtedly indicate whether this was the next stage in His plan for him or not.

In early January, Jeffrey decided that he would endeavour to call and visit as many of the delegates as possible, rather than merely writing to them. He felt that this would serve a positive purpose in that it would allow them to express their opinions and concerns to him while affording him the opportunity to present his case in person to them. He had always considered it important to hear what the 'grass-roots' of the party were thinking and making one-to-one contact with them in their own homes was one of the most effective ways of achieving this. As he moved from town to town and from one delegate's house to another within the constituency Jeffrey felt that there was a growing groundswell of support for his position, but it would be unwise to take anything for granted.

The opposition hadn't gone away.

As the date of the meeting drew nearer they became ever more diligent in their attempt to derail his campaign. With just one week to go to the crucial meeting, the banner headline on the front page of the local newspaper, the 'Ulster Star,' brought disturbing news for Jeffrey. Ivan Davis had announced that he was withdrawing from the race for the nomination for Lagan Valley and had declared his support for David Campbell.

So that was why both of them had put their names forward initially, Jeffrey Donaldson and his followers concluded. They suspected that it was little more than a calculated, cynical ploy to have one withdraw to focus attention on the other, and away from Jeffrey, in the run up to decision day. It was becoming clear that these people would stop at nothing in order to make sure that Jeffrey Donaldson would not be chosen as the constituency's candidate to fight the General Election later in the year.

All this apparent conspiracy and undisguised hostility was to prove counter-productive, however, for it made Jeffrey's followers all the more determined that their candidate **would** secure the nomination.

The battle lines had been drawn for yet another potentially bruising encounter.

With David Campbell, Jeffrey Donaldson and two other less prominent contenders in the field, the scene was set for a nail-biting showdown.

Lisburn Orange Hall was packed to the doors on the evening of Friday, January 17, 1997. Over three hundred delegates had assembled for what they all knew would be a significant, and possibly difficult, meeting.

The candidates drew lots for the order of speaking and Jeffrey was to be the final speaker just as he had been in the Forum election meeting the previous year. This meant a long wait in the anteroom of the hall while the other candidates addressed the meeting in turn, but it allowed him time to reconsider the main points of the speech he had prepared, and commit himself and his future to God in short, silent prayer.

When eventually it came his turn to speak Jeffrey began by detailing what he considered to be his suitability to represent the gathered company, and the people of the entire constituency, as their Member of Parliament. He focussed both on his senior position within the party and the valuable experience gained while working with two of its former MPs, including the outgoing Member for Lagan Valley. There could be no doubt in anyone's mind, as he presented the width and depth of his involvement in the party's affairs over the preceding sixteen years, that it was an impressive track record for a thirty-four year old.

Switching then from the past, and his personal background, he went on to deal with some problems which were currently causing concern within the constituency and his proposals for tackling these issues.

The remainder of his speech was spent in outlining his vision for the future of Northern Ireland. This contained two elements. There had to be, initially, an end of all terrorist activity and that in turn would create a situation in which his second goal could be realised. That was a country at peace with itself and secure within the United Kingdom.

His remarks were well received by the majority of the audience and the questions that followed were generally helpful with the exception of a couple that had probably been planned and planted by the opposition. When Jeffrey had dealt effectively with all the questions posed to him, whether out of a desire for information or an attempt at defamation, it was time for the all-important vote.

The half an hour it took for the votes to be counted seemed like half a day.

Jeffrey moved around the hall with Eleanor, chatting to a number of their friends. It was difficult, for no one dared anticipate the result of the vote, but Jeffrey was encouraged by the number of people who voiced support. There were others, though, who weren't speaking to him at all, and those were the people whose votes he had to worry about.

All eyes turned towards the door of the kitchen when, at last, it opened. People who had been circulating in the hall scurried back to their seats as the scrutineer emerged to hand the result to the Chairman of the Association.

The room, which had been buzzing with friendly chatter two minutes before, fell suddenly silent. The chairman unfolded the piece of paper, slowly and deliberately. He glanced at it for a few seconds, cleared his throat, stood to his feet and reached for the microphone.

The moment of truth had arrived.

In true electoral style the total vote recorded for each candidate was to be read out in alphabetical order. This meant that the vote for David Campbell, Jeffrey's only realistic rival for the nomination, would be announced before his, and thus allow the delegates waiting in the hall to come to an immediate conclusion on the outcome.

They didn't have to be brilliant mathematicians to work it out either.

When the chairman read out the result for 'Donaldson, Jeffrey,' a spontaneous cheer broke out and rang around the hall until the walls seemed to vibrate. Jeffrey had been accorded the vote of two thirds of the delegates present for the second time within a year.

The jubilation subsided briefly to allow the chairman to complete his announcement. All that remained for him to do was to formalise what everyone already knew. Jeffrey Donaldson had been selected as the Ulster Unionist Party candidate to contest the Lagan Valley seat in the next General Election.

After the meeting had been formally closed Jeffrey's supporters crowded around the new parliamentary candidate with their congratulations. There were hugs and handshakes all round. People were reacting as though he were already on his way to Westminster, but Jeffrey kept reminding them that this was only the first stage on that journey.

He had been selected.

But would he ever be elected?

His name would appear on a ballot paper.

But would he ever sit in the House of Commons?

20
THE CANVASS, THE CONTEST
AND THE COUNT

There was now a lot of hard work to be done.

Within the next few weeks Jeffrey began assembling a campaign team to help him prepare for the General Election which was due to be held later that year. The former election agent to Enoch Powell knew the demands of the job better than most and he appointed Barry Fitzsimons, the UUP constituency vice-chairman to act in that capacity for him.

Jeffrey found it helpful during that early planning period to dip into the fund of experience gained during his days in South Down. It was also most encouraging to receive a letter of support from the former MP who had taught him so much about the practicalities of politics. The short note from his London address read,

> *Dear Jeffrey,*
>
> *This brings my best wishes for your success in the coming election and thereafter. I am delighted you have the opportunity to contest Lagan Valley.*
>
> *Yours ever,*
>
> *Enoch Powell.*

The pressure of preparing for an election campaign came in addition to Jeffrey's already busy round of engagements and against a background of continuing sporadic terrorist activity. He was drafting out leaflets, holding planning meetings with his team, and addressing campaign meetings in hotel rooms and local halls while still engaged in a full programme of discussions at Stormont.

The ongoing violence gave those involved in the peace talks a powerful incentive to succeed. The Forum met in plenary session on Fridays to debate the issues that had emerged during the week, and the current security situation was kept under review in those sittings.

On February 12, 1997, less than a month after Jeffrey had been selected to stand as the Ulster Unionist candidate in Lagan Valley, Lance-Bombardier Stephen Restorick was murdered. The twenty-three year old soldier from the Royal Horse Artillery was shot dead by an IRA sniper as he was speaking into a car to a lady motorist at a security checkpoint in Bessbrook, County Armagh.

When the tragic death of this young soldier was raised at the full session of the Forum a few days later the delegates from the unionist parties recorded their sympathies to his family while pointing out the pathos of such pointless killings. This they said was best demonstrated by the words of the woman who had been with him when he was shot. In a poignant radio interview, broadcast the morning after the murder, she said, "He was there smiling, and a little while later he was dead. I watched that young man dying. It's the saddest thing I have ever seen."

Meanwhile back at Westminster, Prime Minister John Major had lost his majority in the House of Commons. He continued in power for a few weeks but soon recognised that it was impractical to attempt to carry on in that position. On Monday, March 17 he called a General Election.

Electioneering could now begin in earnest. All the careful, tentative preparations that had been made were about to be put to the test.

The finely tuned high-powered racing car that had been idling over on the starting grid was about to hit full throttle. The race was on.

Jeffrey Donaldson had been so accustomed to organising campaign strategy for others that he couldn't help but take a hands-on approach with his own.

He helped supervise the printing of posters and organise teams of volunteers to have these put up all over the constituency. He helped design a promotional leaflet and arrange to have thousands of these produced and then hand-delivered across Lagan Valley.

When Jeffrey was satisfied that his picture was high up on nearly every lamppost, and that there was a volunteer assigned to every letterbox, Barry and he sat down with their next goal in view.

Since Jeffrey had always maintained that it was more profitable to meet potential voters in person on the doorsteps than to preach to the converted in Orange Halls, they drew up a canvass schedule to cover the whole constituency in the time that was left. This was not an easy task given that Lagan Valley had one of the largest concentrations of population of any constituency in the United Kingdom. They were helped by the fact that British Summer Time had just begun, and banking on longer evenings they worked out an extensive programme of canvass. This was designed to make use of every possible hour of daylight from mid-morning until dusk, six days a week.

It was physically challenging but politically gratifying to be out meeting the constituents. Jeffrey reckoned that he couldn't profess to represent people whom he had never met. Nor could he realistically expect the electorate to cast their votes for someone who showed no interest whatsoever in them as people, however sound and acceptable his policies.

He began his intensive canvass of Lagan Valley in Lisburn, the large town at the heart of the constituency. One day he could be working in a large housing estate in the town and the next in a more modern development of privately owned dwellings on its fringes. These newer building programmes had sprung up on every main road out of the town, gradually swallowing up a few of the many fertile farms in its hinterland.

With Lisburn adequately covered it was then time to concentrate on the other main towns and villages in the constituency. These included the historic town of Dromore, the large village of Hillsborough which contains the official residence of Her Majesty The Queen in Northern Ireland, and his home village of Moira. It was particularly pleasant to be out and about on his 'home patch' meeting many of his neighbours and others whom he had got to know at church or met at local events, in the course of a day's canvass.

By the eve of the election Jeffrey had called on most of the homes in Lagan Valley and had visited many contrasting places, witnessed a range of widely differing life styles and listened to all shades of political opinion from possible constituents. He was generally encouraged by the canvass, for whether in the village of Dromara, nestling amongst the drumlins of County Down and overlooked by the gentle slopes of Slieve Croob, or in Dunmurry, situated on the southern edge of the city of Belfast and overlooked by its towering high-rise flats, the response was the same. People thanked him for taking the time to call with them and assured him of their vote.

It was one thing to say it, though.

Only polling day would reveal if they were prepared to put their promise into practice.

Jeffrey was up early that May Day morning. He, his agent and the army of tireless volunteers who had helped him throughout his campaign had done what they could in the previous six weeks. Now it was all down to the voters. And Jeffrey still wanted to meet as many of them as possible as they cast their vote.

Barry had planned a route that would allow Eleanor and he to visit every polling station in the constituency together in the course of that decisive day. It was an onerous undertaking but they managed it, taking time to speak to presiding officers, poll clerks and party representatives as well as the most crucial group of all, the men and women who were coming to cast their vote, as they went.

The count was held the next morning in Dromore Leisure Centre which is located on the banks of the River Lagan, just outside the town. Ironically, the count for South Down, Jeffrey's former Assembly constituency, was also taking place in the same building.

Again it was an early start. Jeffrey and Eleanor were joined by Jeffrey's parents and a few other family members, and his election agent and key members of his campaign team to observe the progress of the count. The media were also present in force, ready to broadcast the result of two crucial constituencies to the nation as soon as they were announced.

As the first boxes were opened the signs looked good for Jeffrey. There seemed to be a fair proportion of the votes for him. It was too early by far to be anything resembling confident, however. The Ulster Unionist Party candidate was always aware from his experiences with Enoch that boxes from different districts within the constituency were liable to contain an alternative voting pattern, and this was unpredictable. There were two other factors, the effect of which it would be impossible to assess, and which caused him some nagging concern.

The first was that he was unsure what impact the recent redrawing of the constituency boundaries would have on the unionist vote within Lagan Valley. The other was the fact that the Democratic Unionist Party had fielded a candidate against him. This party hadn't opposed James Molyneaux in the previous election but since Jeffrey Donaldson was 'the new boy on the block' they decided to put someone up against him. It was difficult to predict the outcome of that intervention also.

As the morning went on the ballot papers, bound together in bundles of a hundred, began to pile up steadily in the box marked DONALDSON. Clearly Jeffrey didn't need to have worried unduly about what would now appear to have been little more than minor considerations. The result, though still not predictable, had begun to look hopeful.

By lunchtime the turnout across the constituency had been calculated at just over sixty-two per cent with a total poll of 44310.

There followed another tense period of agonising waiting during which the total vote for each candidate was being counted, checked and recorded. It was mid-afternoon before the Returning Officer was ready to declare the result for the Lagan Valley constituency. Before making his public announcement for the benefit of all the anxious family members, party workers and assembled media, he took the candidates and their election agents aside in a corner of the room to tell them first.

Jeffrey was very nervous. As he crossed to where the Returning Officer was waiting he was aware of a sense of destiny. This was the precise moment he had been anticipating for the past four months and which he felt God had been guiding him towards for the last six years.

The words, 'I know the plans I have for you,' flashed across his mind momentarily.

Was this to be the final unfolding of that promised plan?

It was!

The Returning Officer informed the small group of people clustered around him, officially, of something which they had long since come to suspect unofficially. Jeffrey Donaldson had been accorded the highest number of the votes cast and would thus be announced as the Member of Parliament for Lagan Valley.

It was difficult to keep his whole being in control and prevent his demeanour from betraying his secret until the Returning Officer made his public declaration. Again the votes were announced in alphabetical order and again the vote for 'Donaldson, Jeffrey,' was the second to be declared.

His vote of 24560 was greeted by enthusiastic and prolonged cheering and applause.

When this subsided the Returning Officer continued reading out the result for the remaining candidates but in truth nobody except themselves and their supporters was paying much attention. Jeffrey Donaldson had won more than half of the votes cast and more than all of them put together.

As the Returning Officer was announcing his majority of almost seventeen thousand and declaring that 'the said, Donaldson, Jeffrey, has been duly elected to serve as the Member of Parliament for this constituency,' 'the said Donaldson, Jeffrey' was overcome.

The result was astounding, far beyond anything he had ever expected or anyone had ever predicted.

Standing on the platform, waving to his supporters, he recalled the sentiments of a verse from the Bible, which he had found particularly reassuring during difficult, doubting days. He couldn't remember the exact words amidst all the jubilation erupting around him but the gist of it was that God was able to do far more for us than we could ever ask or hope.

It was true. He had just demonstrated it in a very practical way.

There was no time to dwell on it, however.

His supporters rushed forward to shake him by the hand, slap him on the back and congratulate him on his resounding success.

Reporters from various newspapers, radio programmes and TV channels were waiting patiently for him to extricate himself from the crowd of well-wishers so that they could interview him.

"What is your vision for Lagan Valley?" they were anxious to know.

"How do you account for your massive majority?" they asked.

"Will you still be involved in the talks at Stormont now that you have been elected to Westminster?" others enquired.

The Honourable Member of Parliament for Lagan Valley had begun his first formal interviews, but he couldn't afford to delay long.

There was more to be seen to now than ever before.

Jeffrey Donaldson was on his way to The House of Commons.

21
ADDRESSING THE HOUSE

Within a week of the election Jeffrey was travelling to London to commence what was to be a completely new and immensely challenging phase of his life.

His close friend, and now Lord, James Molyneaux, whose wise counsel Jeffrey had so much appreciated in the past few years, helped him make the transition. It was a mighty one, too, from life in Northern Ireland to life in London, and from discussions and sessions in the recently constituted Forum at Stormont to the world of debate and tradition in the Mother of all Parliaments, the British House of Commons. Jim was glad that Jeffrey, whose attitude and ability he greatly admired, had been elected to assume his mantle as the Member of Parliament for Lagan Valley, and was more than happy to introduce him to the requirements and responsibilities of the position.

They crossed to London together on Tuesday, May 6, 1997. Jim had offered Jeffrey a bed for the night in the spare room of his flat in the capital and they chatted together late on into the evening before retiring. Jeffrey had many questions to ask, and his mentor had much practical advice to offer, in relation to the busy days ahead.

Jeffrey was amongst the first to arrive at Westminster early next morning, anxious to learn as much as possible about his new vocation. He was soon shown to the office that he had been allocated and began to try and make himself at home there. It was like being a senior pupil from a remote, but efficient, rural school or college arriving, armed with commendable qualifications, to begin a degree course at a distinguished university. No matter how much information he thought he had already gleaned from personal experience or from the recommendations of his colleagues, there was still so much to learn.

On that afternoon of Wednesday, May 7, Jeffrey attended his first formal sitting of the House of Commons where the business of the day was to elect the Speaker. He was intrigued by the various procedures that took place before the Right Honourable Betty Boothroyd MP was re-elected to the position she had performed so ably prior to the dissolution of the previous Parliament.

On the next day all the MPs had to file past the Government front bench and then sign the register on the Dispatch Box, but before signing they were required to swear the oath of allegiance to The Queen.

Jeffrey found this quite an exhilarating experience when it came his turn to step forward, for more than one reason. It was true that this symbolic act, for which he had been selected by almost twenty five thousand of the voters from Lagan Valley, signalled the opening of the door to an enormously responsible and important career. On a purely personal level, however, he was overtaken, for an instant, by a strange combination of spiritual reassurance and national pride when a copy of the Bible was handed to him to hold as he took the oath. His mind flipped back to the number of times he had been convinced that he was being directed towards that moment, by that Book. Wasn't it thrilling, too, he mused, to recognise that the handbook of Christianity, whose precepts and principles had been so diligently upheld by so many of the former Honourable Members, was still acknowledged as the ultimate icon of truth and justice?

He felt particularly honoured to swear the oath, as the words were presented to him. 'I swear by Almighty God that I will be faithful and bear true allegiance to Her Majesty Queen Elizabeth, and Her heirs and successors according to law, so help me God,' Jeffrey vowed, not only in word but also in heart.

Having taken the oath, he then proceeded to the front of the House where he shook hands with the Speaker, Betty Boothroyd. Hers would be the task of matching his name to his face during Commons debates in days to come, along with matching the names to the faces of all the other six hundred and fifty-eight MPs.

Such was the perceived fascination of the general public in Northern Ireland with the life of this new Member of Parliament that Radio Ulster sent an interview team over to London to follow him around on this, his first full day, in Parliament.

There was much to report as Jeffrey gave his reactions to the events and emotions of the day.

One of the most moving moments he had to recount for the listeners 'back home' was when he took his seat amongst the Ulster Unionist group on the shiny, green leather benches for the very first time. The General Election earlier in the month had seen the former Conservative Government defeated and a new Labour Government elected with a huge majority. The Ulster Unionist benches were on the Opposition side of the House, just across the aisle from the Conservatives and immediately behind the Scottish and Welsh Nationalists and the Liberal Democrats. Across the floor and slightly to the right of him, the new Prime Minister, Anthony Charles Lionel Blair, 'Tony' to his friends, had taken his seat amongst his chosen Ministers on the Government front bench ready to start his first full day in the country's top job.

It was all so thrilling. There was an obvious air of anticipation in the chamber. This was tinged by a certain anxious edginess arising from the unfamiliarity of it all in the new members and an eagerness to be getting on with it by the 'old hands.'

In the days that followed, Jeffrey sat engrossed as he listened to the exchanges across the floor in the course of the debate on the Queen's Speech, in which the recently elected Government had outlined its programme for that session of Parliament. There were times when he felt like pinching himself to make sure that he wasn't dreaming, and that this was actually happening. The sense of honour with which he had first entered the House, and the glow of pride with which he had taken the oath while holding the Bible, gradually gave way to an inexpressible awe that verged on disbelief. His thoughts floated off down memory-lane again, back to his childhood in Kilkeel. What, he wondered, is the eldest of a family of eight from an ordinary hard-working home away over there in the beautiful Kingdom of Mourne doing sitting on this privileged bench in the Mother of Parliaments?

It was a difficult sensation to shake off, but it wore away as Jeffrey gradually became more accustomed to an environment which seemed to be one magic mix of history and ceremony, authority and responsibility.

As he heard one new member after another give his or her maiden speech, his inevitable return to reality was greatly accelerated by the growing realisation that his turn would be coming up very soon. The day was fast approaching when he would have to stand up and address the House himself!

When allocating posts to his Westminster team, the party leader, David Trimble, had appointed Jeffrey Donaldson as the Ulster Unionist spokesman on Trade and Industry. With a debate on the Economy and European Affairs scheduled for Tuesday, May

20, it seemed an ideal time for the new Member for Lagan Valley to address the House of Commons for the first time.

He sought advice from Lord Molyneaux and David Trimble on procedure, and what he was expected to include in the speech, then set to work. It was obvious that he needed to include something about the location of his constituency, about those who had helped and advised him all along the way so far, and since the debate was on the Economy and European Affairs it might just be a good idea to mention something about the economy, or Europe, or both. But what, if anything, else?

Jeffrey had a week to consider these matters and decide upon the content of his speech, and when the big day came he was ready.

This was an outstanding event in the history of the Donaldson family and a number of them made the journey across from Northern Ireland to the capital for the occasion. Eleanor led the contingent to the visitor's gallery. His father and mother were there, too, and so were his sister Diane and brother Kingsley, and Diane's husband William. Aunt Mavis, his mother's sister who had settled in Luton travelled down to London by train to be with them all. It had to be something really special, she reckoned, to bring so many of her relations whom she saw so seldom, over to her 'side of the water.' And her nephew was speaking in the House of Commons too! She certainly wanted to be there for that!

All seven of them sat savouring the atmosphere of that impressive forum of political deliberation and debate, paying close attention to all that was going on, waiting for their big moment.

It came at 7.42 p.m. when the Speaker called upon 'Mr. Jeffrey Donaldson' to address the House.

Standing to his feet Jeffrey began by thanking the people of Lagan Valley who had elected him. He then gave a detailed description of the constituency with its pattern of market towns and picturesque villages, all set among the small fields of the many farms which dotted the surrounding countryside.

There followed a tribute to the two former MPs who had been instrumental in helping to mould him for that moment. They were Sir James Molyneaux, his predecessor, who had served in the House for more than twenty-five years, and 'another illustrious Member of the House, the Right Hon. Enoch Powell,' for whom he had acted as election agent when he was M.P. for South Down.

As spokesman for Trade and Industry he continued by making a plea on behalf of Northern Ireland's largest indigenous industry, agriculture. "The (farming) industry has suffered greatly in recent years, most recently because of the BSE crisis," he explained. "I urge the Government to give priority to the lifting of the ban on Northern Ireland beef... It is unjust that the previous Government was not prepared to allow Northern Ireland to take the lead towards the lifting of the export ban. I hope that the new Government will end that injustice and will give Northern Ireland agriculture the confidence that it so badly needs by urging Europe to lift the ban on Northern Ireland beef as soon as possible."

He went on to relate how that a group of staff and pupils on an educational visit to London from Wallace High School in Lisburn had been the first of his constituents to meet him in 'the precincts of the House.' Wallace High School's motto is 'esperance,' which means hope, and the MP for Lagan Valley focussed on the subject of hope for the remainder of his speech.

"That is what the House must offer the people of Northern Ireland," he told the assembled Members, "hope for a future free from the scourge of terrorism, where our people can enjoy full equality of citizenship within the United Kingdom.

Some people are cynical and say that great aspirations always come to a hopeless end. I rather like to think that great aspirations bring not a hopeless end but an endless hope. Hope is not just a nice option; it is essential to survival. It lifts our spirits and helps us to keep going."

It was then that Jeffrey, anxious to become publicly associated with the Bible and its teachings, quoted a set of promises from the Old Testament. They were the words from the reference Tommy Latimer had written on the flyleaf of the New Testament he had given to the seventeen year old in Hugh J. Scott's in Belfast, eighteen years earlier.

"According to Solomon's ancient Proverbs," he went on, "hope tells us to *'Trust in the Lord with all our heart, and lean not on our own understanding.'* It tells us to, *'In all our ways acknowledge Him and He shall direct our paths.'*"

Jeffrey then shifted the emphasis from Scripture quotation to an eminent Christian parliamentarian of a previous century by carrying on, "When William Wilberforce addressed the House 207 years ago this month for three and a half hours with what the great orator Edmund Burke called the greatest speech he had ever heard, he had an aspiration to see the practice of slavery banished from British dominions. He faced incredible opposition and his aspirations seemed hopeless, yet Wilberforce was drawn by hope based on his Christian convictions and he campaigned on until the House passed the Slavery Abolition Bill forty-four years later."

Having thus highlighted the triumph of hope against 'incredible' odds, Jeffrey concluded his maiden speech by outlining his desire for the people of his home province. "Northern Ireland, too, faces great problems," he said. "Its divisions have defied some of the greatest political minds in the world, but the problem is not hopeless. We, too, have a dream that peace may come and that all our citizens may learn to do justly, to love mercy, and to walk humbly with their God. We shall seek with all out heart and strength to bring about such a peace. I urge the Government to work towards that end in Northern Ireland, a fair and just peace, a real peace that recognises the rights of the people of Northern Ireland to determine their own political future, free from the threat of terrorist violence and political interference. That is the way to ensure that the hope for which the people of Northern Ireland yearn will not be snuffed out."

That was it. Jeffrey Donaldson resumed his seat. It was exactly 7.52. He had spoken for ten minutes. Seven people in the visitor's gallery beamed with pride as they looked down on this historic moment for their family.

The Speaker had invited Judy Mallaber, the newly elected MP for another Valley, Amber Valley, to follow Jeffrey and present her maiden speech to the House. The Donaldson contingent weren't particularly concerned about what she had to say, however, although another small group, who had been sitting eagerly waiting across from them, undoubtedly were.

Jeffrey's wife, parents and family members felt so proud of their man.

"Didn't he do well?" they whispered to each other with broad smiles.

Jeffrey sat below them, in a daze of relief and realization.

He wasn't paying a lot of attention to what Judy was saying either.

When standing for election he had vowed that if elected he would seek to serve God and Lagan Valley, in that order, to the best of his ability. And now he had been able to mention both of them in his first speech in one of the world's most respected government institutions.

His political career had stepped up a gear.

22
THERE'S ONLY ONE ANSWER

Shortly after that initial speech in the House of Commons Jeffrey received this most encouraging letter.

27 / 5/ 97
Dear Jeffrey,

*Thank you **SO** much for sending the Hansard. Congratulations on your speech and both of us thank you for what you said about Enoch.*

It was lovely to see you last week and it is splendid to be able to put the magic initials (MP) on your envelope now!

Love to you both, and come again when you can,

from

Pam.

Jeffrey greatly appreciated the continued support of his former mentor and his wife. Their obvious interest and enduring friendship were most gratifying.

He was now busier than ever in his dual role as Member of Parliament for Lagan Valley at Westminster and senior party representative for the constituency at Stormont. The talks in

Northern Ireland had been suspended in the run-up to the General Election but now that a new Government was in place they were set to resume.

The Prime Minister, Tony Blair, had appointed Mo Mowlam as the new Secretary of State for Northern Ireland and within days of arriving in the province she began meeting the political parties. She was anxious to evaluate their position and plan a programme to have the talks reconvened as soon as possible.

As part of this introductory and exploratory exercise she arranged to meet the Ulster Unionist Party's senior negotiating team in Parliament Buildings, Stormont, at 12.30 p.m. on Monday, June 16, 1997.

Jeffrey was listening to the midday News on the car radio as he motored up the long straight drive to the impressive building when he had the experience yet again of being stunned by an incomplete announcement.

"News is just coming in of a shooting in Lurgan," the newsreader began. "Two policemen on foot patrol have been shot at close range by gunmen who came up behind them. Their condition is not yet known."

Before attending any meeting with the Secretary of State, Jeffrey was sure that his fellow-members of the UUP talks team would want to know more about the circumstances surrounding this attack, and the condition of the two policemen. He made directly for David Trimble's room as soon as he entered the building, for Lurgan was one of the larger towns in his Upper Bann constituency.

The party leader made a number of phone calls and gradually the full horror of what had occurred began to unfold.

Constable John Graham and Reserve Constable David

Johnston, who worked as community policemen, had been on foot patrol in Church Walk, Lurgan, just yards from the RUC station where they were based. At around 11.45 a.m. two IRA gunmen had approached them and shot each of them in the head. Doctors from a nearby surgery had rushed to the aid of the police officers but it was too late. They were already dead.

The news of that shooting cast an ominous shadow over the UUP team's first meeting with the new Secretary of State. She had requested the meeting to acquaint herself with the party's vision for the way ahead in Northern Ireland. Any formal agenda had to be abandoned, however, as the party delegates were most anxious to urge upon her the need to deal effectively with the security situation and the continuing sporadic terrorist violence.

Later that week Jeffrey Donaldson MP attended the first funeral of a constituent. Although stationed in Lurgan, thirty-year old Reserve Constable Johnston, who had been married with two young children, had lived in Lisburn. As he sat with hundreds of other numbed mourners in St. Columba's Church in the town, Jeffrey heard the minister describe the killings as 'a slap in the face for those people of goodwill seeking peace.' He also found himself identifying entirely with the sentiments he went on to express when declaring that he 'would like to drag the killers by the scruff of the neck to face the questions of this grief-stricken family.'

As the heartbroken widow followed the coffin of her husband out of that church, amidst audible sobs from the huge crowd, Jeffrey Donaldson wondered where this was all going to end. He had asked himself that so often before, at a series of funerals that had marked him so deeply on a number of occasions right since childhood. There had been his two cousins, Samuel and Alex.

Donaldson, the politicians Robert Bradford and Edgar Graham, UDR Lance-Corporal Alan Johnston and now RUC Reservist David Johnston.

What of the hope he had spoken about to the House of Commons six weeks before? What of the 'dream that peace may come and that all our citizens may learn to do justly, to love mercy and to walk humbly with their God?'

He had vowed to work for a 'fair and just peace, a real peace...free from the threat of terrorist violence.'

What could possibly be done to bring that about, given that one of his first official engagements as Member of Parliament for Lagan Valley was to attend the funeral of a victim of terrorist violence?

Could the statement issued by the IRA on July 20, announcing a second ceasefire, be the first welcome glimmer of that hope he had been talking about, the first step towards 'real peace?'

Mo Mowlam monitored the ceasefire during August and then announced that Sinn Fein would be admitted to the talks in September, provided they signed up to the Mitchell Principles of democracy and non-violence.

This was a bitter pill for the Unionist parties to swallow and they were left with an unpleasant choice to have to make. The Prime Minister proceeded to turn what was already a difficult situation for them into a detestable one by becoming the first British Prime Minister since the 1920's to meet an Irish Republican, when he shook Gerry Adams' hand in Belfast and then in 10 Downing Street. The unionist community, many of whom had been on the receiving end of IRA violence for nearly three decades, found such deeply symbolic gestures highly offensive.

It was make your-mind-up-time for unionists. Did they pull out of the talks against this backdrop of perceived 'concessions to republicans,' or did they stay in and seek to have at least some influence on the outcome?

A round of intense soul-searching and often-heated debate followed. There were meetings within the Ulster Unionist Party. There were meetings within the Democratic Unionist Party. There were meetings between the DUP, the UUP, and some of the other smaller unionist parties.

The DUP delegation's decision to pull out of the talks put even more pressure on their UUP counterparts. They held further discussions and decided that there were a number of reasons why the cause of Northern Ireland would be better served if they were to remain within the structure of the talks process, rather than withdraw.

Jeffrey Donaldson was quite happy with these reasons, for he and his colleagues felt that the voice of unionism ought to be heard. They recognised that there had been, in the unsettled climate of Northern Ireland politics in the latter half of the twentieth century, instances of different British Governments taking decisions without unionist consent, for example at the time of the Anglo Irish Agreement. With Labour's unassailable majority it would be doubtful if they would be unduly concerned whether there was a unionist presence in the talks process or not. If they were absent the Labour Party was in a strong position to carry on regardless, with an outcome that could prove totally unacceptable to them, but which they would be forced to accept, having let it be made, unchallenged.

Secondly, they felt that Sinn Fein needed to be confronted. Were they truly committed to exclusively peaceful means of solving their country's problems? If they were, that would be welcome, if a little surprising, but if they weren't, they needed to be exposed. And the best way of doing that, they reckoned, would be to be in there, hearing their suggestions, analysing their intentions and challenging their violent ideology.

Perhaps the most compelling reason of all for Jeffrey was the possibility of seeing peace after thirty years of conflict. He had been upset, as a child, by his cousin's death and funeral, and he had been just as upset at the death of one of his constituents, a young husband and father, three months before. Whether as a boy in Kilkeel, a man in Moira, or an MP in Westminster, he had always been determined to pursue the possibility of a just peace for the province. And if these talks offered any prospect of achieving that aim were they not worth participating in, no matter how difficult that proved to be at a personal level?

The decision of the Ulster Unionist Party to remain in the negotiations caused a bitter rift in unionism, as the Democratic Unionist Party adamantly refused to meet Sinn Fein at any point or for any reason.

The talks resumed in their new format in October but progress was painfully slow. There were deep divisions in the country, rooted in both history and tradition, and these led to the expression of strongly held convictions from both sides. The Ulster Unionist Party team and the Sinn Fein group continued to make demands of each other and lay down conditions, which the other side immediately labelled as 'unrealistic', for the advancement of the talks. There was no direct engagement between the two parties as they kept an uneasy distance, and so proximity talks, or mediation, formed the basis of the discussions.

What was the answer to all the animosity, the remedy for all the resentment?

Could the situation in Northern Ireland ever be satisfactorily resolved?

Jeffrey Donaldson had been agonising over that problem for years and he was interested to hear the view of his friend Enoch Powell, an astute politician, and someone with first-hand knowledge of the complexities of the issue.

Responding to Pam's invitation to 'come and see them again when he could' Jeffrey went to visit them in their London home in January 1998.

The once dynamic and brilliant MP was by then very weak and ill.

On entering the upstairs living room where Enoch was sitting in an armchair in the corner, Jeffrey noticed immediately how frail he had become. Pam and he both expressed their delight at seeing their young friend, nonetheless, and they enjoyed a conversation together. It was pleasant to reminisce about old times over a cup of tea, but when Jeffrey saw that the concentration was making the obviously very weak man weary, he stood to take his leave.

They had been discussing the progress, or lack of it, in the talks at Stormont, just before he had risen to his feet.

"I really must be going now," Jeffrey said, "I don't want to stay too long and tire you out, Enoch. I can see that you are not feeling great."

Enoch Powell chose to ignore his friend's remark about his condition, but he looked up, his face pale and drawn, and fixed his gaze on the MP he had helped groom for Lagan Valley.

"You know, Jeffrey, there's only one answer for Northern Ireland," he declared with the finality of a barrister submitting a conclusive summing up to his case, "That's God."

23
THE GOOD FRIDAY DISAGREEMENT

Those were the last words Jeffrey was to hear his erstwhile tutor say. Enoch Powell, parliamentarian and statesman, died on February 8, 1998.

A great politician had made his final exit, but negotiations on the way forward for Northern Ireland, the province he had come to love, continued. Jeffrey Donaldson and his colleagues in the UUP's senior talks team carried on the endless round of meetings, both with members of their own, and other parties, but they were still making very little headway.

Having seen several deadlines extended already, Senator Mitchell and the British and Irish Governments intensified the negotiations with the aim of making Easter 1998 their target date for completion. It was going to be difficult, and they knew it. There were still deep differences to be resolved on some of the core issues.

With just a week to go to their deadline George Mitchell and his two assistants, Harri Holkeri and John de Chastelain, spent the weekend prior to Easter putting the finishing touches to their 'Draft Paper for Discussion.' They had promised the parties that this would be with them on Monday, April 6, but they weren't in a position to present it to the party leaders until the early hours of Tuesday morning. The leaders were pledged to secrecy but they were asked to share the document with the other members of their negotiating teams and present an initial response to it as soon as possible.

The members of the UUP senior talks team were very concerned about some key elements of the draft paper when they met to discuss it later that morning. They were particularly unhappy about the sections outlining the proposals for dealing with the decommissioning of terrorist weapons, policing, and arrangements for North / South cooperation.

It was clear that all were agreed the proposals set out in the draft document were unacceptable and this led to a discussion, which ended up in a debate, as to how to respond. Jeffrey argued that the party should reject the document outright, making it clear that it did not even constitute a basis for discussion, never mind agreement, and that radical changes would have to be effected in it before they could consider it further. Others, however, including the party leader, considered an absolute dismissal of the proposals as unnecessary and a step too far. They contended that the UUP delegation should point out their concerns to those who had compiled the document, asking to have fundamental changes made in some areas causing particular unease, and this policy was finally adopted.

On leaving the talks venue that evening David Trimble's deputy, John Taylor, was interviewed by the waiting media and asked for his reaction to the 'Draft Paper for Discussion.'

"I wouldn't touch it with a forty-foot barge pole!" he declared, in a concise but mischievous manner.

Recognising the depth and extent of the unionist concerns, for they ranged over a number of basic items in the draft document, the two Governments realised that it was time to take decisive action. It was like a football match that was balanced on a knife-edge. They were well into the second half and the result could still go either way, so it was time to introduce their star players.

The first of these was Tony Blair. He was summoned and left London for Belfast later that evening, praising the work of George Mitchell and his team and saying that he 'felt the hand of history upon our shoulders.' The Prime Minister took up residence in Hillsborough Castle where he met a number of key negotiators soon after his arrival. Jeffrey Donaldson and some of his colleagues were concerned that their leader had been invited to see him, for what were obviously crucial discussions, unaccompanied.

Bertie Ahern, Taoiseach of the Irish Republic, joined Tony Blair just before breakfast time next morning, Wednesday, April 8. It was planned that he too would take an active part in the discussions and help pressurise the parties, especially the recalcitrant unionists, into reaching an agreement.

Having secured the services of the leaders of both Governments, George Mitchell was determined that there would be no turning back. He told the Prime Ministers, then all the parties involved, that they were going to meet the Easter deadline, and there would be no breaks until something definitive was achieved.

This declared resolve by the talks facilitator introduced a further sense of urgency and tension to the situation. The teams were now all fielding their top players and the match had gone into extra time. There was no promise or possibility of a replay, however, regardless of how tired the individual players became. They were there to come up with a result.

On Thursday a series of important meetings took place in the afternoon and evening between the Ulster Unionist Party, the British and Irish Governments and the Social Democratic and Labour Party. These were geared towards addressing the lingering anxieties of the UUP delegation.

The lights burned late in rooms all over Castle Buildings as the discussions continued between the two Prime Ministers and their aides, and the representatives of all the political parties present, well into the night.

Around 3.00 a.m. on Good Friday morning, Jeffrey returned from a meeting with the Irish Attorney General, where he had been seeking confirmation of promised changes to the Irish Constitution. He was soon followed into the room, which the UUP was using as its 'base camp' during the prolonged negotiations, by three other members of the party's senior talks team. David Trimble, John Taylor and Reg Empey informed him, and the few others present, that they had reached an agreement with the SDLP, the largest nationalist party, on a form of devolved government for Northern Ireland. There were, David Trimble explained, other issues still to be resolved but he felt that it would be best to leave these to the two Governments to sort out. The party leader then left to cross to the nearby Stormont Hotel where he hoped to snatch a few hours sleep.

Jeffrey, however, was still worried about these unresolved issues and too keyed up to even contemplate going to bed. He was well aware that such matters as the decommissioning of terrorist weapons, the policing issue, and Sinn Fein demands for prisoner releases, had the potential to create enormous difficulties for unionists. When he learnt, towards daybreak, that the Sinn Fein delegation was still in negotiations with the representatives of both Governments, and that they had at one stage threatened to pack their bags and go home if some of their demands weren't met, he felt increasingly ill at ease.

At 6.30 a.m. Jeffrey decided to take an hour or two out and go home to Moira for a wash and change of clothes. He returned to Stormont as soon as possible to find the world's media, which had been encamped outside Castle Buildings for days, being briefed by the Prime Minister's spin-doctor-in-chief, Alistair Campbell. They were being told that the negotiations were in their final stages, and to expect an announcement that an agreement had been reached, by mid-morning.

As Jeffrey pushed past them to re-enter the building he knew that this hype would soon be broadcast around the world. He could imagine audiences being urged to 'stay tuned for news of an imminent breakthrough in the Northern Ireland peace talks.'

On re-entering Castle Buildings he was to discover that matters were not just quite so far advanced as the media outside were being given to believe. Red-eyed delegates were preparing themselves for a final push for a resolution. George Mitchell had advised the parties that he would have the final text of the agreement with them for their perusal, and hopefully approval, by mid-morning. Perhaps that was what Alistair Campbell had been talking about, but presenting the text of an agreement, and persuading parties with such diverse views to endorse it, were two entirely different things!

And finally it came! David Trimble arranged for each member of his negotiating team to have a copy of the prepared text at once. They were then instructed to find a quiet place where they could read through it from cover to cover and draw up, as they did so, a list of any issues they considered to be of particular concern.

Jeffrey Donaldson went off to one of the small meeting rooms that had been reserved for the UUP delegation. He shut himself in, alone, and feeling the burden of the moment, with that important text on his knee, prayed for guidance and discernment before beginning to read it. Jeffrey was aware that although this promised to be an arduous occupation it was also a very responsible one. It would be arduous because the text was couched in such unfamiliar, legalistic language. It would be responsible because he felt accountable to so many of the good people in his constituency. What would they think about it if they had the opportunity to read it? Could he honestly gauge the nature of their response?

As Jeffrey read carefully through page after page of text he made a note of the items that he felt would create problems in the implementation of the agreement.

When he came to the section on policing his mind went back once more to the deaths of his two cousins and those of David Johnston and John Graham less than a year before. What would their families think of this, he wondered. Or indeed the current serving officers, many of whom had faced death or sustained injury over the previous thirty years. How would they react to the potential demise of the revered Royal Ulster Constabulary?

The question of prisoner releases caused him deep concern also. All paramilitary prisoners were to be released over a period of two years, during which time the IRA and loyalist terrorists were to decommission their weapons. There were no guarantees that they would, though. And what if they didn't? Would Sinn Fein representatives still be allowed to hold office in the proposed power-sharing Executive at Stormont?

The agreement he was reading through served only to provide him with difficult questions rather than satisfactory answers. He felt that it was creating, rather than solving, problems for the unionist community.

When the team members had been given ample time to study the agreement individually, David Trimble summoned them together again for a crucial session. As the party leader went around the table, speaking to them one by one to ascertain their response, each of them outlined his deep reservations about certain aspects of the document. There were many similarities in the concerns expressed and the discussion concluded with the group deciding to request a meeting with Prime Minister Blair so that they could apprise him of their heartfelt anxieties about a number of the basic issues contained in it.

A meeting was hastily convened and Jeffrey Donaldson was one of those who used the opportunity to spell out to the Prime Minister their personal reservations about, and in some cases objections to, certain features in the agreement. He referred to the list he had compiled in the period he had been given to read through it, as he argued very strongly that many of the people he represented would find such terms unacceptable.

The Prime Minister was dogmatic that the text of the document could not be altered because it was his judgement that if it were, there remained the possibility that other parties could withhold their support. He undertook to discuss the matter with his officials, however, and promised to be in touch with David Trimble again as soon as possible. His response, when it came some time later, was in the form of a letter, as follows:

Dear David,

I understand your problem with paragraph 25 of Strand 1 is that it requires decisions on those who should be excluded or removed from office in the Northern Ireland Executive to be taken on a cross-community basis.

This letter is to let you know that if, during the course of the first six months of the shadow Assembly or the Assembly itself, these provisions have been shown to be ineffective, we will support changes to these provisions to enable them to be made properly effective in preventing such people from holding office.

Furthermore, I confirm that in our view the effect of the decommissioning section of the agreement, with decommissioning schemes coming into effect in June, is that the process of decommissioning should begin straight away.

Yours ever,

Tony Blair.

David Trimble provided all the members of his team with a copy of this letter and the discussions entered an even more earnest and anxious phase.

The other parties in the building had already expressed themselves ready to endorse the agreement and were becoming increasingly frustrated with the prevarication of the Ulster Unionist Party.

The party leader was clearly inclined to accept the letter as an assurance from the Prime Minister that all would be well in the days to come. He appeared ready to join the other parties in giving a final assent to the agreement and tried eagerly to persuade his dubious colleagues that the letter should allow them, as a party, to overcome their perceived concerns.

Tension had begun to mount, both inside and outside the room. Having been interrupted so often in the earlier stage of their critical discussions by Government officials, anxious to know if they had reached a consensus of opinion yet, the delegates locked the door.

This didn't stop the interruptions, though.

Jonathan Powell just rapped on the door periodically, and when this evoked no response from those closeted inside he began to shove notes under it. These, too, were largely ignored.

It was clear that those waiting outside, including the world's media, couldn't understand why this small group of politicians could choose to be so unaccommodating as to hold up their 'historic announcement.'

The reason was simple. Deadlock had been reached. Some of the team were inclined towards David Trimble's views and the others shared the concerns that Jeffrey had previously articulated. Some were prepared to allow the Prime Minister's letter to dispel their earlier fears. Others dismissed it as a 'fudge,' devoid of concrete assurances.

The pressures had risen to their highest level ever.

Just when it seemed that matters were approaching a supercharged stalemate someone came to the door with a request that David Trimble thought it best not to ignore. Could he come to the telephone to speak to President Clinton for a few minutes?

The meeting was hastily adjourned while the leader went off to take the President's call and the remaining delegates were left to reflect on the developments, or lack of them, up until that point.

One of Jeffrey's colleagues, Ken Maginnis, MP for Fermanagh and South Tyrone, saw the unexpected interval as a welcome opportunity to take him aside to one of the rooms. There they could be together alone to discuss the current impasse, which he reckoned was threatening to discredit their party.

It was an emotional encounter because both had served in the

Ulster Defence Regiment and both had lost friends and comrades as a result of terrorist violence. Ken Maginnis identified with Jeffrey's 'understandable concerns' but implored him to set them aside, and back the leader, nonetheless. At one point he broke down in tears as he begged him to consider his position very carefully for the sake of party unity.

Whilst appreciating the strength of Ken's argument Jeffrey felt the need to present his point of view in equally forthright terms. "Look, Ken, that is all very well, but my conscience is more important to me than party unity," he declared. "How can I leave this building to go out and walk the streets of Lisburn or Moira and look the people I represent straight in the eye and tell them that this is a good agreement when I am sure that it isn't? How can I urge them to support something which I believe in my heart to be fundamentally flawed? How can I? Tell me how..."

When Ken Maginnis recognised the strength of Jeffrey's conviction he left the youngest member of the delegation alone while he returned to discuss the matter further with Reg Empey and John Taylor.

Jeffrey Donaldson found himself in a dilemma.

He had no desire whatsoever to create division in the party he had served so diligently for so many years. On the other hand he would never be happy or have peace of mind with the terms of that particular agreement, and so why should he back it, just to save face?

Jeffrey prayed for further guidance and then, realising that he had a few minutes to spare and a telephone at hand, he rang his friend and mentor, Jim Molyneaux, to update him on the situation and seek advice. When Jeffrey had given him a brief summary of the moral and political predicament he faced, Jim came back with his counsel.

"You've got to be true to your conscience, Jeffrey," he said.

It wasn't long before David Trimble reconvened his team and it soon became evident that he had changed his tack. Someone out there had been putting further pressure on him to deliver his party's response so he called a meeting of all the Ulster Unionist Party officers in the building. Having sought the views of each officer in turn he declared that he would shortly be making a second round and this time it would be to record a vote. He made it clear that all he would require from each of his colleagues would be a simple one-word response.

It was to be a straightforward Yes or No to the agreement.

On doing this David Trimble secured a majority by the narrowest possible margin as the divided party officers gave their assent to the final agreement on a split vote.

Suddenly it was all business in the room where the atmosphere had been so terribly strained just minutes before. The leader brought what had been a dramatic and draining day's discussions within his party to a rather abrupt conclusion by announcing, "It's my intention to call George Mitchell and tell him that we are ready to proceed."

And he did. It was 4.45 p.m.

As David Trimble prepared to lead his delegation upstairs to the conference room to join the other parties in endorsing the agreement, he approached Jeffrey and asked, "Are you coming up?"

"No. Leave me out this time, David," Jeffrey replied. "You know that I do not approve of what you are doing and therefore feel it would be farcical for me to join you in the plenary session as you endorse this agreement."

David Trimble merely shrugged his shoulders before leaving to go upstairs with what remained of his team. Jeffrey, and those other party members who had expressed their dissent and proved impossible to win over, decided that it was time for them to go home.

Jeffrey left the building to walk across to the car park, in the full gaze of the waiting media, but without making any comment about what had happened inside.

As he approached Moira in the car he heard on the radio George Mitchell's announcement to the world of an agreement that 'was good for the people of Ireland, North and South.' His speech concluded by praising the political leaders of Northern Ireland for their 'sense of purpose.' They had, he claimed, 'delivered an agreement that's fair and balanced and offers hope to the people of Northern Ireland. For that they deserve the gratitude of their people and the just verdict of history.'

Where, Jeffrey wondered, does all of that leave me?

What will history's verdict be on my decision?

What kind of a price am I going to have to pay for simply obeying my conscience?

24
THIS IS DOWNING STREET

Later that evening, Jeffrey, Eleanor and the girls drove to the airport to catch a flight to London where they had planned to spend a few days together over the Easter holidays. The trip to the capital did not remove them from the political hype that had reached fever pitch back in Belfast, however.

The flight proved a welcome respite, for Jeffrey was obliged to keep his mobile phone switched off. Right up until he stepped on to the plane, and just as soon as he switched it on again after arriving at Heathrow, his mobile had been ringing incessantly. The calls were flooding in from journalists, and party colleagues who had not been involved in the talks at Stormont, all anxious to know what had happened a few hours earlier.

Many of the calls he received from party members were very supportive of his position. This gave him some encouragement. It was reassuring to learn that he was not alone in his deep concern about the terms of the Agreement to which David Trimble had signed up on behalf of the Ulster Unionist Party.

It was difficult to relax on Saturday for there were still periodic phone calls from reporters keen to hear Jeffrey's version of events. It was quite clear that the media speculation about his personal decision to withdraw from the talks, late the previous afternoon, hadn't abated.

When Easter Sunday came, though, there were very few telephone calls and the family began to relax and appreciate the opportunity to be together, largely uninterrupted. Obviously all the journalists and party members had reverted to their holiday plans for the weekend leaving Jeffrey to enjoy his.

Next morning he walked the short distance to a local shop to pick up the national papers, and began reading them eagerly as soon as he returned. Jeffrey was keen to keep himself updated on the latest reaction to, comment on, and analysis of what the media had styled, 'The Good Friday Agreement.' It was going to take him some time, for there was a lot of it. Most of the papers carried copious columns of appraisal and Jeffrey was interested to know what they all had to say.

He had plenty of time and was determined to read every reaction. A glance up at the clock told him that it was eleven o'clock and he was thankful that up until that moment there hadn't been one phone call of any sort.

Where is everybody? he thought, wryly. The tranquillity of that Easter Monday morning was such an unbelievable contrast to the hectic succession of phone calls on Friday night and Saturday.

It was interesting to read about the responses of the various parties to the Agreement, which required to be ratified by public referendum at a later date.

Sinn Fein had failed to declare their position, having stated that they were waiting until they had called a special party meeting before making any final decision. It was also becoming clear that David Trimble was planning to convene further meetings with senior party members to seek endorsement of his commitment to the Agreement.

Jeffrey was absorbed in the papers and was mildly startled when the phone did eventually ring. He hadn't been expecting anyone to call and he certainly hadn't been expecting the call he was about to receive.

When he answered, a lady announced in a very polite voice, "This is Downing Street," before going on to ask in the next breath, "Can you take a call from the Prime Minister?"

Jeffrey was conscious that his throat had all of a sudden dried up as, in shock, he stammered out his response, which was, "Yes. Of course I can."

"Then just hold please, until I put you through. It may take a moment," the lady went on to say.

What's all this about? Jeffrey had time to reflect briefly as the silence at the other end of the line was broken by a series of clicks. He had just been reading in one of the papers, about ten minutes before, that Tony Blair and family were spending Easter at the King of Spain's holiday residence. Was the Prime Minister really phoning him from such a salubrious location?

The connection took much shorter than Jeffrey had anticipated and it wasn't long before a familiar voice came on the line.

It was indeed the Prime Minister who greeted Jeffrey in surprisingly friendly terms, considering that the last time they had met was in a stern encounter back at Stormont the previous Friday. Perhaps the fact that both of them were on holiday and had managed to wind down to some degree after the strains and stresses of the previous week, had led to this much more informal approach.

The young MP suspected, however, that Tony Blair hadn't called him on an Easter Monday morning just for a friendly little chinwag. There had to be more to it than that and the purpose of the call became evident when the Prime Minister enquired, "And so, Jeffrey, what are your main concerns about this Agreement?"

Having been offered the ear of the Prime Minister, Jeffrey seized the opportunity to outline in detail his strong reservations about key elements of the Agreement to him yet again. He had done so in no uncertain terms before it was signed and this surprise contact gave him another chance to express his anxieties about the sections relating to decommissioning, policing and prisoner releases particularly.

The Prime Minister listened carefully to what Jeffrey had to say and undertook to consider the issues he had raised before suggesting that they meet at Westminster after the Easter recess.

As their conversation was coming to a close Jeffrey thanked the Prime Minister for his unexpected personal interest and quipped, "You know, Prime Minister, a backbench MP like me wouldn't normally receive a call from you unless he were going to be made a Minister!"

"Well you know, Jeffrey, anything's possible," the Prime Minister replied after a momentary pause, and with just the slightest hint of enticement in his voice.

With that the two men said their goodbyes and each returned to the relative normality of his Easter break.

When the Donaldson family arrived back home in Moira later in the week Jeffrey found that there were a number of letters waiting for him. Many of these were from party members in Lagan Valley and farther afield, and a high percentage of them expressed their approval of the stance he had taken on Good Friday.

There were a few, however, that were of a bitter, critical nature. He had expected that there would be those in the party who would disapprove of his attitude and actions, however motivated, and if past experience were anything to go by they would probably make their feelings known to him.

The first of such scathing letters was one he opened that morning on his return from London, from a senior party member in Coleraine. He was an ardent supporter of David Trimble's position and suggested that Jeffrey should reflect on his decision to withhold his support for the Agreement, and fall in behind his leader, for the sake of party unity.

At one point in the letter the writer quoted the famous lines from Shakespeare's play 'Hamlet':

'This above all – to thine own self be true,
And it must follow, as the night the day,
Thou canst not then be false to any man...'

The aggrieved member used this quotation to argue that Jeffrey was doing himself a disservice, in that by being disloyal to the party position he was, by association, betraying himself.

Jeffrey saw it completely differently, though, and when he sat down to write his response to the letter, argued that William Shakespeare had stated his personal position more eloquently than he could have done it himself. That was exactly what he had been doing throughout those agonising and arduous days of negotiations. Being true to himself. Simply obeying his conscience.

Another point made by the correspondent from Coleraine was that if the Agreement opened the door of opportunity towards peace in Northern Ireland how could Jeffrey be seen to be turning his back on it?

The letter contained more than one reference to the prospect of peace in the province, and Jeffrey was determined to answer his critic, not from Shakespeare, but from the Christian's main handbook, the Bible. He knew that it contained many references to peace, but how was he to find the most appropriate one to include in his reply?

Taking down his Cruden's Concordance he turned to the word 'peace,' only to find that there were hundreds of references to it. The lists stretched across pages! Scanning down the columns, however, two references below each other caught his eye. They both seemed to be exactly the same, and what was more , each of them contained the word 'peace' three times within the compass of seven words!

Turning immediately to Jeremiah 6 : 14 and then Jeremiah 8 : 11, which were just a few pages apart in his Bible, he discovered two things, one interesting, the other inspirational.

The first was that the text of both verses was practically the same, and the other that they summed up precisely the sentiment he wanted to put across.

They said:

'They have also healed the hurt of My people slightly, saying, 'Peace, peace!' when there is no peace.'

Using this verse as a theme for the latter half of his reply Jeffrey stated that in his opinion the terms of the Agreement would only 'heal the hurt' of Northern Ireland 'slightly.' It was, he contended, like sticking a strip of Elastoplast on a gaping, festering wound and expecting it to disappear miraculously overnight.

It was futile to go around hailing the prospect of peace in the province when in fact there was 'no peace,' and there wouldn't be lasting peace either, Jeffrey went on to say, until the root cause of the problem was tackled.

In echoes of 'the solution on the scrap of paper,' which had so puzzled him on his visit to Tullyhappy Orange Hall years before, Jeffrey went on to outline what he believed to be the ultimate answer. It would only be when the people of Northern Ireland, of all shades of political allegiance, humbled themselves and returned to God, that He would completely 'heal their land.'

The composition of that letter took some time, but when Jeffrey had it finished and began reading it over to check that it contained all the thoughts he wanted to express, it afforded him a slight, but strange, sense of satisfaction.

It had been spiritually restorative to turn to the Bible for answers and politically exacting to be compelled to condense his convictions into a concise written form.

And it was good that he enjoyed the challenge.

For there were lots more letters to come.

Jeffrey age 3.

Jeffrey ready to leave for his first 'Twelfth' L-R Elaine, Diane, Jeffrey and James Donaldson.

Constable Samuel Donaldson
murdered by the I.R.A.
August 1970.

Chief Inspector Alexander
Donaldson murdered by the I.R.A.
February 1985.

Lance Corporal Alan Johnston
(UDR) murdered by the I.R.A.
February 1988.

The final hours of the prorogued Northern Ireland Assembly. June 1986.

After handing in Nomination Papers in Banbridge as a Candidate for the Assembly By-Election. October 1985.

At a U.D.R. Association parade in Co. Down with Dad and brother James.

As Election Agent with Pam and Enoch Powell. January 1986.

Wedding Day at Mourne Presbyterian Church. Eleanor receives a congratulatory kiss from Enoch Powell. June 1987.

The Youth Fellowship of Kilkeel Presbyterian Church where Jeffrey and Eleanor served as leaders. Summer 1991.

First meeting with Tony Blair and Mo Mowlam in Belfast. 1996.

The Donaldson Family, Back L-R, Glen, Julie-Anne, Jeffrey, James, Elaine and Kingsley. Front L-R, Diane, Jim (Dad), Annie (Mum) and Andrew. Summer 1996.

The member for Lagan Valley making his first intervention at Prime Minister's Question Time, House of Commons. July 1997.

Meeting President Clinton in The White House. St. Patrick's Day 1997.

With Lord Molyneaux and Lord McConnell after Election to The House of Commons. June 1997.

Meeting Nelson Mandela in South Africa. Summer 1997.

*Outside the Waterfront Hall after a meeting with the
Ulster Unionist Council. May 2000.*

*David Trimble shows the strain after facing yet another Ulster Unionist
Council meeting. November 1999.*

Jeffrey and Eleanor meeting Her Majesty the Queen at the opening of the new Civic Centre in Lisburn. November 2001.

Receiving the Charter for City Status at Hillsborough Castle. May 2002.

The Donaldson Family. L-R, Laura, Jeffrey, Eleanor and Claire. August 2002.

Facing the press at Stormont after having been welcomed into the DUP by party leader Dr Ian Paisley.

With Peter Robinson, Arlene Foster and Norah Beare in Lisburn Orange Hall after joining the DUP January 2004.

Visiting a Primary School in his Lagan Valley constituency.

Canvassing in Lisburn during The Assembly Election. November 2003.

*With Ann Graham Lotz on the terrace of the House of Commons.
October 2002.*

*With Jim Allister, Nigel Dodds and Peter Robinson before meeting
President Bush in Washington. March 2004.*

Addressing the Orangemen at the 'Twelfth'.

Taking the unionist message to the West Belfast Festival. August 2004.

25

HOW CAN A CHRISTIAN BE AGAINST PEACE?

There was intense political activity and increased public awareness of political matters in the week immediately following the endorsement of the Belfast, or 'Good Friday,' Agreement.

The Prime Minister announced that every household in Northern Ireland would be supplied with a copy of the Agreement. They would then be afforded the opportunity to give their verdict on it in a referendum to be held on Friday, May 22.

With every adult in the province being given the prospect of having a say in the matter the already unusually high level of interest in the political situation increased even further.

'The Agreement' became a regular topic of conversation. With copies of it dropping through letterboxes all over Northern Ireland, people began to talk about it everywhere. In homes and restaurants, on the streets and in the shops, in the workplace during the week and church car parks after services at the weekend, it became the focus of prolonged consultations.

What began as amicable discussions occasionally ended as acrimonious debates.

Friendships suffered because of it.

Households often differed over it.

It was against this background of deliberation, speculation and occasional confrontation that Jeffrey Donaldson had to prepare to address the eight hundred delegates of the Ulster Unionist Council on Saturday, April 18. This meeting had been convened to seek the party's approval for the 'Accord.'

The ripples of unrest about the Agreement had spread out to, and then in through, all the Ulster Unionist Party branches across the province and so the ballroom of Belfast's Europa Hotel was packed with delegates well before the meeting was due to commence on that date.

The speeches that were made as the morning progressed only served to highlight the sharp differences of opinion within the party.

The leader and a number of others expressed the view that the Agreement represented the best deal that could be negotiated, and if implemented, could lead ultimately to peace within Northern Ireland. Jeffrey, and a number of his colleagues failed to be convinced by their claims, however, and as their reservations had never been satisfactorily addressed, argued strongly against the motion to approve the terms of the Accord.

When the vote was taken after a series of impassioned outpourings, both for and against, David Trimble won a significant victory by securing the support of just over seventy per cent of the delegates present.

Jeffrey was not happy, though. Nor were a number of other senior figures in the Ulster Unionist Party. As far as they were concerned the Agreement may have been given party approval but it did not have their personal acceptance. It had been ratified by the party, but they reckoned it wasn't right for the people of the province.

They were given the chance to air their concerns at a meeting of the Ulster Unionist Parliamentary Party at Westminster the following Wednesday. Lord Molyneaux, Rev. Martin Smyth MP, (South Belfast) William Ross MP, (East Londonderry) William Thompson MP, (West Tyrone) Clifford Forsythe MP, (South Antrim) and Roy Beggs MP, (East Antrim) all joined Jeffrey Donaldson in expressing their dissatisfaction with the situation.

They were particularly anxious to have their own personal position clarified in relation to the forthcoming referendum in light of the decision that had been taken by the party's governing body. There had been a precedent established in previous referendum campaigns when MP's were free to vote according to their consciences.

They were anxious to know if this would still apply on May 22.

Confronted with the former party leader and six uncompromising MPs, and presented with such convincing evidence of past convention, David Trimble eventually conceded, with some reluctance, that his dissenting parliamentary colleagues would be free to vote No in the referendum in just over four weeks time.

The Prime Minister obviously hadn't forgotten his Easter Monday morning promise to meet Jeffrey 'at Westminster after the holiday,' and he arranged to see him just after Prime Minister's Questions on Wednesday, April 29. They met at 3.40 p.m. in the Prime Minister's office in the House of Commons.

It was a short but productive meeting.

Recognising the depth of Jeffrey's personal and often-articulated concerns, and the extent to which these echoed the sentiments of the grassroots of the Ulster Unionist Party, Tony Blair proposed coming to Northern Ireland to meet the Lagan Valley MP and a wider group of disenchanted party members face to face. He would, he said, be willing to listen to their concerns and then consider what the Government could do to allay their fears.

Within days it was decided that Prime Minister Blair would meet a delegation, led by Jeffrey Donaldson, at Stormont on Wednesday, May 6, at 8.00 p.m.

When the evening came around, those who accompanied Jeffrey to the meeting, which was held in the Secretary of State's office, included Arlene Foster who had backed his stance on Good Friday, his long-time friend and Lagan Valley colleague, Drew Nelson, as well as David Brewster, Peter King, John Hunter and Peter Weir who were all UUP members of the Forum.

The group presented the Prime Minister with a paper outlining their profound disquiet at a number of the fundamental elements of the Agreement. In the detailed discussions that followed Tony Blair gave them time to explain their genuine anxiety about the main issues which they felt would prove unacceptable to many in the unionist community. Those particularly highlighted were the proposals in relation to policing, the decommissioning of terrorist weapons, and the early release of paramilitary prisoners.

As the meeting came to an end, Tony Blair undertook to consider, and then respond to, each of the points raised.

This response, when it came a few days later, was in the form of a draft speech the Prime Minister was preparing to give at Balmoral, on the outskirts of Belfast, as a keynote address in the referendum campaign.

Jeffrey studied the text of this reply very carefully, first with the members of the delegation who had been with him that Wednesday night in Stormont, and then with his fellow-dissenting MPs in the Ulster Unionist Parliamentary Party.

When both groups had examined the Prime Minister's reaction to their expressed reservations, they all agreed that he had singularly failed to assuage any of their concerns. They concluded that his attempted clarification of certain aspects of the Agreement amounted to little more than a fudge.

Since he was considered to be one of the leaders of 'the No camp' within the UUP, Jeffrey was seldom out of the media spotlight.

In one TV interview, less than a week before the referendum was due to take place he described the points the Prime Minister made in response to his group's heartfelt concerns as 'blurring the lines between democracy and terrorism.' When pressed on his personal intentions Jeffrey went on to state that he felt that he had been left with no other option but to vote 'No' on May 22.

This very powerful and very public declaration of intent evoked a flood of response from people in Northern Ireland. This took different forms. Some wrote to him, some phoned him, and others spoke to him in the street, all airing their point of view.

It was clear from those who contacted him that there was strong support for his stance on the Agreement amongst the Ulster Unionist Party voters in Lagan Valley. He had many encouraging letters and phone calls from constituents, and supporters from all six counties of the province, some of them even reiterating the opinion that he was just 'the kind of man this country needs.'

There were some others, though, including a number of fellow-Christians, who voiced their unease with his open opposition to the Agreement. Their unease was usually expressed in the form of letters to Jeffrey's constituency office in Lisburn and had as their underlying theme the basic question, 'How can a Christian be against peace?'

These letters came in varying degrees of length, detail, and candour, but a common feature of all of them was that they were copiously interspersed with quotations from the Bible in support of their argument. Two of those most frequently used seemed to be the proclamation of the angels at the birth of Jesus, who, they firmly believed, had come to bring 'peace on earth, goodwill toward men,' and Jesus' words to a multitude on a mountain one day, 'Blessed are the peacemakers, for they shall be called the sons of God.'

Another argument that cropped up in a number of the letters was, 'Christians all over the world have been praying for years that God would bring peace to Northern Ireland. Now that their prayers are about to be answered how can you, as a Christian yourself, justify opposing the Agreement which will deliver that long-awaited peace?'

They were difficult, probing questions affecting the two consuming passions of Jeffrey Donaldson's life, his faith and his politics.

The Lagan Valley MP considered it important to answer every letter or give an explanation, when given the chance, in every phone call, clarifying his position.

His approach varied according to the text of the letter received or the tone of the phone call being taken, but he was careful to include in each answer, what he considered to be the root cause of all the trouble in the province, and the only possible solution to it.

Beginning with the references he had previously discovered in Jeremiah, when preparing to reply to the critic from Coleraine, he referred to the fact that this Agreement would only heal the hurt of the Northern Ireland people 'slightly.' Continuing with his 'Elastoplast on the festering wound' analogy, he would then contend that the fundamental error that all the well-meaning, peace-seeking Government agencies had made was that they had made a misdiagnosis of the cause of the malady.

Why, he asked, would a man want to carry a bomb into a fish shop on the Shankill Road in Belfast on a Saturday afternoon in the autumn of 1993 and kill nine innocent shoppers and injure over fifty more?

Or why would gunmen burst into a Hallowe'en dance in Greysteel, Co. Londonderry about a week later and spray the hall with bullets killing and injuring many innocent revellers?

These murderers would claim to have a political motive, Jeffrey argued, but that was not the reason for their actions. They had acted as they did because of the evil that was in their hearts. The Bible called it sin.

Jeffrey would then go on to explain that the peace Jesus had come to bring to earth had been made possible when He died on the cross. The original Good Friday Agreement had been made between God and mankind when Jesus cried out 'It is finished!' Under the terms of this Accord, all people had to do was believe that Jesus had died there, as a substitute for their sins, and those sins would be forgiven. Anyone who believed would become a child of God, and have in his or her heart the peace that Jesus had come to bring to earth.

This peace deal had been awaiting personal endorsement for nearly two millenia and had been neglected, despised or just simply ignored by the people whom it had been designed to help. And if the only absolutely faultless Agreement ever formulated for the good of mankind had been so utterly rejected by those set to benefit most from it, had he not the right to say 'No' to a deal he considered to be fundamentally flawed?

This led him on to giving his reaction to the 'blessed are the peacemakers' quote. In doing this Jeffrey often referred to further words of Jesus on the same subject, when He proclaimed to a different audience, under different circumstances, 'Do not think that I came to bring peace on earth. I did not come to bring peace but a sword.' Here He was referring to the division that would follow when some would gladly accept the terms of the treaty He had come to implement, and others would utterly reject it.

It wasn't a good thing to become totally carried away with the 'Gentle Jesus, meek and mild,' image either, Jeffrey would contend. Certainly Jesus was the most gracious Man who ever graced this planet with His presence, but when He saw the ordinary people being misled by religious leaders, or swindled by unscrupulous traders, He was quick to jump to their defence. Was it not He who had branded a group of sanctimonious but hypocritical Jewish religious leaders as 'whitewashed sepulchres,' beautiful on the outside, but rotten on the inside? Had he not also made a whip and chased a crowd of swindlers, who had been cheating foreign visitors at their currency exchange booths, right out of the temple courtyards?

And if Jesus had been justified in opposing what He knew to be wrong for His people, could Jeffrey Donaldson not be seen to be justified in opposing what he believed most strongly to be wrong for his? Did the honest, hard-working, law-abiding citizens of Northern Ireland not need someone to stand against what he believed was undoubtedly not in their best interests?

Jeffrey was at pains to point out that he was not against peace in the province. Nobody wanted it, or had longed for it throughout his lifetime, any more than he did. What he was against was the terms of this particular Agreement which he considered to be unfair to the people he represented.

Although Jeffrey campaigned strongly to put his case across, others who believed just as strongly in the merits of the Agreement, as they saw them, promoted their side of the argument with equal vigour. The days leading up to the referendum were particularly tense with both sides putting their point of view very forcefully to the electorate. One of the decisive factors during those politically pressurised days was a speech made by Prime Minister Tony Blair during a visit to Coleraine, when he wrote a number of 'hand-written pledges to the people of Northern Ireland' on a roller-board.

When the vote was taken on May 22 just over seventy per cent of the population of the province voted to accept the Agreement with slightly more than a quarter of them voting 'No.'

Jeffrey Donaldson was disappointed, but recognised that he would still have the opportunity to continue his campaign on behalf of the disaffected unionist community in the new Assembly which was to be set up.

Immediately after the date was announced for the election to this new body at Stormont the Ulster Unionist Party began arranging selection meetings in each constituency to choose a series of candidates.

After consulting with some of his colleagues Jeffrey decided to submit his name for selection in Lagan Valley. However, a party rule prohibited a member from holding two elected offices and he would therefore have to seek special dispensation from the Party Officers, to stand as a candidate for the Assembly whilst remaining an MP.

A meeting of the Party Officers was convened and there were three applications for dispensation on the table. David Trimble and John Taylor were both seeking special dispensation to go forward for selection, in addition to Jeffrey.

After some discussion the Party Officers decided to grant David Trimble and John Taylor, as leader and deputy leader of the party, a special dispensation to put their names forward for selection. Jeffrey's application, though, was refused on a split vote.

The MP for Lagan Valley was later to learn that the group on the senior management committee in the constituency, who had so vehemently opposed his selection at the General Election, had made a prior approach to David Trimble with what amounted to an ultimatum. They warned him that if he were to allow 'that man Donaldson,' to stand, they would withdraw their support for the leader's position.

This was both annoying and hurtful. Jeffrey tried hard, however, to keep his annoyance from giving way to anger, his hurt from breeding bitterness.

On the night of Thursday, May 28, Jeffrey and Eleanor went along to the selection meeting, as members of the Lagan Valley UUP Constituency Association, to support those candidates who had stood by him in earlier difficult days.

As soon as Jeffrey Donaldson entered the Pond Park Hall in Lisburn that evening most of the delegates already present stood up and cheered spontaneously. The few left sitting kept their heads down and looked decidedly uneasy.

Soon after the meeting began a number of the delegates challenged the chairman from the floor. They demanded to know why the Party Officers had refused to allow their MP to stand for election to the new Assembly when two other sitting MPs had been granted permission to go forward. Their views were enthusiastically endorsed by the majority of the members present, and with the meeting threatening to end in uproar if immediate action were not taken on the matter, a motion was passed instructing the constituency officers to petition the Party Officers to rescind their decision. The meeting was then adjourned for forty-eight hours to await their response.

A further meeting of Ulster Unionist Party Officers was hastily convened the following day and representatives from Lagan Valley conveyed the Constituency Association's request to them. It would appear, though, that Jeffrey's opponents had succeeded in increasing the pressure on the party leader, for David Trimble adamantly refused to rescind the Party Officers' original decision. This was in spite of the two facts that the delegation took great pains to point out to them.

The first of these was that it was the expressed desire of at least two thirds of the local association, and the other that a refusal to accede to their request could cause serious unease and considerable division amongst them.

When this decision was conveyed to the Lagan Valley Constituency Association many members were incensed, and Jeffrey Donaldson was inundated with pledges of support. Most of those who contacted him on the Saturday evening, and in the days immediately following, urged him to stand as an independent candidate. It would be vital, they said, to show Jeffrey's opponents, who were as determined as ever to see him sidelined and undermined, who had the real backing of the constituency.

Amongst those who offered to stand with Jeffrey, if he would agree to do so, was a Presbyterian minister who volunteered to mobilise a campaign team from his congregation to canvass on his behalf.

This overwhelming demonstration of support was most gratifying. It was encouraging to know that he was so highly respected amongst the people whom he had been representing as a Member of Parliament. It was also challenging, however.

It placed him in a moral and spiritual dilemma.

The people who were phoning him night and day, or calling at his constituency office in Lisburn, all spoke with one voice. They all had the same message.

It was, "Get out there and fight them! You can win a seat. Thousands will back you. We need you to represent us."

His conscience, though, was telling him something different.

If he stood as an independent, he would split the Ulster Unionist Association in Lagan Valley. And he had no desire to do that. Nor did he want to come out fighting, all guns blazing. That wasn't his way.

Jeffrey prayed long and hard about it. He asked God to guide him through the situation, and He did.

As he reflected on his position, Jeffrey became convinced that he should not force the issue. He felt the echoes of Psalm 37 flood over him again.

'Trust in the Lord…Commit your way to the Lord…wait on the Lord…' were three phrases that flashed into his mind on different occasions. And there was another one to add to the list. Jeffrey had heard it often in sermons, and had committed it to memory for use in times of turmoil, such as this.

It was from Psalm 46, and said, 'Be still, and know that I am God.'

His supporters were urging him to, 'Push forward and fight…'

Whereas God seemed to be saying, 'Be still, and know…'

Before the end of the next week Jeffrey told all those who had so generously pledged him their support, that he would not be standing as an independent candidate in the Assembly elections.

And from the moment he made his final decision public, he felt assured that he had done the right thing.

How, he reflected afterwards, could a man who enjoyed lasting, inner peace with God, and who yearned for that same peace to descend on his native province, be seen to disrupt the peace by causing division in his own constituency, however just the cause?

He was a Christian.

And he was definitely not against peace.

26

IGNORED, APPRECIATED, AND REASSURED

Elections to the Northern Ireland Assembly took place on Thursday, June 25, with the Ulster Unionist Party emerging as the largest party, having gained twenty-eight seats. Of the three other main parties, SDLP won twenty-four seats, the DUP twenty and Sinn Fein eighteen.

The first meeting of this new body took place a few days after the results were declared, in the conference room of Castle Buildings, where the negotiations, which had led to its establishment, had taken place some weeks before.

Before any formal business could be conducted the Assembly had to elect a First and Deputy First Minister. This required a majority vote of both unionist and nationalist members and when the names of David Trimble and Seamus Mallon were submitted, the votes of the UUP, SDLP and some of the smaller parties were sufficient to ensure that majority

The leadership of the Ulster Unionist Party made it clear at that stage that they would be abiding by the manifesto commitments they had made in the run-up to the elections. They would not, they maintained, be sitting in an administration that included Sinn Fein ministers until the IRA had begun to decommission its illegal weapons.

This policy was encapsulated in the party's oft-repeated slogan, 'No guns, no government.'

A period of protracted negotiation, aimed at resolving the resulting impasse, took place at Stormont over the summer, and then on into the autumn of 1998. Since Jeffrey Donaldson had not been allowed to stand for election to the new Assembly, he was not a member of it, and hence was excluded from the discussions.

He found this difficult at first.

Having once been cast in a leading role in all of the Ulster Unionist Party's major productions it was discomfiting to be relegated to the front row of the audience to sit, silent and shunned, watching this latest drama in which his party had major parts, unfold. There were times when he wondered why some of those with whom he had worked so closely in days gone past, were so determined to maintain that exclusion. They must have been aware that this could only lead to a widening of the rift within the party, thus making it infinitely more difficult to heal.

Although not involved in the business of the Stormont Assembly there were two other areas where Jeffrey was kept constantly busy. These were his work in his Lagan Valley constituency and his work for the people of his constituency, and the province, as a Member of Parliament at Westminster. The intensity and variety of the activities and consultations in which he participated, and the people and issues he encountered, are best illustrated by outlining the events of a typical week in his life in mid-June 1999.

The Assembly elections, which had been held a year before, were by then little more that a distant, if disturbing, memory for Jeffrey as there were so many different matters demanding his attention, virtually every hour of every day.

Jeffrey began the week, as he did every week when at home,

by going along to Moira Baptist Church with Eleanor, Claire and Laura on Sunday morning. In the afternoon he travelled back to the Kingdom of Mourne to attend a church service organised by the Co. Down UDR Association in Annalong. It was pleasant, and occasionally poignant, to recall his experiences in the Regiment with his dad, Jim Donaldson, his brother James, and many of the others who had served with him.

Sunday evening was spent with the family and then on Monday morning, June 21, Jeffrey began working in his study at home around 6.30 a.m. While there he drafted some replies to letters he had received and dictated some work for his secretary. At nine o'clock he went into his constituency office in Lisburn and spent half an hour going through the diary for that day, and then the remainder of the week with his secretary, Norah Beare.

Having left a number of matters in Norah's capable hands it was then off to Belfast for an interview with the BBC for its local current affairs programme, 'Spotlight.' Despite his apparent isolation from the political scene at Stormont, Jeffrey still enjoyed a high media profile with newspaper and TV journalists seeking his opinion on a wide variety of topical issues.

At eleven o'clock Jeffrey led a delegation from the group FACT, to meet Adam Ingram, the Minister for Victims in the Northern Ireland Office, at Castle Buildings in the Stormont estate.

FACT (Families Against Crime by Terrorism) was a Lisburn based group, which Jeffrey had helped to form to support those of his Lagan Valley constituents who had suffered as a result of terrorism. The meeting had been convened to allow some of those whose families had been devastated by terrorist activity to meet the Minister and discuss a number of subjects including the early release of paramilitary prisoners.

Thelma Johnston was one of those who met Jeffrey up at Stormont that morning and accompanied him into the meeting with the Victims Minister. Thelma was the mother of David Johnston, the young policeman who had been murdered by the IRA in Lurgan, and this was the second time that Jeffrey had offered her his support in less than two months. At the end of April he had arranged for her to visit the Headquarters of the Royal Ulster Constabulary on the Knock Road in Belfast to see her son's name in the Book of Remembrance.

That had been a most moving experience. When Thelma had seen David's name in that book she had been overcome by a sense of grief and loss. It was all so final.

She had been happy to accept Jeffrey's invitation to join the group on this mission to meet Adam Ingram, seven weeks later. She felt that she would be doing something to enhance the memory of her son if she could somehow ensure that David's assassins would be compelled to serve a sentence that reflected the cruel, callous nature of their crime.

Joseph and Annie Mc Ilwaine, and their daughter Janet were also present at that meeting. Joseph and Annie's son, and Janet's brother, Joseph Mc Ilwaine junior, had been a part-time member of the Ulster Defence Regiment, and was murdered by the IRA at his regular place of work in Aberdelgy Golf Club, Lambeg.

Another member of the delegation at Stormont that morning was Michelle Williamson, from Lisburn, whose father and mother, George and Gillian Williamson, had been killed in the bomb on the Shankill Road in Belfast in October 1993.

Having experienced at first hand, and since childhood the heartfelt anguish felt by grief-torn families decimated by terrorist activity, Jeffrey had made it a priority in his role as an MP to highlight the position of these families and enable them to obtain all the assistance possible from government and other agencies. The meeting at Stormont was but a link in that chain, a contribution to help heal the deep wounds that thirty years of terrorist violence had created.

During the course of the discussions Jeffrey took yet another opportunity to express his strong opposition to the provision for the early release of convicted terrorist prisoners as outlined in the terms of the Good Friday Agreement.

Later in the meeting Michelle reminded Adam Ingram of the words of the judge at the trial of Sean Kelly, the IRA bomber who had been found guilty of the murder of her parents and seven other innocent victims. Sentencing Kelly to nine life terms in prison he had said that this should mean that the bomber would spend the remainder of his natural life behind bars.

Michelle then went on to point out that under the terms of this 'ridiculous' Agreement, instead of Kelly serving out that recommended sentence, he would be out of jail in six years. This would mean that he wouldn't even have to serve one year in prison for each life that he destroyed. Michelle felt passionately about this, describing such a decision as, amongst other things, 'unjust, insulting and degrading.'

The Minister listened carefully to what Jeffrey, Michelle, Thelma and all the others had to say, but despite appearing sympathetic ended the meeting by asserting adamantly that the Government would not be renegotiating the terms of the Agreement.

When the FACT party dispersed after their encounter with Mr. Ingram, Jeffrey went to Hillsborough for a lunchtime meeeting before travelling on for a 2.30 p.m. appointment in the District

Planning Office in Craigavon.

Two of Jeffrey's constituents, David and Wendy Cairns, had applied for permission to build a new bungalow on a site near Dromore but this had been recommended for refusal by the Planning Office. At that meeting David and Wendy's MP put forward their case and set out a number of special reasons why this young couple should be granted permission to build a home on their preferred site. When all the arguments had been put forward and vigorously debated the planners relented and agreed to grant David and Wendy the planning approval they so much wanted.

Jeffrey's next call that afternoon was in the Boxmore Plastics factory in Lisburn to discuss the problems they were having with high energy costs and then it was on from there to meet an elderly lady in Dunmurry, on the outskirts of Belfast. This lady was living in unsatisfactory, temporary accommodation and was anxious to obtain a house or flat in the nearby Seymour Hill Housing Estate. Jeffrey saw where she was living, understood her desire to move to somewhere with more modern facilities, and promised to contact the appropriate housing authority on her behalf.

When he returned to his constituency office in Lisburn it was just after 5.30 p.m.

His desk was covered with messages to be attended to and letters that Norah had left for him to sign, and when he was finished all of that he took an hour off to have a meal.

That evening Jeffrey visited an Art Show in Lisburn Institute of Further and Higher Education and it was well after ten o'clock before he made it home for the night.

Tuesday morning began in much the same way as Monday morning had done. Jeffrey spent some time at home catching up with correspondence and compiling a list of calls to make in relation to the previous day's meetings and visits.

When he arrived in his constituency office he began to work his way through the pile of letters on his desk. One of them gave him a particular sense of satisfaction.

A few months earlier Nigel and Marion Jackson had called to ask for Jeffrey's advice and help with some difficulties they were experiencing with their small business in Lisburn. Their MP had done what he could to assist them and this was their note of thanks. It said simply:

Dear Jeffrey,

We would like to thank you for what you have done for our family and us.

We didn't think anyone would care enough to help us in our hour of need.

What we are trying to say is, that in a thankless job as yours must be, you can be sure that at least one family in your constituency really, really appreciates what you have done for them.

'And the King shall answer and say unto them, Verily I say unto you, Inasmuch as you have done it unto one of the least of these my brethren, you have done it unto me.'
Matthew 25: 40

Nigel & Marion Jackson

It was most encouraging to receive a letter like that at the beginning of what promised to be yet another routinely busy day, and to be reminded from the scripture quotation that what he was attempting to do for the people of Lagan Valley was also recognised as part of his service for God.

At 9.30 a.m. a group of residents from the north side of Lisburn came in to see their MP to voice their concerns about the plans by the Ministry of Defence to build a large number of houses in the area. They were particularly worried, they said, about the effect that this proposed development would have on the roads network in the surrounding district. An increased volume of traffic would make the roads more dangerous for their children.

This was but the first of a series of appointments that morning and Jeffrey remained in the office, dealing with issues raised by a succession of groups of constituents until lunchtime.

He held a staff meeting with Norah, his secretary, and David Archer, his assistant, over lunch. They reviewed all the ongoing casework, deciding how the different items should be dealt with. David and Norah would have a full afternoon's work on what had been delegated to them. There would undoubtedly be new cases coming in throughout the week, too, and relevant information about each of them would be compiled to await the attention of the constituency MP on his next full day in the office, which would probably be Friday.

With the staff meeting complete it was time for Jeffrey to drive to Belfast International Airport to catch the 3.30 p.m. flight to London, where another round of engagements awaited him at Westminster.

On the flight, Jeffrey was seated next to a Belfast businessman who proceeded to take him to task for his very public stance on the Agreement. The businessman argued that the Agreement was good for the economy and that political stability was essential if

Northern Ireland was ever to see a revival in its economic fortunes.

It was not the first time that Jeffrey had encountered such attitudes in the confines of an aeroplane cabin, but at least this man had confronted Jeffrey face to face and given him the chance to reply. The MP responded to the points that the man had made by saying that he remained convinced that the Agreement was fundamentally flawed and was incapable of delivering the political stability which its supporters had promised, and which everyone in the province craved.

While such encounters were difficult, Jeffrey felt satisfied when he had been able to at least express his point of view. What he found much more hurtful was when those whom he knew well, and with whom he had often travelled back and forward to London on flights, chatting amicably, before the Agreement, now ignored him completely.

It was hard to come to terms with.

As the plane began its descent into London and the MP and the businessman sat silently side by side, everything said that could be said, Jeffrey wondered how many more of these men there were in Northern Ireland. Then he brought it closer to home and began to speculate on how many of the businessmen in his constituency didn't agree with his perspective of the Agreement. How many of them were there living beside him in Moira, for instance? Or working in the shops and factories in Lisburn?

There couldn't be all that many when one considered his massive majority at the General Election.

The voice of a senior member of the cabin crew, welcoming everyone to 'London, Heathrow,' diverted his mind on to a different, and immensely more reassuring, track.

The people of Lagan Valley had elected him as their MP, to

represent them at Westminster, and so when he stepped off the plane in London he was there on behalf of the twenty four and a half thousand people who had voted for him, plus every other man, woman and child in the constituency.

He was struck yet again with the awesome responsibility and tremendous privilege of it all.

When he had first stood up to speak in the House of Commons he had been convinced that his path to that point had been directed by God.

Now, two years later, Jeffrey believed even more strongly that he was where God had planned for him to be, doing what He had prepared him to do.

And he would do it, with all his ability and with every ounce of his energy, for as long as his Heavenly Father and his earthly constituents wanted him to.

27
FROM G6 TO UNION FIRST

On arriving in central London, Jeffrey went straight to the House of Commons where he had arranged to have dinner with Rev. Francis Pym. This prominent Church of England minister spent a lot of time working alongside Christian Members of Parliament, both from the Commons and the Lords, affording them spiritual counsel and support.

Rev. Pym had requested this meeting with Jeffrey Donaldson for he had a proposal to put to him. He would like to see a group formed to meet regularly in the Palace of Westminster and pray specifically for Parliament in its role as lawmaker for the country.

As Francis outlined his vision to the MP for Lagan Valley he explained that he had already approached a number of interested prayer leaders from the Greater London area who would be willing to come in to pray with and for the Christians in Parliament.

Jeffrey found the prospect of forming such a group most appealing and agreed to put Francis' proposal to a meeting of the Parliamentary Christian Fellowship, which he planned to attend on Thursday morning.

At 8.30 a.m. on Wednesday, Jeffrey arrived back at Westminster to participate in what was one of the most important, and most inspiring, appointments of his week.

He made his way to room W1, off Westminster Hall, where he found three members of the G6 group already waiting. The remaining two came in within minutes to complete the company.

This partnership consisted of six Members of Parliament, from across the political spectrum at Westminster. They had one common bond that united them, despite differences in party perspective, and that was their Christian faith. The group had been formed during Jeffrey's first year in Parliament, and had been the vision of Anthony Cordle, a Christian with a keen interest in politics, and who worked closely with the Parliamentary Christian Fellowship. Anthony appreciated the pressure that many Christian MPs were under and recognised that they could benefit from meeting each other on a regular basis to pray, read the Bible, and discuss matters both spiritual and parliamentary, together.

The term G6 had been borrowed from the world of international leadership and represented the number of MPs who had agreed to support one another in prayer and fellowship. The G6 comprised two Labour MPs, Stephen Timms, (East Ham) and Andy Reed, (Loughborough), two Conservative MPs, Gary Streeter, (Devon South West) and Caroline Spelman, (Meriden), one Liberal Democrat MP, Steve Webb, (Northavon) and the Ulster Unionist Party MP from Lagan Valley.

Jeffrey had always found this appointment with his Christian colleagues every Wednesday morning most encouraging, and that morning was no exception. It was comforting to engage in prayer and Bible study with people of like mind. Parliament, although a constantly busy place, can still be a lonely environment for an MP who is removed, perhaps hundreds of miles, from his or her constituency. Jeffrey found this loneliness particularly acute when excluded from much of the political activity in Northern Ireland following the Belfast Agreement, and at that time the prayerful support of his friends in G6 had proved invaluable.

When the G6 meeting ended in W1 it was up to the UUP office where Jeffrey went through the mail with Margaret Mc Kee, the secretary to the Ulster Unionist Parliamentary Party. Margaret, who came originally from outside Newry, Co. Down, is a committed Christian and had worked in the Youth Board of the Presbyterian Church in Ireland and with Evangelical Alliance, both in Belfast, before moving to the capital to take up her post with the UUP at Westminster.

As a member of the well-known church, All Souls, Langham Place, Margaret was well acquainted with Christian activity in London and was very supportive of Jeffrey's Christian interests in Parliament. She provided administrative support for the Parliamentary Christian Fellowship, in addition to her normal duties, and the PCF meeting, due to take place the following morning, was amongst a number of matters they discussed in the half-hour they were together.

At 10.20 a.m. Andy Atkins from Tear Fund called to meet Jeffrey in his private office at Westminster to discuss the possibility of developing parliamentary support for the work of this Christian relief organisation. Jeffrey undertook to highlight some of the issues of prime concern to Tear Fund, including the pressing need of that particular period which was death by famine in some of Africa's most impoverished countries, in the House of Commons. He would urge the UK Government to provide immediate aid to these drought-stricken regions, where people were dying daily in their hundreds from hunger and malnutrition.

On a personal level, Jeffrey enjoyed working alongside Tear Fund as he recognised that it presented a Christian MP with an opportunity to afford practical support to the work of a relief organisation with a strongly Christian ethos.

Long before he had become an MP Eleanor and he had signed up for Tear Fund's child-care partnership programme in which people wishing to provide practical support can make regular contributions to help children from deprived backgrounds. Jeffrey and Eleanor had decided to support two girls, reflecting their own family. One of these girls was from Kenya, the other from the Philippines. All four members of the Donaldson family enjoyed receiving letters from the girls and learning how their monthly donations had made a tremendous difference in their lives and circumstances.

In one particular instance they were made aware of a special need in the life of the girl in Kenya. Her home had burnt down, and Jeffrey and Eleanor had sent a special one-off donation to help the family relocate. The very grateful letter that they received some months later was most moving. It was marvellous what a few pounds, properly channelled by Tear Fund, could do for a family in need.

With such a wealth of experience of the practical benefits of the ongoing work of the organisation, Jeffrey was happy to assure Andy that he would do all he could to raise, and develop, parliamentary backing for its valuable, often life-saving, operations.

There was little time to spare before Jeffrey's next meeting, which was a briefing by leading members of the Down's Syndrome Association in one of the committee rooms above the chamber in the House of Commons. There were a number of MPs from different parties present to hear the two speakers outline the extent of the condition across the country and seek Government support for research into it.

This was yet another instance of a case where Jeffrey's interest in, and willingness to become involved with, an organisation, stemmed from his earlier life and experiences in Northern Ireland. He had become acutely aware of the field of disability, having grown up with, and often helped to care for, his brother Andrew who was quite severely disabled with cerebral palsy. Jeffrey had often felt perturbed by the way his parents had to struggle to obtain proper help and support for Andrew, and was determined to do everything possible to make it easier for others coping with disabled children.

After lunch and further paperwork the Lagan Valley MP went down to the Chamber for the start of the day's business, which began with prayers, conducted by the Speaker's Chaplain. Not all MPs attend for prayers but Jeffrey Donaldson had made it a policy to be present, wherever possible, for this brief, but nonetheless important, recognition of God in the proceedings of Parliament.

A series of departmental questions followed immediately after prayers and lasted up until Prime Minister's Questions at three o'clock. The House was full for this event and all across the democratic world people would be turning on their TV sets to watch this political drama unfold.

Jeffrey rarely missed this gladiatorial contest of finger-pointing debate between the Prime Minister and the Leader of the Opposition, and on that particular day one of the points at issue was of special significance to all the Northern Ireland MPs.

The Leader of the Opposition, William Hague, reminded the Prime Minister of his commitment to the people of Northern Ireland on the morning of the referendum the previous year. This was that 'representatives of parties intimately linked to paramilitary groups can only be in a future Northern Ireland Government if it is clear that there will be no more violence and the threat of violence has gone. That doesn't just mean decommissioning...but all the structures of terrorism.'

He then proceeded to pose some pertinent questions.

"Does the Prime Minister agree that the beatings, shootings and mutilations continue and are being carried out by organisations that actually signed the agreement?" he enquired. "Terrorist structures remain fully operational and fully armed and 277 terrorists are back on the streets, including yesterday the Brighton bomber walking free. Do not these grim facts show that the real obstacle to progress is not the Ulster Unionist Party, the SDLP, the Government or the Opposition, but the refusal of terrorist groups to decommission their illegal weapons?"

The Prime Minister responded by saying, "Well, they have to decommission their weapons; that is clear. These judgements on ceasefires are very difficult indeed..."

"They are difficult decisions," William Hague admitted in reply, before continuing, "The Conservative Party and millions of people across the country support the Good Friday agreement and want it to succeed, but look with dismay on the early release of terrorists and their possible inclusion in Government when not one gun or one ounce of Semtex has been handed in. However, I am pleased to hear the Prime Minister say that they must decommission. As we approach next week's deadline, will he give an undertaking that until there has been a credible and verifiable start to decommissioning, he will not ask the First Minister of Northern Ireland to enter an Executive with Sinn Fein?"

After the Prime Minister had responded to this direct examination of his intentions by saying that he did not intend 'to end up negotiating the terms of the agreement in the next few days,' two other MPs, David Marshall, Labour, (Glasgow,

Shettleston) and the leader of the Liberal Democrats, Paddy Ashdown, both spoke in support of the Government's stance.

This lively exchange on the future of the province set the scene for two further meetings that Jeffrey Donaldson was to attend later in the day.

The first of these was a meeting of the Northern Ireland Select Committee at 3.45 p.m., immediately after Prime Minister's Questions. This Committee was chaired by Peter Brooke, former Secretary of State for Northern Ireland, and was made up of thirteen MPs. Seven of these were Labour, and the remaining six were from the Opposition parties. Northern Ireland was represented by four of its MPs, Peter Robinson (DUP), Eddie Mc Grady, (SDLP) and Roy Beggs and Jeffrey Donaldson, from the UUP.

The two main items on the agenda for that afternoon were reports on the seemingly ever-contentious Parades issue, and the future of the Prison Service in Northern Ireland, following the release of so many paramilitary prisoners under the terms of the Belfast Agreement. Having been involved in mediation at Drumcree nearly four years earlier, and with his current work in support of the families of those maimed or murdered by terrorist activity, Jeffrey had strong views on both matters and contributed enthusiastically to the debates and questioning in the Committee.

At 6.30 p.m. Jeffrey joined all his UUP colleagues for a meeting of the Parliamentary Party in David Trimble's office in the House of Commons. This was the second occasion on which William Hague's probing questions on Northern Ireland was to give rise to some animated argument on the outcome of the 'Good Friday' Agreement.

Jeffrey Donaldson and a number of the other MPs present took the opportunity to express their frustration at the complete lack of progress on the decommissioning of paramilitary weapons and the continuing acts of terrorism in parts of Northern Ireland.

The Lagan Valley MP had met, just a few weeks earlier, with some of the families of the victims of the Omagh bombing. This act of barbarity, which had occurred the previous August, had resulted in the loss of twenty-nine innocent lives. Jeffrey conveyed something of the sense of devastation felt by these people at their loss and also their exasperation at the apparent failure of the authorities to apprehend anyone for the bombing. He went on to say that it was ironic that this worst atrocity of what had become known as 'the Troubles,' had occurred after the Agreement, in a period when its advocates had forecast that it would have delivered peace.

Recalling the encounter with Adam Ingram on Monday, Jeffrey described the sense of betrayal felt by people like Michelle Williamson and Joseph and Annie Mc Ilwaine and which they had expressed in forthright terms to the Minister. They had told him how they had been forced to watch in horror and disbelief as the terrorists who had murdered their loved ones were released from prison.

Jeffrey urged David Trimble to stand by the party pledge of 'No guns, no government,' and refuse to form an administration that included Sinn Fein in the absence of actual decommissioning by the IRA. He was not the only one who felt that way either. Others of his colleagues, and particularly William Ross and Rev. Martin Smyth, backed his point of view, citing instances from their own constituencies to support their argument.

When the meeting of the Ulster Unionist Parliamentary Party finished Jeffrey returned to the Chamber, where the debates were continuing, and he remained there until the House rose at 10.00 p.m. for the adjournment.

There was a meeting of the Executive Committee of the Parliamentary Christian Fellowship at 9.30 a.m. on the Thursday morning and that was Jeffrey's first appointment of the day.

The Parliamentary Christian Fellowship is a group of evangelical Christian MPs and members of the House of Lords who seek to maintain a Christian witness in Parliament. There has always been a strong Christian influence at Westminster down the centuries with men like William Wilberforce and Lord Shaftesbury having made a significant contribution to the life and laws of the nation. The members of the PCF endeavour to ensure that such a vital influence continues to be kept to the fore in the national legislature.

It was Jeffrey's colleague, Rev. Martin Smyth, who had introduced him to the PCF when he had first been elected to Parliament, and such was his enthusiasm for the activities of the Fellowship that he was soon appointed to the Executive Committee.

The Committee planned a number of events during the year and the main item on the agenda that morning was the next National Prayer Breakfast. During the course of the meeting Jeffrey informed the other members of the proposal from Rev. Francis Pym to form an intercessory prayer group, bringing together parliamentarians and prayer leaders from across the capital and beyond, to pray regularly for Parliament. This suggestion was warmly welcomed by the Committee who saw it as a natural extension of their witness.

Jeffrey Donaldson spent the rest of that day involved in various items of parliamentary business before catching a late afternoon flight back to Belfast. Later that evening he addressed Portadown Unionist Branch in Carleton Street Orange Hall.

On Friday morning when he went into his office in Lisburn to begin another round of engagements there were two most gratifying 'Thank You' cards awaiting him in the mail.

The first of these was from David and Wendy Cairns, who wrote: -

Dear Mr. Donaldson,

We are very pleased to inform you that our planning application has finally been accepted.... We would like to express to you our deepest appreciation for all your help in this matter, and cannot begin to describe how pleased we both are.

Once again, many thanks for your time and energy given to us.

David & Wendy.

The other card was from Michelle Williamson, who said: -

Dear Jeffrey,

Just a little card to say 'Thank you' for all your help and support throughout the whole campaign for justice.

You have always stood beside me when I stood alone, and I appreciate that.

I wish you all the very best in your political career.

Many thanks again,

Michelle.

Jeffrey had always found it uplifting when those for whom he had provided some help took the trouble to say, 'Thanks,' and he began that Friday morning of appointments with constituents in his office with renewed zeal.

Some might have had the impression that because Jeffrey Donaldson was a unionist politician he only worked for Protestant people. He had always made it clear, however, that if elected he would represent, and work diligently for, every member of his constituency, irrespective of their political or religious affiliations. This was well illustrated that morning when one of those who came to see him was a Roman Catholic gentleman from just outside Lisburn. He was interested in extending his bed and breakfast business and was anxious to obtain the help of his MP in seeking assistance from the Northern Ireland Tourist Board to allow him to proceed with his plans.

Jeffrey gave him some advice on procedures and then assured him that he would contact the NITB on his behalf.

It was off to Belfast in the afternoon for a meeting of Party Officers in Ulster Unionist Party Headquarters in Glengall Street. Ever since the signing of the Belfast Agreement these meetings had become increasingly contentious affairs, with two distinctly different opinions emerging as to its importance and possible effectiveness. Jeffrey, and those who shared his perspective on the matter, consistently maintained that it could never deliver a just and lasting peace in Northern Ireland.

On his way back home to Moira, Jeffrey called with a group of pensioners in Glenburn Road, Dunmurry, to discuss the possibility of having central heating installed in their homes, and other improvements, which the residents described as 'long overdue,' carried out.

Having spent an hour at home for a meal Jeffrey was on the road again, this time to speak at the ceremony for the unfurling of a new banner for one of the local Orange Lodges near Aghalee.

On Saturday morning the Lagan Valley MP had two constituency calls to make, one in his home village of Moira and the other in Hillsborough, before attending the opening of a new shop for the mobile phone company, Orange, in Bow Street, Lisburn, at noon.

It was a pleasant change for Jeffrey to relax at home with his wife and daughters on the Saturday afternoon. It had been a busy week. Many matters had been seen to, and settled. Others had just been raised and would require a lot more time and effort expended upon them before they could be considered closed. All such issues could be set to one side for five or six hours, though, as the family spent time together before husband and father welcomed a number of important visitors to the Donaldson home in Moira that evening, for his final engagement of the week.

Those who had come to call were the leading members of Union First.

This group had been launched by senior figures in the Ulster Unionist Party who continued to oppose the Belfast Agreement. Those present included Lord Molyneaux, Rev. Martin Smyth MP, Arlene Foster, Peter King and Peter Weir. An apology had been received from William Ross MP, another ardent member of the dissenting alliance.

The purpose of that evening's meeting was to plan the way forward for the group, focussing particularly on how best to maximise their strength within the party to prevent David Trimble from reneging on his election pledges. They were aware that support for their position was increasing month by month but concerned that time might run out before they could convince a majority within the party of their belief that the 'Good Friday' Agreement was deeply flawed and incapable of delivering long term stability for Northern Ireland.

It was difficult to interpret the ongoing political manoeuvrings, including discussions between the Prime Minister, Sinn Fein, and David Trimble, as hopeful signs. These different leaders and groupings were obviously making every effort to break the political impasse and see a power-sharing Executive created and power devolved to the Northern Ireland Assembly.

Jeffrey warned his colleagues that whilst the political scene would quieten down during the summer they needed to be prepared for an increase in momentum leading to a significant sequence of events in the autumn.

Before the host bade his guests goodbye later on that evening, at the end of what had probably been a full week for all of them, the members of Union First had come to an unwelcome, but inescapable, conclusion.

It was that the prospect of a showdown within the Ulster Unionist Party was drawing ever closer.

28
WE HAVE JUMPED

Jeffrey had been correct in his prediction. Political activity began to tone down over the summer holiday period.

This did not mean that the Lagan Valley MP became suddenly and involuntarily inactive, however. His work in the constituency continued as usual and he also began to focus his attention on other more seasonal matters, including the Orange parades in July, which had been synonymous with summer in Northern Ireland for many generations.

Monday, July 12, 1999, was a particularly significant day in the lives of thousands of members of the Orange Order, for that was the day of their traditional parade, but it was unusually memorable for Jeffrey Donaldson for two reasons.

Firstly he had been the main platform speaker at the Orange Demonstration in Magheragall, outside Lisburn. It was a very pleasant day and the crowd, comprised of Orangemen and the members of all the accompanying bands, with their relatives and friends, was, according to organisers, amongst the largest they had seen for many years.

As he sat on the platform, waiting his turn to speak, Jeffrey listened to the resolutions being passed. One of these was a resolution of loyalty to the Queen. Thinking forward to his next appointment, Jeffrey made a mental note to tell Her Majesty about that one.

When he had finished speaking to the huge crowd, who either

stood or sat around, enjoying the summer sunshine, Jeffrey left the platform and was driven away with a motorcycle escort. He was on his way to the airport to catch a flight to London where he had an extremely important appointment.

He had been invited to attend a reception, hosted by Her Majesty The Queen, at Buckingham Palace at 6.00 p.m.

Having made it, with little time to spare, Jeffrey mingled with the other guests as Her Majesty moved from group to group speaking to everyone. When she came along and stopped with Jeffrey, the Lagan Valley MP said, amongst other things, "I'm glad to speak to you in person, ma'am. I was pledging loyalty to Your Majesty earlier today."

The Queen smiled knowingly, no doubt well aware of the importance of the date, July 12, to many of her subjects in Northern Ireland.

When Parliament resumed in October, after the summer recess, the political talks resumed in earnest, with David Trimble engaging in discussions with the other parties and the British and Irish Governments in an effort to break the deadlock which had occurred in the wake of the Belfast Agreement. Jeffrey and his colleagues surmised that this could not occur without further compromising the democratic process, and this would prove totally unacceptable to them.

It was clear that the inevitable moment of open confrontation was almost upon them.

While he continued to monitor the progress of these talks very closely, Jeffrey was still engaged in the daily round of activities in Lagan Valley. One of the most exciting challenges in which he was involved in that autumn of 1999 was the initiation of a campaign to have Lisburn promoted from borough to city status.

On Thursday, November 4, the MP for the area attended, and contributed enthusiastically and constructively to, a meeting at which the case for Lisburn was outlined.

The Government had written to towns of a certain size throughout the United Kingdom inviting them to apply for elevation to city status and they would award this honour to one town only to mark the dawn of the new millennium. The representatives of a number of local public bodies, gathered at that meeting, decided that Lisburn had a very strong case to present, and agreed unanimously to support the application.

On the following Sunday, November 7, Jeffrey returned to his native Mourne district to attend a ceremony during which a memorial to the victims of terrorism in the area was unveiled. When the formal proceedings were over Jeffrey stepped forward to read the list of names inscribed on the memorial and he hadn't gone far down it until he came to his cousins, Alex and Samuel Donaldson. He could barely believe that it was almost thirty years since Samuel had been murdered. He remembered it as though it were yesterday. The knock at the door, his father's shocking announcement, the inconsolable grief, the funeral, and the sense of numbness that had beset the family circle for months.

Having paused for a moment to relive one of his most realistic and horrific memories of childhood, Jeffrey read on down the list and it wasn't long until he came to the name of Alan Johnston. As soon as he reached Alan's name he lifted his head instinctively and looked across the road at Mourne Presbyterian Church.

Jeffrey remembered both happy and challenging days in that building. The day of his wedding, when he and Eleanor had paused on the steps that he could see clearly from where he stood, to allow Enoch Powell to give the new bride a hearty congratulatory kiss, had been a day of unrestrained joy and gladness.

By contrast, the day of the funeral of the man whose name had inspired him to glance across at the church, had been a day of unrestrained grief and sadness. And for Jeffrey it had been even more than that. As he had sat looking at his UDR colleague's coffin he had been struck, through the singing of the well-known hymn, 'Abide With Me', by the uncertainty of life, the inevitability of death, and the necessity to prepare for the hereafter. It was on that day that he had made up his mind to make his peace with God, whatever the cost.

On the way home, as he reflected on the hurt inflicted on the Mourne community, as it had been on so many other communities in Northern Ireland, Jeffrey wondered if all the killing and maiming had honestly come to an end.

It was by then eighteen months since the 'Good Friday' Agreement and there was still no sign of the IRA beginning the decommissioning of its illegal weapons. Support amongst unionists for David Trimble's strategy was beginning to wane and the UUP leader knew that he had to take unprecedented steps to try and move matters forward. Senator George Mitchell had been invited back by the two Governments to conduct a review of the Agreement and under his renewed chairmanship the talks gathered momentum.

The British and Irish Governments were both putting pressure on Sinn Fein to deliver an IRA statement of their future intentions. This would enable David Trimble to enter a power-sharing Executive with Sinn Fein for the first time in the history of Northern Ireland. The leader of the Ulster Unionist Party was shown a draft IRA statement which he rejected at first, but when the IRA agreed to appoint an interlocutor to liaise with the

International Independent Commission on Decommissioning, (IICD) headed by General John de Chastelain, he decided that this might form a basis for recommending to his party that they enter an Executive with Sinn Fein. In doing this he hoped that it would prove sufficient to persuade the republican leadership to decommission at least some of its weaponry.

Senator Mitchell announced the conclusion of his review on Monday, November 15, and there followed a series of statements by each of the parties involved. When he had analysed all the declarations that had been made, David Trimble concluded that they provided a basis on which the Ulster Unionist Party could proceed with the establishment of the power-sharing Executive. He convened a special meeting of the Party Officers who agreed to call an extraordinary meeting of the Ulster Unionist Council on Saturday, November 27, to take a final decision.

Jeffrey Donaldson felt that the deal on offer was totally inadequate and he and his fellow-dissenting MPs from the Ulster Unionist Parliamentary Party issued a statement rejecting it.

Intense lobbying took place on both sides of the divided party over the next ten days. There were over eight hundred delegates entitled to attend, and cast their votes at, the crucial meeting on the last Saturday of the month and each side was anxious to secure a council majority on that date.

The strain and tension within the party was evident as the tight-lipped delegates arrived at the Waterfront Hall in Belfast at 10.30 a.m. that morning for the commencement of this critical meeting of its governing body.

Nobody was in any doubt that the day they had all seen coming had at last arrived. It was now time to address all the issues that had split the party so deeply, out in the open.

The days of hectic lobbying were over.

The hour of confrontation, and then decision, had arrived.

Shortly after the meeting began David Trimble made a gesture in an attempt to win the support of the delegates who still remained undecided on how to vote. Some of them had been bombarded by the propaganda from both camps and were vacillating.

Recognising the perceived weakness of what was on offer from the IRA, the party leader proceeded to alter his proposal to the meeting by adding an offer to reconvene the UUC in February 2000, should the IRA fail to decommission its weapons following the establishment of an Executive.

The debate within the hall became increasingly passionate as the morning wore on, despite this concession from the party leader. Feelings were running high as speaker after speaker addressed the gathering, giving his or her tenaciously held reasons for accepting or rejecting David Trimble's motion.

Jeffrey was chosen to wind up the debate on behalf of 'the opposition,' and he spoke forthrightly about what he believed to be the futility of the UUP abandoning its manifesto pledge of 'No guns, no government,' in return for what could only be described as a very vague and non-committal statement by the IRA. He predicted that the IRA would not decommission within the time-frame set by David Trimble and that the Ulster Unionist Party would pay a heavy price at the next election for welshing on its promises to the unionist people. The electorate would not take kindly to 'allowing Sinn Fein to corrupt the democratic process by acting as law-makers by day and law-breakers by night,' he contended. His closing words came in the form of an impassioned appeal to the delegates to stand by their principles and vote against the motion.

When the speeches were over, however, and the votes were counted, 480 delegates had voted for the motion with 349 against. It appeared as though David Trimble's 'post dated cheque,' had proved crucial in persuading a majority of those present to support him in his decision to enter into Government with Sinn Fein. At a press conference after the meeting the leader of the Ulster Unionist Party had 'a message for Gerry Adams.'

It was, "We have jumped. Now you follow."

A few days later the first local administration to be set up in Northern Ireland since 1974 was formed. To the horror of many unionists, Martin Mc Guinness was appointed as Minister of Education in the new power-sharing Executive, and his colleague Bairbre de Brun became Minister of Health. This sense of outrage in the unionist community was made even worse by the fact that these two Sinn Fein Ministers now controlled more than half of the Northern Ireland budget and yet there appeared to be no sign whatsoever of the IRA fulfilling its obligations.

With party members feeling particularly irritated by the IRA's failure to commence the process of decommissioning, as promised, the Ulster Unionist Council was reconvened on Saturday, February 12, 2000 to review the situation. It had been intended that the Council would vote to withdraw the UUP Ministers from the Executive, in keeping with David Trimble's pledge made at the meeting in November.

This decision had been pre-empted by Peter Mandelson, who had been appointed Secretary of State for Northern Ireland in succession to Mo Mowlam, however. He announced the suspension of devolution and a return to direct rule from Westminster. This move meant that all of the Ministers in the Executive had their powers withdrawn.

Before the end of the meeting that day Jeffrey argued that the events of the previous few months proved that he and his colleagues had been vindicated in their stance and that David Trimble had been foolish to put his trust in an IRA statement that was so clearly short on commitment and clarity.

With the Annual General Meeting of the Ulster Unionist Council just six weeks away, and with the posts of all the Party Officers, including David Trimble's position as leader, up for re-election at that meeting, the tension failed to ease.

There was growing pressure from within Union First, and also from many dissatisfied members of the Ulster Unionist Council, for a leadership challenge. Jeffrey and his parliamentary colleagues met at Westminster early in the week in which the election was to be held, to formulate a plan of action.

It was agreed that Rev. Martin Smyth, who was the most senior member of the group, should announce that he was challenging David Trimble for the leadership of the Ulster Unionist Party. The group also discussed their reaction to another item on the agenda for Saturday's AGM, and that was the report by the former Tory MP and Governor of Hong Kong, Chris Patten, on the future of policing in Northern Ireland.

Jeffrey and his colleagues were opposed to certain key elements of the Patten Report, regarding it as effectually marking the end of the Royal Ulster Constabulary, the force which had served so courageously for many years. Its contribution had been particularly commendable during the thirty years of 'the Troubles' when so many of its officers had lost their lives in protecting the entire community from terrorism. The MPs meeting in Westminster decided to support a motion which would require a guarantee of the retention of the title of the RUC as a condition of any resumption of the power-sharing Executive.

Following another spell of intense pressure on the delegates by the two factions within the UUC, they all reassembled, for the third time in four months, on Saturday, March 25, at Balmoral in south Belfast.

When it came to the vote on the leadership issue that day, David Trimble was re-elected as leader with a majority of 457 to 348 over Rev. Martin Smyth.

Later in the meeting, though, the members of Union First secured a significant victory in relation to the Royal Ulster Constabulary. After the motion had been debated at some length the Ulster Unionist Council voted by a majority of fifty three per cent to forty seven per cent to press for the retention of the title of the RUC.

This was the first defeat that David Trimble had suffered within his own governing body for some time.

He had jumped, along with more than half of the party.

Who, though, was following?

And were some of the original jumpers now deciding to jump back?

More importantly, where did all this constant in-fighting leave Jeffrey Donaldson, sympathetic supporter of the victims of terrorist violence and uncompromising campaigner for the decommissioning of terrorist armaments, in his desire to see a just and lasting peace return to Northern Ireland?

29
FORGOTTEN FAMILIES

The death of a mutual friend can often have the effect of causing people to acknowledge the relative insignificance of their differences, whether political, cultural, or religious, when jolted into an unwelcome recognition of their own mortality. A shared sense of grief can lead to those of varying opinions forgetting their disagreements, at least temporarily, on such occasions.

This happened to members of the Ulster Unionist Party and particularly those in its Parliamentary wing in the spring of 2000.

Life for Jeffrey Donaldson and all the other Westminster MPs had settled into its established pattern after the Annual General Meeting of the party in March. They were all busy, both in their constituencies and in the Houses of Parliament, where their regular meetings could be either quite relaxed or unbearably strained. A lot depended on the topic under discussion at the time.

Then Clifford Forsythe, MP for South Antrim, and one of their respected colleagues, died suddenly. This came as a shock to the members of the Parliamentary Party and they all shelved their differences on Saturday, April 29, as they assembled at his funeral to mourn Clifford's passing and extend their sympathy to his grieving family.

Jeffrey felt his loss very keenly as Clifford had shared his views on the Agreement and other political matters, and they had worked closely together on a number of issues.

Clifford's was not the only funeral Jeffrey had to attend that week. Samuel and Alex Donaldson's mother, Isobel, who had lived at Ballinran, was buried two days earlier, on Thursday 27. The minister at the funeral that afternoon reminded the congregation of Isobel's unswerving Christian faith, which had been an example to many after she had suffered the double blow of losing two sons to terrorism.

The political battle to remove the threat of that terrorism continued in the days that followed, with constant pressure being exerted on the paramilitary organisations to decommission their paramilitary weapons. The IRA, in response, made a statement on May 6, in which they agreed to re-engage with the independent decommissioning body to discuss putting their arms 'beyond use.' They also consented to allow some arms dumps to be inspected by two international inspectors, who, it subsequently emerged, were to be the former ANC Secretary-General, Cyril Ramaphosa from South Africa, and the former Finnish President, Martti Ahtisaari.

Having consulted with his closest allies in the senior levels of the party, David Trimble again announced that he was calling a special meeting of the Ulster Unionist Council to recommend that the Ulster Unionist Party return to a power-sharing Executive with Sinn Fein.

Jeffrey and his partners in Union First held meetings with delegates in a number of towns across the province prior to this meeting of the UUC, which was scheduled to take place on Saturday, May 27. In addition to this the Lagan Valley MP spent a lot of time talking to party members on the telephone in an effort to persuade them to vote against the proposal to re-enter government with Sinn Fein. This, he argued, would be a mistake for the party and bad for the country.

On the day of the meeting Jeffrey once again opened the debate on behalf of those in opposition to the party leader's policy. He proposed that rather than coming to any immediate conclusion on the matter the delegates should delay making a decision until the IRA had actually begun to decommission its illegal weapons.

Another vigorous, and at times acrimonious, debate ensued, in the prestigious surroundings of Belfast's Waterfront Hall, with the world's media encamped outside awaiting the outcome.

When the vote was finally taken, those present voted by the narrow margin of 459 to 403 in favour of Mr. Trimble's recommendation to return to devolved government. However, the party leader recognised that the gap had closed significantly, and that the Ulster Unionist Party was split, virtually down the middle. Fully aware that if this trend were to continue there would come a day, at one of these by now painfully regular meetings, that his stance would be rejected. With that possibility in mind he had a blunt message for the IRA when speaking to the assembled media after the meeting. It was simply, "There is a limit to the extent we can stretch ourselves without an adequate response being made in the circumstances."

With Parliament in recess over the summer, Jeffrey turned his attention to a subject about which he felt very strongly. He had been contacted by a number of RUC widows whose husbands had been murdered in 'The Troubles,' but prior to 1982 when the Government had introduced enhanced compensation and pension arrangements.

Jeffrey agreed to meet a small delegation of these women and he listened carefully as they outlined their plight. They explained what it was like struggling to rear a family, having been deprived of the help of their husbands, and with little financial support. The Lagan Valley MP could identify with them completely. His cousin Alex's wife, Ida, was an RUC widow and he was well aware of what she had come through trying to bring up her three children, and that was after 1982. He had no hesitation in undertaking to help them highlight their case with the Government.

He advised the ladies to contact all the widows affected and arrange for them to form an action group to pursue their case. They did this within weeks, and adopting the title, 'Forgotten Families,' set about lobbying both politicians and senior Government officials.

In response to their continual, and often emotional, representations, the Government appointed a senior civil servant, John Steele, to look into the matter. His brief was to investigate the circumstances of the pre-1982 RUC widows and prepare a report.

The Lagan Valley MP joined a small deputation of the widows as they presented the submission, which they had prepared carefully over the summer, to John Steele in September 2000. He urged the Government's representative to recognise the hurt that had been inflicted on the widows as a result of the Patten Report and in particular the decision 'to remove the proud title of the Royal Ulster Constabulary.'

When the widows were given the opportunity to speak, one of them told Mr. Steele how slighted they felt. "The title and insignia of the RUC are engraved on my husband's headstone," she informed him, "and it is an insult to his memory that both of these things should now be discarded by the Government."

Jeffrey pressed John Steele, who had listened to the ladies with obvious sympathy, to recommend to the Government that they should establish a special fund to assist the RUC widows, ensuring that they received both adequate recognition and compensation for their suffering and loss.

The group left the meeting heartened by the promise of the senior civil servant to give all aspects of the matter the most careful consideration.

Prior to the resumption of Parliament in October, a by-election was held in the South Antrim constituency to elect a new Member of Parliament, following the death of Clifford Forsythe in the spring. In a major upset for the Ulster Unionist Party, Rev. William Mc Crea of the Democratic Unionist Party won the seat by a margin of less than a thousand votes over the UUP candidate, David Burnside. Jeffrey Donaldson was not surprised at this result as it reflected what he had recognised as a significant shift in opinion amongst unionists across Northern Ireland. It was, as far as he was concerned, yet another indicator that 'grass-roots' unionism was becoming increasingly sceptical of David Trimble's policies.

With another winter season of heightened political activity about to commence, Jeffrey and his colleagues in Union First began to contemplate the fact that it was now five months since the UUP had re-entered government with Sinn Fein and there had been no discernible progress on the decommissioning issue. They decided that it was time to call the leadership to account on the matter once more, on behalf of the delegates who were constantly telling them that they were unhappy with the situation as it stood. It was not difficult to collect the sixty signatures required to convene a special meeting of the Ulster Unionist Council and the date for the meeting was set as Saturday, October 28, and the venue was to be the Waterfront Hall, overlooking the River Lagan.

With the defeat of the Ulster Unionist Party candidate in the South Antrim by-election fresh in the minds of many within the party, a bruising next round of 'the blame-game' began. Tensions continued to mount and the party's annual conference, which was also held in the Waterfront Hall on Saturday October 7, took on the appearance of a dress rehearsal for the main event. There was heated debate that day, but it was more like a sparring contest at the weigh-in rather than an all out full-blooded contest for a coveted title.

It was obvious that the protagonists were holding back on their knockout punches until the star bout on the bill, and that was scheduled for three weeks later.

A series of Union First meetings took place in the run up to the UUC meeting as Jeffrey Donaldson formulated his plans for that crucial encounter. Since his group had called the meeting they would be responsible for preparing the motion for debate, and he would present it on the day.

Business at Westminster resumed in October, and all the Ulster Unionist MPs returned to London for the opening of the new parliamentary session. One of the first items on the agenda, and one in which they would all probably be anxious to be involved, was the election of a new Speaker for the House of Commons on Monday 23, following the retirement of the popular Betty Boothroyd MP. A series of votes were held that afternoon, with a Scottish Labour MP, Michael Martin from Glasgow, finally emerging as the victor.

The Ulster Unionist Parliamentary Party were quite happy to accept Michael's appointment and congratulate him on it. In the long run it didn't matter to them who won the vote that day, provided he conducted the business of the House in an efficient and orderly fashion.

What was uppermost on their minds was who would emerge

as victor that coming Saturday. Who would win the vote then? That was of more vital and immediate concern to all of them.

As the date of the meeting approached, David Trimble recognised the growing level of dissent within the party and realised that he would once more have to come up with some alternative proposals to avoid defeat.

On Saturday, October 28, and for the fifth time inside a year, more that eight hundred delegates assembled in the by-now familiar surroundings of the Waterfront Hall. Many of them had travelled considerable distances to converge on Belfast from every county of the province, for yet another critical encounter.

Jeffrey spoke first in proposing the motion, which called upon the party to withdraw from the Northern Ireland Executive unless the IRA had begun to decommission its weapons by the end of November that year. David Trimble immediately tabled an amendment demanding that Sinn Fein Ministers be excluded from the North – South Ministerial Council unless the IRA engaged constructively in the process of decommissioning.

The debate that followed was highly charged, with speakers from both sides putting forward their arguments in clear and unequivocal terms, expressed in increasingly harsh and bitter tones.

After more than two hours of such uncompromising debate the first vote taken was on David Trimble's amendment and this was carried by a margin of 445 votes to 374.

With the amendment having been carried a vote was not taken on the main motion that had been proposed by Jeffrey Donaldson and his colleagues in Union First. The Lagan Valley MP was disappointed at this outcome but maintained that the move to call a special meeting of the UUC had been justified, for it had forced the party leader to reconsider, and then move, his position.

In an interview with the media after the meeting, Jeffrey gave his reaction to the morning's events. "In the end I think we have won some sanctions," he said. "At least we are coming away with something out of this meeting. Obviously I would like to have seen these sanctions being tougher and stronger, but we will give it a few months to see what happens. If there is no decommissioning we will be back here again, you can be sure of that."

30
FACE TO FACE

With the two distinct groupings within the Ulster Unionist Party having maintained an uneasy standoff during the winter, the following spring brought some welcome news for Jeffrey Donaldson.

On Wednesday, March 21, 2001 the Government issued the following statement:-

'The Secretary of State today announced progress on two Police-related proposals- lump-sum payments to RUC widows and the establishment of the RUC George Cross Foundation.

The first of these, which stems from John Steele's review of the recommendation for the creation of a new Police Fund, is for RUC widows whose husbands were murdered by terrorists before November 1982 to be paid lump sums to show the State's concern for this special group. The Secretary of State has decided to set these payments at double the level recommended by John Steele (£1,000 per annum of widowhood). The payments will be made in the next few days. Each widow will receive £2,000 for every year they have been widowed to date or up to remarriage. This means that the average payment to those who have not remarried is £50,000 ..

The lump sum payments will be tax-free...

The cost of the lump sum payments will be £4.2m...'

This was heartening news and Jeffrey was satisfied that his

work with and for this group of RUC widows had not been in vain. Although the Patten Report had spelt the end of the Royal Ulster Constabulary, as it had been known for so many years, it was pleasing to help ensure that these widows had been given a measure of recognition and that their families were not entirely forgotten.

It was also encouraging to know that any little he had been able to do for them had been appreciated The gratitude of the widows was expressed in a letter he was to receive from the chairman of the group a week later.

The commitment Jeffrey had shown in helping them achieve a satisfactory resolution of their situation was reflected in such comments as, 'Just to say thanks to you seems very inadequate when we are aware of how unstinting your efforts have been on our behalf,' and, 'At all times we have appreciated the way in which you responded to any queries and also how you followed up each query and got back to us. You were patience itself when I had to contact you on your mobile....'

With Easter approaching, press speculation began to mount about the prospect of the Prime Minister calling a General Election in the near future. This tentative prediction was to prove well founded, for at the beginning of May Tony Blair announced that he was 'going to the country,' with polling day set for Thursday, June 7.

As it was anticipated that a General Election would take place at some point in the year 2001, a selection meeting had already taken place in the Lagan Valley Constituency Association, and the sitting MP had been reselected as their candidate. This meant that Jeffrey had his campaign team already in place, even before the date of the election was announced, and so he considered himself reasonably well prepared to contest the seat.

With a majority of more than sixteen thousand votes when first elected as a Westminster MP, and with four years of hard work in the constituency behind him, Jeffrey might have expected an easier contest second time around.

Times had changed, though. A lot had happened in four years.

Given the deep divisions among unionists, and in the Ulster Unionist Party in particular, over the Belfast Agreement, and the Lagan Valley MP's high-profile role in leading the opposition to David Trimble's policies, it was hard to know how the electorate would respond. One thing was abundantly clear. It was that there were still those in the local Association who backed the party leader and were decidedly reluctant to support Jeffrey's candidature.

Their negative attitude was more than compensated for by the commitment of Jeffrey's growing band of supporters, however. Many of these people were not affiliated to any political party but came forward and expressed their willingness to help the MP who had worked so tirelessly on their behalf, to retain his seat.

As Jeffrey engaged in his tried-and-tested method of campaigning, that of knocking doors and talking to people, he was greatly encouraged. He hadn't visited many doorsteps before discovering an interesting, and reassuring, attitude amongst a high percentage of the electorate. It appeared that it was not his position that was being questioned by potential voters, but that of his party leader.

With the local council elections being held on the same day as the General Election there was a good turnout at the polling stations. As Jeffrey toured the constituency, endeavouring to visit every station, he was warmly received by those he met and had a feeling that his position was probably secure.

His premonition turned out to be correct.

When the count took place in Dromore Leisure Centre the following day Jeffrey Donaldson was re-elected as Member of Parliament for the Lagan Valley Constituency. His total vote of 25966 saw his majority increased, quite remarkably, to 18342.

These figures were significant, whether considered politically, by the array of political analysts who make a living from trying to explain voting patterns across the country, or personally and spiritually, by the re-elected MP himself.

It was politically impressive for at least two reasons. One was related to the situation in Lagan Valley, the other to the province as a whole.

Firstly, it was achieved in spite of the unwillingness of a number of the party members in the constituency to accord him any kind of support. The pundits could explain this by agreeing that 'Jeffrey Donaldson was a hard-working MP who was highly respected by his constituents,' and that 'many who wouldn't even bother to vote for someone less conscientious, had turned out for him.'

They had bigger problems equating Jeffrey's result with what had happened in other constituencies in Northern Ireland, where an Ulster Unionist majority had once been virtually a foregone conclusion. In many areas, that anticipated endorsement of the party and its policies at the polls didn't materialise. The UUP vote slumped to an all-time low. This led to the loss of seats in East Londonderry, West Tyrone, Fermanagh / South Tyrone, Strangford and North Belfast. Even in David Trimble's Upper Bann constituency the party leader's previously comfortable majority was slashed to two thousand votes.

On a purely personal level, Jeffrey felt that the huge contrast between his vote in Lagan Valley and that for the candidates in some other constituencies had justified his warnings to the party that their current policy of support for the 'Good Friday' Agreement did not reflect the thinking of the bulk of the unionist electorate.

Spiritually, it was both humbling and heartening. Jeffrey took his re-election with an increased majority as a clear indication that he was where God wanted him to be, doing what He wanted him to do, for Him, and all the people of Lagan Valley.

The State Opening of the new Parliament took place on Wednesday, June 20, and a week later Jeffrey and his Christian colleagues met to renew their fellowship in the little committee room off Westminster Hall. As he had watched the General Election results from the mainland coming in during the early hours of the morning following the poll, nearly three weeks earlier, the declarations Jeffrey had most keenly awaited were those from the constituencies of his five fellow members of G6.

'Will we all make it back?' had been the question uppermost in his mind.

They had, and as the six of them sat down together for the first time since the election Jeffrey discovered that he wasn't the only one who had been waiting eagerly for the results of the other five. Every member of the group admitted to having done likewise, and with the same level of enthusiasm.

Andy Reed, Labour MP for Loughborough, raised a hearty laugh when he recalled how he had been given strange looks by Labour supporters at his constituency count centre. He had cheered as the TV presenter announced that Caroline Spelman had held the Meriden seat for the Conservatives!

A Labour colleague who had witnessed this reaction eyed him rather quizzically before enquiring, "Do you not realise that Meriden was one of our top target seats in the Midlands?"

As they came to catching up together on the events of the previous few months when they had been 'at home' in their constituencies, preparing to contest the General Election, a most amazing fact emerged. They discovered that, in spite of the varied electoral fortunes of their respective parties, all six members of G6 had been returned to Parliament with increased majority votes.

In their prayer session that morning each one of them in turn thanked God for two obvious blessings. The first of these was that they had all been returned with such resounding votes of confidence from their constituencies. They took this as a sign of God's guidance in their lives and approval of their witness, not only individually, but also collectively, as they met to pray and study His word in the heart of the Mother of Parliaments. The other blessing was the reassurance of knowing that they would have each other to rely on for spiritual support as another parliamentary session stretched out ahead.

With the election over, the focus returned to the faltering political process in Northern Ireland, where David Trimble had warned that he would resign as First Minister on July 1 if there had been no decommissioning by the IRA.

His deadline passed with no movement from the republican side on the arms issue and he duly resigned as he had forewarned. With the departure of the First Minister the power-sharing Executive and the Assembly were once again plunged into crisis.

Confronted with yet another red light on what had become for him a somewhat torturous road called, 'The Peace Process,' the Prime Minster responded by convening a conference involving all the political parties and the British and Irish Governments. This was to meet at Weston Park, a seventeenth century stately home in Shropshire.

Recognising the strengthened position of the Lagan Valley MP within the party, following the General Election, David Trimble invited Jeffrey Donaldson to join the negotiating team to participate in the conference. Jeffrey replied by saying he would give the invitation some careful consideration before making a definite response. He needed to think it over as he had many reservations about returning to the centre of political discussion and decision-making.

After consulting with his senior colleagues in Union First he came to the conclusion that on balance it would be better to be on the inside track where he could monitor the progress of the negotiations. Jeffrey accepted the invitation, for to do so would place him in a position to oppose any further unnecessary concessions to the IRA.

Soon after the conference began the UUP delegation held a meeting with the Sinn Fein leadership in the rather grand old building on the morning of Tuesday, July 10. This was a momentous occasion for Jeffrey as it was the first time that he had been involved in a face-to-face encounter with the Sinn Fein leaders, who included, on that occasion, Gerry Adams, Martin Mc Guinness and Gerry Kelly.

This was to prove one of the most difficult meetings that Jeffrey Donaldson had ever attended to date, for he was chillingly conscious that the men facing him across the table were more than merely politicians. They had also strong connections with the Provisional IRA, a terrorist organisation to which he had been strenuously opposed all his life.

As he had prepared to enter the first floor meeting room that morning Jeffrey had felt a powerful surge of emotion well up within him. It was then, in the midst of all the preparations going on around, that he had taken a few seconds to pray earnestly that God would guide him through what would undoubtedly be a challenging, and possibly even painful, experience. He knew there were things that he felt he needed to say, and which Sinn Fein needed to hear, on behalf of all the people who had suffered so grievously at the hands of the IRA.

The meeting began with a general, but restrained, exchange of views between David Trimble and the republican delegation. This low-key opening interchange continued until the Lagan Valley MP cut in.

Anxious that the impact of what he had to say should be neither minimised or misunderstood, having been cloaked in a cloud of pleasantries, he went courteously, but directly, to the point.

Jeffrey began by chiding the Sinn Fein representatives for the IRA's failure to live up to its obligations on issues like decommissioning. He reminded those present of the pain the IRA had inflicted upon the whole Northern Ireland community for almost thirty years.

The moment of face-to-face encounter had arrived. It was not an experience to which Jeffrey had been looking forward with any great enthusiasm, but as he began to speak he became possessed by an unexpected sense of calm. With the emotions, which he had been afraid would overcome him in such an encounter, held well in check, he continued by giving a poignant example of what he meant.

"My family has experienced that pain," he told those present. The message was addressed to the Sinn Fein group, but of interest to all. "Constable Sam Donaldson was the first RUC officer to be murdered by the Provisional IRA, the organisation you represent, in the current 'Troubles.' That was in 1970 in Crossmaglen, South

Armagh.

The Donaldson family will never forget the letters and cards that were received from ordinary, decent Roman Catholics living in that community, expressing their sorrow at what had been done, supposedly in their name. They even held a special service in the chapel to demonstrate their abhorrence at what had taken place in their midst. That wouldn't happen today, simply because the IRA has left that community so traumatised and intimidated, as you have dispensed your terror through the bullet and the bomb.

That's why decommissioning is so important.

It will convey a clearer message than any of your words could ever express, that your so-called 'war' is over, and the siege of the community has been lifted.

You have accused me, and others like me of not wanting 'a Fenian about the place,' but the truth is that we just don't want a terrorist about the place. If you want to win the trust of the people that I represent then you must recognise their pain and take decisive steps to remove the gun from the politics of Northern Ireland.

I have every confidence that if you take those steps then unionism will be generous in its response, and the entire population of the province, whether Protestant or Roman Catholic, or whether living in Lagan Valley or South Armagh, will reap the benefit in this and future generations."

When Jeffrey had finished speaking it was to become clear from the response of the Sinn Fein delegation that his intervention in the discussions had made an impact. Their leader, Gerry Adams, declared that he and his colleagues were endeavouring to bring about an end to what he described as 'physical-force republicanism.'

With all parties having stated their positions, the talks at Weston Park adjourned for two days to allow the unionists to participate in the annual Orange Order celebrations.

During this interval, Gerry Adams was interviewed on BBC Radio Ulster on the morning of Wednesday, July 11, about the Weston Park discussions with the Ulster Unionist Party. In the course of that interview he described the talks as having been 'vigorous,' and confessed to having been particularly intrigued 'by what Jeffrey Donaldson had to say.'

When the talks resumed on July 13 it soon became evident that there was not going to be all-party agreement on the way forward. Key issues such as decommissioning remained unresolved, and so, beset with a sense of frustration at the lack of progress, the British and Irish Governments closed the talks and decided to take their own initiative. Within days they had issued a joint statement outlining their suggestions for solving the outstanding problems.

The officers of the Ulster Unionist Party did not regard their statement as a basis for further progress, however, as it included controversial proposals for an amnesty for IRA terrorists 'on the run.'

Although this attempt, by the two Governments, to bring about a resolution of this latest crisis in the process to restore lasting peace and political stability to Northern Ireland had ended in deadlock, Jeffrey felt that he had been right to attend the talks at Weston Park. He was sure that his presence in, and contribution to them, had been, at least to some degree, influential in deterring the party leadership from signing up to yet another unsatisfactory and unsustainable agreement.

Crucially, it had also given Jeffrey the opportunity to bring the republican leadership face to face with the depth of unionist concern about the current direction of the 'peace process.'

31
WHERE WAS GOD?

The media were not the only people to notice Jeffrey's increased political profile in the weeks following the General Election. It was soon to become clear that there were others who had been monitoring his movements with a more sinister motive.

One Thursday afternoon as Jeffrey sat in his office in Westminster preparing to return to Northern Ireland, he received an urgent telephone call from the Police Commander in Lisburn. Although it was obvious that he was not going to give details over the telephone, Jeffrey sensed from the gravity of his tone and the nature of his instruction that something was causing him deep concern. He told Jeffrey that he was not under any circumstances to return home that evening but he should, instead, proceed directly to Hillsborough Police Station where he would be waiting.

Jeffrey was alarmed by the seriousness of the call and was left wondering what it could mean, but he recognised that it was important that he followed the instructions he had been given, exactly. On arriving back in Northern Ireland he drove directly to Hillsborough, and as he pulled up in the car park at the front of the appointed police station he was somewhat surprised to see the Superintendent himself emerge from the redbrick building to meet him. The senior officer came out to Jeffrey's car and accompanied the MP, who had by then become rather anxious, into the station. When inside, the Superintendent lost no time in directing Jeffrey to a vacant interview room where he could reveal the purpose of his earlier telephone call.

A chill ran down the spine of the Member of Parliament for Lagan Valley as the police officer revealed that they had become aware that a dissident republican group had been 'targeting' him for some time. They had been monitoring his every movement for months and were in the advanced stages of planning an attack. The police were thoroughly convinced that an assassination attempt was imminent.

Jeffrey Donaldson had become accustomed to living with threats on his life. He had already been the target of terrorist activity. The first of a number of curtain-raisers had occurred just after he had become an MP. On that occasion a letter bomb had been addressed to him at his constituency office.

This, though, was different. Jeffrey recognised the seriousness of the situation, which the Police Commander had gone on to describe in some detail. This was no mere curtain-raiser. This was the main event, the big show. A well-organised, well-armed, ruthless group out there somewhere was preparing to kill him in the near future.

It was frightening. Jeffrey had always known that his strong opposition to terrorist activity, from whatever quarter it came, would be liable to produce threats of recrimination. He could cope with those when they existed only as vague, distant, unpleasant prospects in the subconscious. To have a high-ranking police officer sitting across a table from him, spelling out the specifics of an imminent attack on his life, was something altogether more alarming.

The Superintendent assured Jeffrey that the police would do everything possible to protect him and his family, and that from the following morning he would be provided with an armed police escort in a specially protected vehicle.

Having worked closely with some of his colleagues who had required this level of protection in the past, Jeffrey knew immediately what this would mean, not only for himself, but also for Eleanor and the girls.

As the weeks passed and Jeffrey adjusted to life with an armed escort, he was greatly impressed by the professionalism of the officers who had been assigned to protect him. They very quickly became 'part of the family,' and did all they could to limit the level of intrusion into the Donaldson domestic scene. Despite their very best efforts to remain as low-profile as possible, while still performing their function efficiently, there was no doubt that the greatly heightened level of security that had become essential to ensure Jeffrey's safety, was going to impose unavoidable restrictions in his everyday life.

After the summer holidays Jeffrey was invited to be part of an Ulster Unionist Party delegation travelling to Washington to brief the United States administration, and Congress, on the current unionist position. As he and his colleagues Ken Maginnis, former MP for Fermanagh/South Tyrone, and Belfast Councillor Chris Mc Gimpsey were flying across the Atlantic on September 11 their aircraft was suddenly diverted to make an unscheduled landing at Gander airport in Newfoundland, off the Canadian coast.

The captain gave no explanation for this change of flight plan at first other than to state that American airspace had been temporarily closed. When the plane touched down at Gander less than an hour later Jeffrey could see that there were a number of large passenger aircraft already parked up on the tarmac.

The passengers were instructed to remain in their seats and the pilot then came on to explain that there had been 'a number of serious incidents,' in the United States. These had led to the grounding of all flights in America and the shutting down of its airspace to incoming flights. No further information was available at that time and Jeffrey and all the other passengers on the virtually fully booked flight remained on the plane for hours before being finally allowed to disembark.

As they entered the airport terminal they could see that there were passengers from many nationalities being 'processed' through a hastily improvised system. It must have been a nightmare for the authorities, for the queue ahead of Jeffrey and his colleagues seemed to stretch on forever before reaching any point of action, and yet weary passengers by the planeload were still joining it from behind!

Although it would probably be ages before they would be given any official information as to what had happened to cause this current crisis, the rumours that began to circulate amongst the waiting passengers were barely believable. If they were true, and they must be, for nobody, surely, could have contrived to make them up, they were to give Jeffrey his first sense of the enormity of the events that had unfolded in the country of his destination. It appeared that there had been simultaneous attacks on the Pentagon in Washington and the World Trade Center in New York, involving hi-jacked aircraft.

The details of these attacks were still incomplete and it was not until the UUP trio and the other passengers from their flight were transported to the Primary School in Gander that they saw for the first time the TV pictures of aeroplanes crashing into the twin towers of the World Trade Center in New York.

One of the tiny classrooms in the Primary School was to be the temporary home of the UUP delegation, and as many other passengers as it would hold, for the next three days. They slept on makeshift camp beds and were fed by the local community who had rallied around in true Canadian style. The generous hospitality of the Newfoundland people was a welcome reminder that there was still a kind and caring side to humanity, and more than compensated for the cramped and Spartan conditions of their temporary accommodation. One of the most trying aspects of the entire experience for all the residents at the Primary School was the fact that they had not been permitted to remove any of their bags from the plane and so were forced to spend much of this time in the same set of clothes in which they had disembarked.

On the fourth day after landing at Gander the flight was cleared to continue and Jeffrey and his UUP colleagues found themselves eventually in Washington D.C. Their stay was to be brief, however, as the US Government was entirely focussed on framing its response to the catastrophic loss of life that had occurred in their country. The three trans-Atlantic delegates from the Ulster Unionist Party recognised from their experience of death and destruction in Northern Ireland, the worst of which seemed small in relation to the scale of the carnage which had taken place in the United States just a few days before, that it would be totally inappropriate and unrealistic to expect anyone from the administration to meet them. All that remained for them to do, in the circumstances, was to return home as soon as possible.

On the return flight to London Jeffrey considered the impact that President George Bush's declaration of an all out war on terrorism would have on the American attitude towards terrorist activity in Northern Ireland. He concluded that America's terrible experience of the effects of global terrorism would make them much less sympathetic to Irish terrorism in the future. With Britain standing shoulder to shoulder with the American people there should be no sympathy for an IRA that exploded bombs in the city of London in years to come. It would, he mused, be the ultimate irony if it were terrorism itself that would rob the IRA of its greatest potential weapon in extracting concessions from the British Government.

When he returned to the UK, two things, one of which gave Jeffrey Donaldson a bright idea for the other, occurred almost simultaneously.

The first of these was that following the National Prayer Breakfast in October he had been appointed to organise and lead the annual event the following year. This presented him with the responsibility of securing the services of a suitable speaker as soon as possible, even though the next Prayer Breakfast was still more than eleven months away,

As he was considering this matter he received an E-mail entitled, 'Where was God?' It was a copy of an extract from a TV interview given by Anne Graham Lotz, the daughter of the well-known American evangelist, Billy Graham, in the wake of September 11. The content of this brief message struck Jeffrey Donaldson so forcibly that he sent off for a transcript of the entire interview.

When this arrived Jeffrey discovered that Anne Graham Lotz had been interviewed by Jane Clayson on 'The Early Show,' with CBS News, on Thursday, September 13.

When the interviewer had asked the Bible teacher about her father's reaction to Tuesday's horrendous happenings, and then proceeded to enquire how it was possible to 'keep faith at a time like this,' she went on to put the question she claimed many were already asking.

It was simply, "If God is good, how could God let this happen?"

Jane Clayson then invited an answer by concluding, "To that, you say...?"

It was Anne's response, given as an excerpt in the E-mail but even more meaningful in the context in which it was first elicited, that had such a profound impact on the Lagan Valley MP.

She replied, "I say God is also angry when He sees something like this. I would say also for several years now Americans in a sense have shaken their fist at God and said, 'God, we want You out of our schools, our government and our business. We want you out of our market place.' And God, who is a gentleman, has just quietly backed out of our national life, our political life and our public life, removing His hand of blessing and protection.

We need to turn to God first of all and say, 'God, we're sorry we have treated you this way and we invite You now to come into our national life. We put our trust in You.'

We have, 'In God we trust,' on our coins. We need to practise it in our lives."

As Jeffrey read these words over once more, he recognised that this message would apply to more than the United States. The people, and particularly the leaders, of the United Kingdom needed to hear it as well, and he determined to take steps to make this possible.

He prayed for guidance for a few days before inviting Anne Graham Lotz to speak at the National Prayer Breakfast, which he had been appointed to chair almost a year later, on Wednesday, October 23, 2002.

When she indicated that she would be pleased, and would indeed feel privileged, to bring God's message to the British Parliament, Jeffrey was delighted.

It promised to be a challenging, and possibly inspirational, occasion.

The only problem for Jeffrey was that there were other occasions that would be challenging in a different sense, and probably not inspirational in any sense, looming on the immediate horizon.

32
HOME AND AWAY

In mid-October 2001 Jeffrey Donaldson travelled to Australia with his good friend Robin Fairbairn from Crossgar, Co. Down. The two men had been invited by the Orange Order in Melbourne to speak at a number of Orange events in the city, and then at meetings in various locations in the state of Victoria.

On the second week of their stay, after having received an enthusiastic reception from the members of the Orange Order in Victoria, Jeffrey and Robin flew north to Brisbane to commence a series of visits in New South Wales and Queensland. It would be a shame, Jeffrey reckoned, to travel half-way round the world to the beautiful sun-kissed southern continent and not make contact with the members of the Mourne Donaldson family, whose forefathers had emigrated to Australia about 150 years earlier.

Jeffrey's father was keen that he should do this, and furnished his son with names and addresses of the 'Australian' family. The list had six names on it, and three addresses. Austin and Jenny Donaldson lived in Nerang, Queensland, Betty and Nancy Donaldson came from Warialda, N.S.W., and Michael and Carolyn Donaldson had a farm out in the wide-open spaces of New South Wales.

The two travellers had been pleased to have been accorded such a warm welcome by the Orange Order in Melbourne but they were almost overwhelmed by the warmth of the reception they received from this distant branch of the family tree. The Australian connection were so thrilled to meet a genuine homegrown

Donaldson, all the way from the 'old Kingdom of Mourne,' that they showered Jeffrey and his travelling companion with kindness. They had so much to tell each other, so many questions to ask, so many family ties to sort out in their minds, and so many new names to learn, either from meeting a person or seeing a picture, that the time they had to spend in each home passed almost imperceptibly. It seemed that they had barely arrived before they were packing up to leave again.

After having hired a car Jeffrey and Robin were to discover that driving from one town or city to another in Australia wasn't quite like travelling from one place to another back home in Northern Ireland. Driving from Nerang to Warialda wasn't quite the same as going from Newry to Waringstown. The distances were vast in comparison, but they didn't mind. It was spring in Australia. The sun shone, the jacaranda trees were bursting out into beautiful blue blossom, the kookaburras called, and Jeffrey's relatives hugged them when they arrived and appeared truly sorry to see them leave.

Although unhappy to be separated from his wife and daughters for such a prolonged period, Jeffrey was glad to be away from the darkening evenings of autumn back in Northern Ireland, and happy to be removed, at least for a while, from the political subterfuge developing there.

On October 23, the chairman of the international decommissioning body, General John de Chastelain, announced that the IRA had 'put a quantity of arms beyond use.' On the following day David Trimble rescinded the resignations of his three fellow UUP Ministers, enabling them to return to the power-sharing Executive.

His own position as First Minister was not as easily resolved, however. As he had resigned from that post at the beginning of July, the legislation contained in the Northern Ireland Act, 1998, required that a fresh vote be held in the Assembly. When this took place David Trimble would be required to secure the support of a majority of the unionist MLAs (Member of the Legislative Assembly) before he could resume as First Minister.

Although relaxing at the other side of the planet, Jeffrey was being constantly updated on the political developments back in the province. During one of these long-distance telephone calls, Jeffrey's Union First colleague Peter Weir informed him that both he and another Union First member, Pauline Armitage, Assembly member for East Londonderry, would not be supporting the re-election of David Trimble. Jeffrey agreed with their position that more clarity was required from the IRA as to the nature and extent of the decommissioning that had already occurred, and the timetable for the completion of the process, before they could support the position of the party leader. Their opinion and actions were crucial in this instance, because David Trimble could not obtain the stipulated majority of unionist MLAs to ensure his reinstatement, without their two votes.

The party leader then sought the support of the Alliance Party, who had not designated themselves as either unionist or nationalist under the rules of the Assembly, claiming rather to take a neutral stance. In an attempt to secure the required vote, David Trimble tried to persuade that party to call a number of their MLAs 'unionists,' if even for a temporary period.

Shortly after Jeffrey returned from Australia a vote was taken in the Assembly on Tuesday, November 6, and with three Alliance MLAs having been miraculously transformed into unionists just for the day, David Trimble narrowly won the vote and was duly reinstalled in the office of First Minister.

Jeffrey Donaldson was appalled when he heard of this manoeuvre. He regarded the exercise as downright dishonest and reckoned that it would bring not only the Ulster Unionist Party, but also the entire political process in Northern Ireland, into disrepute. The subsequent reaction of David Trimble and his supporters, which culminated in the expulsion of Peter Weir and the long-term suspension of Pauline Armitage, from the Ulster Unionist Party, only served to make him feel all the more disgusted.

In response to this action by the party, the leadership of Union First once more collected, without any difficulty, sufficient signatures to call yet another special meeting of the Ulster Unionist Council. At this meeting, which was held in Belfast, they put forward a motion, proposed jointly by Arlene Foster and David Burnside, MP for South Antrim, who had assumed a more prominent role in opposition to David Trimble. The motion sought to compel the UUP Ministers to withdraw from the Executive by the early spring of 2002 if there was no further movement towards complete and verifiable decommissioning.

Jeffrey made the wind-up speech in support of the motion and he was followed by David Trimble, who contended that the most effective way to maintain pressure on the IRA was to continue pursuing his present policy.

When the vote was taken David Trimble succeeded in gaining another narrow victory, but Jeffrey and his colleagues vowed to keep up their campaign for the party to adopt a firmer stance.

The reasons for, and results of, the continued divisions within the Ulster Unionist Party and also Northern Ireland politics as a whole, were temporarily set aside when the nation went into mourning in the spring of the following year.

Her Majesty the Queen Mother, who was by far the oldest member of the Royal Family, having lived for more than a century, died peacefully in her sleep on Saturday March 30, 2002. Such was the grief at the passing of this grand old lady that the hours when her coffin lay in state in Westminster Hall had to be extended to accommodate all those wishing to pay their last respects.

A few days later, on Wednesday, April 3, Jeffrey Donaldson spoke in the House of Commons, extending the sympathies of his constituents to Her Majesty the Queen and the Royal Family. They had, as he went on to explain, special links with Lagan Valley.

In the course of his speech he said, "March 2002 will long be remembered by my constituents as a month of mixed emotions. Early in the month, the honour of city status was conferred on the borough of Lisburn by Her Majesty the Queen, in this her Golden Jubilee year. We celebrated the new city of Lisburn, especially in light of our close association with the Royal Family, with the village of Hillsborough being the official residence of Her Majesty the Queen and having played host, on many occasions, to Her Majesty the Queen Mother. We remember those visits with affection.

As my friends and colleagues have said, those visits came at times when the people of Northern Ireland were facing great uncertainty and adversity, with the shadow of violence hanging over our part of the United Kingdom. When the Queen Mother and other members of the Royal Family came to visit Northern Ireland, we took hope from their interest and the time that they spent among us...

As my hon. Friend the Member for South Antrim (David Burnside) said, we were inspired by the Queen Mother's Christian faith and by the fact that she prayed for the people of Northern Ireland. We very much appreciate that, and we appreciate the contribution that she made to the life of Northern Ireland and to the life of our nation. We will greatly mourn her passing… We will miss the Queen Mother. She was a very special lady, and she meant much to my constituents."

Later that week Jeffrey attended the Queen Mother's funeral. He was one of a number of MPs present in Westminster Hall, where the lying-in-state had taken place. It was from there that the funeral procession, led by members of the Royal Family, began, on its way to Westminster Abbey for the service of thanksgiving and commemoration.

Despite the death of her mother, Her Majesty the Queen continued with her planned tour of the United Kingdom to celebrate her Golden Jubilee year. Her visit to Northern Ireland from May 13 – 15 was of particular interest to Jeffrey Donaldson and the people of the borough of Lisburn. On her last day in the province, May 15, Jeffrey and Eleanor attended a special ceremony in Hillsborough Castle when Her Majesty presented a Royal Charter granting city status to Lisburn.

This historic award, which had been announced in early March, represented the crowning moment of a long campaign in which Jeffrey had played a pivotal part in persuading the Government of the merits of Lisburn's case for city status.

This was the second time that Jeffrey had the pleasure of welcoming Her Majesty the Queen to his constituency. On the former occasion, on November 15, 2001, he had attended the official opening of the splendid new Headquarters for the local council. This impressive building at Lagan Valley Island, in the heart of the town-soon-to-become-a-city, had been officially opened by Her

Majesty that day.

Following the celebration of city status for Lisburn and the pleasure of meeting Her Majesty The Queen for a second time, Jeffrey was brought back to the reality of life's ups and downs in the early summer of 2002. During a visit to the United States he heard some news which worried him considerably. This time, though, the message did not relate to the normally turbulent world of Northern Ireland politics but to the health of a member of his happy family. He was on a trip marking the twinning of Dromore, from his constituency, with Drumore, Pennsylvania, when phone calls from Eleanor informed him of disturbing developments.

Their elder daughter, Claire, had been experiencing considerable pain in her pelvis for some time and various medical examinations had not identified the source of her discomfort. An X-ray, taken the previous week, had given Claire's consultant some cause for concern and he was arranging for her to have an MRI scan. This was scheduled to take place on the day following Jeffrey's return from his American trip.

The results of the MRI scan also proved inconclusive although they did reveal a large malformation on the left side of the pelvis. This would require further investigation. The consultant carried out the necessary procedures and Jeffrey and Eleanor were advised that they would have to wait for two weeks before all the test results came back.

It was a worrying time. Other matters seemed to pale into insignificance, as Claire's health became their prime concern. It drew the family together in prayer. Their faith, as a family, and as individual Christians, was tested to the limit. During those anxious days Jeffrey and Eleanor were consoled and reassured by the knowledge that Claire and Laura had both, when younger, made a personal commitment to Christ. This crisis in their lives bonded the family together in a unique way. The concerned parents were encouraged, in the midst of it all, to hear the girls talk openly about their fears, and how they were depending on God to help them overcome these.

In addition to their own family prayer times, Jeffrey and Eleanor and the girls were very aware of the sincere prayers of many Christians, both in local churches and fellowships and further afield. They were most appreciative of the support of many Christian friends, one of whom was Derick Bingham, an evangelist based in Belfast.

Derick, whom Jeffrey had known for many years, made a number of visits to the house during those trying days. The spiritual solace he offered and the spiritual strength he encouraged, through scripture reading and prayer, were most welcome by the family passing through this ordeal.

Finally the day arrived when Eleanor received a call from the consultant at Musgrave Park Hospital, to be given the results of the tests he had conducted some days earlier. Much prayer had been offered for Claire's condition, and healing, and now the moment of truth had arrived. The parents were about to be given the medical prognosis.

It came as a huge relief when the consultant informed them that the malformation was a non-life threatening condition known as chronic osteomyelitis, which is an inflammation of the bone marrow. Claire would, however, require intensive treatment in the hospital over a period of weeks in an effort to alleviate her condition. This would obviously result in considerable adjustments to the rhythm of family life in the immediate future but the fact that Claire's condition was treatable was a clear answer to prayer.

There was to be one long-term and beneficial spin-off from Claire's illness and the tense, nervous wait before the test results became known. They inspired Derick Bingham, who had ministered to the family at the time, to write a short booklet for young people who were afraid of what might happen to them in the future. This booklet, which was widely distributed, told the story of 'The Lamplighter,' and was subtitled, 'For those who are scared of the dark.'

At the end of the story Derick explained that although 'the Lamplighter's footsteps can no longer be heard on our streets today there is One who still brings light into the very darkest of places.

He is the Divine Lamplighter and his name is Jesus, the Son of God.'

33

STANDING IN THE GAP
FOR THE NATION

As the summer drew to a close there was growing unease within the unionist ranks that Sinn Fein had failed to make any move on the decommissioning of IRA weapons. With Parliament still in recess Jeffrey met with a number of his Union First colleagues to review the political scene.

They noted that it had been some ten months since the Ulster Unionist Council had last debated the inclusion of Sinn Fein in the power-sharing Executive, and no significant progress on decommissioning had been made since then. It was the consensus view of the meeting that it was time this situation was again challenged. A requisition for a special meeting of the UUC was duly presented to the party officers and the date for a further meeting of the Council was fixed for September 21.

There was the usual flurry of activity in advance of the Ulster Unionist Council meeting and commentators in the media were in no doubt as to its importance in relation to the infighting within the Ulster Unionist Party. As Jeffrey and his colleagues canvassed support from the delegates it became clear that a number of party members, who had previously supported David Trimble's position, had become thoroughly disillusioned and were thus prepared to back a different approach.

Recognising that these 'floating voters' were going to be a determining factor in the outcome of the meeting, Jeffrey set about drafting a resolution with renewed vigour. He knew from past experience that it would not be sufficient for his side just to make the best speeches. They must also submit ideas that would address the main issues of concern, but also offer a constructive alternative to the fruitless, faltering policies of the party leader.

There was a large turnout of delegates for the Saturday morning meeting in the Ramada Hotel in south Belfast. The atmosphere was electric from the very start. Most people recognised that there had been a shift of opinion amongst some of those arriving for the meeting, but this was impossible to quantify. It was clear that the result of any vote would depend on the arguments advanced in the meeting, and would certainly be 'a close run thing.'

Jeffrey opened the debate and put forward his proposals for future policy. These were designed to introduce a progressive series of sanctions against Sinn Fein within a clearly defined time scale. He advocated that the ultimate sanction should be the withdrawal of all Ulster Unionist Party Ministers from the power-sharing Executive if the IRA failed to decommission its illegal weapons and cease all terrorist activity before the end of January 2003.

As the debate continued it soon became evident that support for Jeffrey's proposition was coming from unexpected quarters. There was an audible gasp from David Trimble's adherents when the previously loyal Bertie Kerr, a Fermanagh councillor, declared his support for the Donaldson motion. It was now very clear that a vote, if called, could go either way. The situation was balanced on a knife-edge.

Recognising this, Sir Reg Empey proposed an adjournment for a brief period to enable both sides to discuss the possibility of formulating an agreed motion. David Trimble was most reluctant to go down that road for he was well aware that it would inevitably end up in more hard-line territory.

He was right.

When the deliberations were completed between the advocates of the opposing views, the resultant resolution encompassed many more of Jeffrey's proposals than had ever before been accepted by the ruling Council. This revised motion was read to the meeting and adopted unanimously by the delegates present. Jeffrey, and the Union First group which had drawn up the original set of proposals, were pleased at having achieved significant advances without the meeting ending in an acrimonious split. Under the terms of the agreed motion Ulster Unionist representatives were to be immediately withdrawn from the North/South Ministerial Council, and the IRA were given three months to complete the decommissioning of their weaponry or the UUP would withdraw from the power-sharing Executive.

Within days of that meeting of the Ulster Unionist Council, however, there was an unexpected development which plunged the already pitching political process in Northern Ireland into even more turbulent waters.

In the early morning of Friday, October 4, the Sinn Fein offices at Stormont were searched as part of a major police investigation into intelligence gathering by the IRA. A number of leading Sinn Fein figures were arrested, and their Head of Administration at Stormont was subsequently remanded in custody charged with having documents likely to be of use to terrorists.

The future of the power-sharing Executive was once more in doubt as David Trimble announced, on October 8, that he would pull his Ministers out of the Executive in seven days time unless the Government proposed the expulsion of Sinn Fein. A week later, when this deadline expired, Dr. John Reid, Secretary of State for

Northern Ireland, forestalled any move by the leader of the Ulster Unionist Party by announcing yet another suspension of the Assembly and Executive. This meant a further return to direct rule from Westminster.

The full impact of what was to become known as 'Stormontgate,' began to be felt in the weeks that followed. When police had processed all the material they had taken away in their dawn swoop they began to call at the homes of hundreds of security force personnel to inform them that their personal details had fallen into the hands of the IRA.

They were not the only public figures to receive such frightening news, either.

Some days after the suspensions were announced Jeffrey received a telephone call from the Police Commander in Lisburn asking him to call in at the city's main Police Station as soon as possible. It sounded like a repeat of the message he had received just over a year before. The Commander's voice sounded just as urgent and earnest now as it had done then, and when Jeffrey attended at the Police Station as instructed the news he was given sent the same unwelcome chill down his spine.

The police had discovered, in the course of their searches, and after subsequent dissemination of the information obtained, that the IRA had been collecting information on him and storing it on their computer records.

Nothing had changed. Jeffrey Donaldson was still living under the threat of assassination.

All of this convinced Jeffrey that his repeated warnings to the Ulster Unionist Party about the inadvisability of sharing power with Sinn Fein in the absence of an avowed end to terrorist activity had been justified.

Conscious that Northern Ireland was not the only country to experience the spectre and self-destruction of internal strife, Jeffrey had always been interested in the study of conflict situations, and their possible solutions, across the world. Two of the regions which he found particularly fascinating, but for different reasons, were South Africa and the Middle East.

On a visit to South Africa in May 1997 he had met some of the key participants in the peace process in that country. Perhaps the most memorable of those interviews was when he was part of a small delegation that had a meeting, lasting almost an hour, with President Nelson Mandela. Jeffrey was intrigued to learn about this man's transformation from being the leader of a political movement with strong links to a terrorist organisation to becoming the President of a fully democratic South Africa.

While Jeffrey recognised that there were some lessons to be learnt from the South African situation, it was back in Europe, in October 2002, that he was brought face to face with what can happen when people's hatred and prejudices are carried to extremes.

He had been working closely for some time with the Holocaust Educational Trust, which aims to promote an awareness of the genocide that took place under Hitler during the Second World War. Jeffrey's involvement in the Trust stemmed from his interest in the ongoing conflict in the Middle East, and his empathy with the people of Israel who had been the focus of repeated terrorist attacks.

On October 17 Jeffrey joined a school party organised by the Trust on a visit to the former German concentration camp at Auschwitz in Poland. His aim was to encourage schools in Northern Ireland to participate in the Trust's educational programme, so he decided to accompany the group of Secondary School children from the south of England to observe the impact the visit had on them.

What he had not reckoned on was the effect it would have on himself.

The children had been laughing light-heartedly on the bus on the way to the former camp, that day. When, however, they had their introduction to what took place in 'the world's largest graveyard,' through archive footage in the film theatre in the visitor centre, Jeffrey was not surprised to witness the group stunned into awestruck silence.

On leaving the film theatre the party moved out into what had once been a camp of death, thronged with thousands of starving, persecuted people, and Jeffrey stood silently below the notice, requesting appropriate behaviour. He felt his blood run cold as he read,

You are entering a place of exceptional horror and tragedy. Please show your respect for those who suffered and died here by behaving in a manner suitable to the dignity of their memory.

As Jeffrey followed the school group around, sometimes listening to what their guide had to say, occasionally veering off on his own to read an inscription, he noticed that nobody had to ask the children to behave in a dignified manner. The appalling awesomeness of the place dictated the tone and nature of their response.

What he saw in that camp made an indelible mark on Jeffrey's memory. He could understand why anyone who dared to speak, did so in hushed tones, why the schoolchildren were subdued, and why many, standing transfixed before heart-rending exhibits in huge glass cases, had tears trickling down their cheeks.

Outside, it was a scripture quotation, on a cracking stone monument at the entrance to one of the many forbidding barrack blocks that caused him to stop and reflect long and hard.

The stone had been set up to mark the visit of the President of Israel, Chaim Herzog, to the camp in 1992. The pitiful appeal of the monument was that its sole inscription was a verse from the Bible written in Hebrew, Polish and English. The words, *'My sorrow is continually before me,'* from Psalm 38, seemed to summarise, for Jeffrey, in a very potent way, not only the unutterable barbarity of Auschwitz, but centuries of suffering by the Jewish people.

In the midst of all this grief and horror, Jeffrey went on to reflect on the fact that the might of a ruthless dictator could not annihilate the Jewish nation. These people were God's people, and Hitler had made a fundamental mistake in pitting his paltry, passing power against that of an almighty and eternal God.

On Wednesday, October 23, just a few days after he returned from his trip to Poland, Jeffrey chaired the National Prayer Breakfast for which he had been preparing for almost a year.

Historic Westminster Hall was filled with more than eight hundred Christian leaders from Parliament, London and across the nation, that morning. Jeffrey welcomed all those present, as did the Rt. Hon. Michael Martin MP, Speaker of the House of Commons.

One of the first to address the invited guests was Rabbi Michael Melchior, Deputy Foreign Minister of Israel, and what he had to say transported Jeffrey back, in thought, to Auschwitz and the endless anguish of the Jews.

"My country is going through a very, very tragic period just now," he told the gathered company. "Instead of rejoicing, we are going to funerals... And what is worse, this bloodshed is being carried out in the name of God."

He concluded his short, but heartfelt message, by reading from Psalm 122 and imploring those attending the National Prayer Breakfast, 2002, to 'pray for the peace of Jerusalem.'

Introducing the main speaker of the morning, Anne Graham Lotz, a short time later, Jeffrey referred to the broadcast that had so much affected him in the wake of the tragedy of September 11, the previous year.

When Anne rose to speak she conveyed the greetings of her father, Dr. Billy Graham to the audience, before going on to make it clear that the message she felt she should deliver that day had come not from her natural, but her Heavenly, Father. She carried such a sense of authority with her presence, and her presentation was so compelling, that everyone was soon hanging on her every word.

Although not reading the passage, she said that her address that morning would be based on the story, which she described as 'Isaiah's wake-up call,' from chapter six of the Book of Isaiah.

This 'wake-up call' for Isaiah, came, she pointed out, at a crisis point in the history of the nation of Israel. It happened 'in the year that King Uzziah died.' The wake-up call, not only to America, but also to all the other nations of the world, had come when they were shaken by the events of September 11, 2001.

Anne described her reaction as she watched TV coverage of planes crashing into the World Trade Center in New York, and the buildings imploding. She thought, 'All those people stepping out into eternity and they were not ready to meet God.'

"And it is still happening," she went on. "In Washington, D.C. people are stepping out into eternity one bullet at a time. In Israel they are stepping out into eternity one busload at a time... And what I ask you, are we in the church doing while all this is going on? I'll tell you! We are arguing about the colour of the carpet! Or whether we should sing hymns or choruses! Ladies and gentlemen, it's time God's people woke up!"

Turning back to the Bible story, the speaker then described what happened when Isaiah was jolted into a consciousness of the serious state of affairs in his nation. When he 'woke up, he immediately looked up, and his eyes were opened to a fresh vision of Jesus Christ.'

"Is it any wonder that he exclaimed, 'Woe is me!'" she asked her audience.

Having acknowledged his sinful nature, and unworthiness to be in the presence of God, Isaiah had his sin and iniquity taken away. When God then enquired, 'Whom shall I send, and who will go for us?' he was in a position to, as Anne described it, 'hold his hand up and say, 'Here I am, send me. I'm a sinner, but I've been to the cross for cleansing, and I'm available.'"

As she went on to outline the solution to the problems of America and the United Kingdom, Jeffrey was moved to hear her quote the verse that he had first read on a scrap of paper, years before.

'If my people, which are called by my name, shall humble themselves, and pray, and seek my face, and turn from their wicked ways; then will I hear from heaven, and forgive their sin, and heal their land.'

Before concluding her address Anne presented her audience of parliamentarians and Christian dignitaries with a very stirring challenge.

"God's people are now being called to stand in the gap for their nation," she declared, her voiced echoing around the nine-hundred-year-old Hall. "God is looking for another Isaiah... And like him, before you stand in the gap for your nation you need to wake up, and you need to return to the cross.

The message of God for some man or woman here this morning is, 'Wake up! Return to the cross. Recommit your life to Christ. And stand in the gap for your nation'"

As Anne resumed her seat, Jeffrey stood up to thank her, and in doing so he reiterated the challenge. "Are we ready to stand in the gap, those of us who bear the name of Christ in this nation?" he asked the audience again. "So often we as Christians look to someone else for the answers. We look to our Government for the answers. We look to Parliament for the answers. Anne has reminded us that God is looking to **us** for the answers. Are we willing to stand in the gap for Him, and for this nation, that through us God will bless this land?"

He had obviously been affected by the thrust of the inspirational address. It had touched him, if no one else.

In his up-and-coming days as a forthright, no-nonsense politician, Jeffrey Donaldson had been described by his followers in the unionist community in Northern Ireland as, 'the kind of man this country needs.'

That morning, at the National Prayer Breakfast, that phrase had taken on a whole new meaning.

Was he prepared 'to stand in the gap for his nation, for God?'

34
SUSPENDED

Wednesday, December 4, 2002, was like any other day at Westminster as Jeffrey carried out his normal parliamentary duties. Having endured the tedium of the routine business conducted at the Standing Committee, which that day had been considering the Harbour (Northern Ireland) Order, Jeffrey made his way through Westminster Hall to a reception hosted by his friend and colleague Mark Francois, Conservative MP for Rayleigh. As he walked across the Hall he remembered the morning of the National Prayer Breakfast, and it seemed that the high walls were still echoing with the challenge of Anne Graham Lotz.

Margaret Mc Kee was waiting for him at the top of the steps leading into the Jubilee Room. Jeffrey thought this rather unusual, and when his Westminster secretary approached him he noticed a distinct glint in her eye. This, with Margaret, was a sure sign that mischief was afoot.

She caught the Lagan Valley MP by the arm and guided him towards the door and when it was opened from inside Jeffrey was to receive one of the most pleasant surprises of his life.

The Jubilee Room, which would normally be a hive of political activity with lobbyists button-holing MPs on some pressing issue, was packed at that moment with a sea of familiar faces. As he stepped into the room a loud cheer went up and this was followed by a spirited rendition of 'Happy Birthday.'

With only three days to go to his fortieth birthday, Margaret had arranged a reception of a different kind to celebrate this milestone in his life. Jeffrey was taken totally by surprise by such a kind gesture, and on glancing around he realised that his secretary had taken great pains to ensure that a wide representation of his parliamentary friends and fellow-MPs were present.

A strong Northern Ireland contingent included Jim Brady from his Close Protection Team, his political mentor Lord Molyneaux, David Burnside and Rev. Martin Smyth from the UUP, and the DUP MP Nigel Dodds. From amongst his friends at Westminster, Jeffrey could see Andy Reed and Steve Webb from the G6 group, Andrew Turner the MP for the Isle of Wight and Laurence Robertson, Conservative MP for Tewkesbury, whom Jeffrey had first met before they were both elected as MPs in 1997. Also present, from his family, was his brother Kingsley who had been promoted to the rank of Captain in the Royal Tank Regiment, and had travelled up from his base for the occasion.

Jeffrey enjoyed the company of his friends that evening and thanked Margaret profusely at the end of it for taking the time to arrange this out-of-the-blue 'birthday treat.'

With birthday and Christmas past and gone Jeffrey and his senior colleagues in Union First began to refocus their attention on the political arena. They were aware that one of the chief criticisms directed at them by David Trimble and his supporters was that they had not been able to come up with a viable alternative to the Belfast Agreement. In order to show that they were not 'devoid of ideas,' as had been claimed, they therefore decided to draw up a set of principles upon which a new agreement could be based.

Jeffrey reasoned that this should be done as soon as possible, for with elections to the Northern Ireland Assembly scheduled for the coming May it would be important for the anti-Agreement wing of the UUP to have a distinct policy to present to the electorate. A number of Ulster Unionist Party candidates, including Jeffrey, who had been already selected to contest the Assembly elections and who shared his views on the Agreement, formed themselves into a group to work together and plan a co-ordinated campaign.

When the final draft of their policy position had been agreed, arrangements were made to launch what had become known as 'The Stormont Principles,' in a meeting to be hosted by the Friends Of The Union group in the Stormont Hotel, Belfast, in mid-February, 2003.

In the document launched at that meeting the Union First Group set out the following summary of 'The Stormont Principles' : -

1.   Peace is the right of every man, woman and child living in Northern Ireland.

2.   The people of Northern Ireland have the right to determine their own constitutional and political future.

3.   The Union provides the best future for all the people of Northern Ireland.

4.   The people of Northern Ireland have the right to good government based upon equality and human rights.

5.   Unionists and Nationalists have a right to be involved in the governance of Northern Ireland at a full and equal level.

6.   Only those Political Parties that have established an unequivocal commitment to exclusively peaceful means can participate in the government of Northern Ireland.

Jeffrey realised that the developing of, and going public with, this policy platform, would inevitably result in further tension between himself and David Trimble, who was still determined to support the Belfast Agreement.

At the same time as this policy paper was being prepared, Jeffrey was also involved in helping expand the vision of the Prayer for Parliament group, which met regularly under his chairmanship. Inspired by Anne Graham Lotz's message at the National Prayer Breakfast, Jeffrey felt that the time had come to reach out from Parliament and seek to involve other Christians across the United Kingdom in interceding for the nation. This vision was described by Julie Anderson of Prayer for the Nations as 'creating a prayer shield for the United Kingdom.'

At a meeting held at the home of Rev. Francis Pym in Bolney, Sussex, also in February 2003, it was agreed to establish a network of prayer intercessors across the United Kingdom. The Prayer for the Nation team planned to use modern technology, such as the world-wide-web and e-mail to provide Christians with prayer bulletins on crucial issues affecting Parliament and the national interest. The group recognised that for the 'prayer shield' to be effective they would have to enlist the support of thousands of Christians prepared to commit themselves to regular prayer, and while this appeared a daunting task, they knew that it would represent a major step towards 'standing in the gap for the nation.'

Following the meeting that evening they began contacting a number of evangelical Christians whom they asked to help compile a network of prayer partners who would be happy to receive prayer-bulletins by e-mail and post.

The 'gap' was filling up. The 'prayer shield' was being reinforced.

By this time there was intense media speculation about the prospect of war in Iraq, and at a meeting in the Ministry of Defence in Whitehall with the Minister, Dr. Lewis Moonie MP, Jeffrey was afforded a timely reminder of the ultimate price that the Armed Forces can be called upon to pay during periods of conflict.

A group of widows, whose husbands had lost their lives whilst serving with the Ulster Defence Regiment in Northern Ireland, accompanied him to that meeting. They had arranged to meet Dr. Moonie in London to ask that the Government recognise their plight, as many of them had suffered significant hardship through the loss of a husband or father who was often the family breadwinner. Jeffrey urged the Minister to set up a special fund that would provide support for UDR widows, similar to that which he had previously helped secure for the RUC widows.

The women were encouraged when the Minister undertook to have his office investigate the matter and make a decision in due course.

With the diplomatic activity over Iraq intensifying, Jeffrey became conscious that while he had been helping a group of widows prepare a case in relation to their husbands who had been killed in the course of their duty, his brother Kingsley was preparing for the possibility of active service with his regiment in that Middle Eastern country.

The Prime Minister announced that the Iraqi regime, under Saddam Hussein, had failed to comply with previous United Nations resolutions and that he intended to recommend to Parliament that the United Kingdom should join with her

American allies in declaring war on this dangerous dictator.

Tony Blair presented the resolution for war to the House of Commons on March 18, and as Jeffrey listened to the impassioned debate on both sides of the House, he was painfully aware that if he were to vote in support of the Prime Minister he would be, in effect, sending his own brother to the battlefront. Sitting in his place on the green benches, and with the debate storming on around him, Jeffrey prayed about the decision he would soon have to make, and for Kingsley's safety should the House vote to go to war.

When the debate ended the Speaker called a division, and with a somewhat heavy heart the MP for Lagan Valley walked through the 'Aye' lobby and registered his vote for war in Iraq. Despite a significant rebellion by a number of prominent Labour MPs, including Clare Short and Robin Cook, when the votes were counted the motion was carried by a majority of 412 votes to 149.

Britain had declared war, and within a week Kingsley was in Basra.

Jeffrey referred to this, when highlighting the part played by soldiers from Northern Ireland in the Armed Forces of the United Kingdom, and the very natural concern of their families, in a debate on the war in Iraq in the House of Commons, on Wednesday, March 26.

"The Secretary of State will be aware of the contribution of hundreds of soldiers from Northern Ireland who are serving in the Gulf," he began. "We were all inspired by the remarks of Lt. Col. Tim Collins, the commanding officer of the 1st Battalion, the Royal Irish Regiment. Of course there are many other soldiers. I have a brother with the Royal Tank Regiment in southern Iraq, and it is an anxious time for families, as they await news of the conflict...'

Whilst the wider Donaldson family had begun to focus on the unfolding events in a far off land, Jeffrey and Eleanor had embarked upon the preparations for the second house move of their married lives. Although they had grown very attached to their home in Moira and enjoyed the relative tranquillity of life beside the demesne, a number of factors, including the increased attention being given to Jeffrey's personal security, had forced them to consider a move. After a brief period of house hunting they discovered that an attractive property, with the beguiling name, for them, of 'Mourne View House,' had come on the market. When Jeffrey and Eleanor went to see the property, which was situated between Moira and Dromore, they recognised that it would be ideally suited to their family's needs. They were so taken by it that they entered into negotiations almost at once, purchased it, and moved into it on Monday, April 28, 2003.

Although they had enjoyed a happy association with Moira Baptist Church during the ten years they had lived in the village, this relocation brought with it a change of church affiliation. Within weeks of coming to live near Dromore, the Donaldson family were warmly welcomed into Banbridge Road Presbyterian Church in the town.

Having been heavily involved with all the practicalities of moving house, Jeffrey had been out of the political limelight for a couple of weeks and was therefore rather surprised when the Prime Minister announced, on May 1, that the forthcoming Assembly elections were to be postponed until the autumn.

The reason Mr. Blair gave for the postponement was the failure of the pro-Agreement parties to reach a settlement that would end the current political impasse. In an attempt to fill this supposed political vacuum, the Prime Minister, together with his Irish counterpart, Bertie Ahern, published a document, which they called 'The Joint Declaration.'

This paper set out in considerable detail what the Prime Minister described as 'a shared understanding' of how the political parties might resolve the outstanding issues, including decommissioning, paramilitary activity, security normalisation, and the restoration of the political institutions. Crucially, the document also contained what many unionists regarded as significant concessions to the republican movement, including an effective amnesty for IRA terrorists 'on the run' from justice.

The two Governments urged the political parties in Northern Ireland to accept the Joint Declaration as a basis on which to move forward, and David Trimble soon called a meeting of the senior members of his party to consider the UUP response to this initiative.

In his initial briefing, the party leader welcomed the decision to postpone the elections and explained the various elements of the Government paper to his colleagues. Whilst reserving his final judgement on the document, he summarised these recent developments as 'a huge success for unionism.' Sir Reg Empey, who had also been involved in the negotiations which preceded the publication of the document, told the meeting that although the party would have difficulty with certain aspects of the Joint Declaration, 'the restoration of devolution will only occur on the basis of considering the total package.' Jeffrey Donaldson was so taken aback by the apparent acquiescence of his two senior colleagues with what he regarded as a totally unsatisfactory political package, that he recorded their comments on the front of his copy of the document.

When he rose to address the meeting, Jeffrey spoke of his 'total disbelief' that the Ulster Unionist Party should welcome the postponement of a democratic election as a result of the IRA's failure to end its terrorism. He contended that in putting off the election, even for a few months, the Prime Minister had effectively handed a veto over the political process in Northern Ireland to the army council of the IRA. In outlining his analysis of the Joint Declaration, Jeffrey went on to express grave concern at the concessions that were on offer to republicans, and contrasted these with the lack of clarity on key issues such as decommissioning. When it came to the summing up of his remarks, a few minutes later, Jeffrey concluded that the document was heavily weighted in favour of the republican position. Then, drawing on Sir Reg's advice that the package should be considered in its totality, he argued that if this were done the Ulster Unionist Party would have no choice but to reject it, 'in its totality.'

This was by no means the first time that David Trimble's recommendations had been at odds with those of Jeffrey Donaldson. The party leader advocated that the Ulster Unionist Party should take more time to consider the Joint Declaration in detail before formulating its response. Thus with one side arguing for outright rejection, and the other for careful reflection, the lines were drawn for another confrontation.

Not surprisingly, another meeting of the Ulster Unionist Council was arranged to debate the matter at length. This was called for Monday, June 16, to allow both factions of the party to air their diametrically opposed perspectives on the Declaration before a full representation of delegates from across the province.

Speaking before the meeting, Jeffrey described it as 'a defining moment for the party,' as the debate on the Joint Declaration encapsulated all of the issues that were at the heart of the division within Ulster Unionism.

The meeting was tense, and the discussion at times heated, as both sides argued their case and sought to counter that of others. Again David Trimble maintained that the party should allow itself time to examine the document in detail and then present a considered response. Jeffrey, by contrast, endeavoured to persuade the meeting that to procrastinate was to create the impression that the party was willing to be complicit in the Government's betrayal of democracy in the veto granted to the IRA, and its abrogation of justice through the ill-conceived amnesty for the 'on-the-runs.'

Despite the strength of the arguments on both sides, the final vote reflected the by-then deeply entrenched position of the delegates, with the result that David Trimble once again avoided defeat by the also-by-then familiar majority of fifty-four to forty-six per cent.

When speaking to the assembled media immediately following the meeting Jeffrey Donaldson said, "This result leaves people like myself and those who support me in a position where we have to decide if this party now represents what we believe in."

The press interpreted this statement as meaning that the Lagan Valley MP was now considering his position in terms of his future with the Ulster Unionist Party. This gave rise to an intense wave of press speculation for the next week, as Jeffrey consulted with his closest colleagues about their next move in the aftermath of the UUC decision.

On Monday, June 23, a press conference was convened in the Rotunda Room of Belfast's Europa Hotel. At this eagerly anticipated gathering Jeffrey and his fellow-UUP MPs Rev. Martin

Smyth and David Burnside announced that they were resigning the Whip of the Ulster Unionist Party at Westminster. This, they declared, would allow them to vote according to their conscience on matters relating to the Joint Declaration. Their decision was endorsed by Lord Molyneaux, who stood alongside them as they briefed the media.

David Trimble and his closest supporters were incensed by this action, as it had the immediate effect of depriving him of his position as the leader of the fourth largest party in Parliament. In the course of one brief announcement by three MPs the Ulster Unionist Party was reduced to the embarrassing position of being the smallest party in the House of Commons, a status it shared with the SDLP.

The party leader reacted swiftly and prevailed upon the UUP chairman to call an emergency meeting of the party officers to deal with the dissident MPs. At that meeting, which was held on June 26, the officers decided, on a split vote, to refer the three MPs to a disciplinary committee to be chaired by Raymond Ferguson, a solicitor and party member from County Fermanagh.

The hastily convened disciplinary body met the following day in Ulster Unionist Headquarters in Belfast, and announced afterwards that they were suspending the three MPs from the party with immediate effect, pending a hearing to be held on July 17.

In this unprecedented move, the Party President, Rev. Martin Smyth, one of its Vice-Presidents, Jeffrey Donaldson, and David Burnside, MP for South Antrim, all found themselves outside the party for which they had worked diligently for many years.

The shock waves from this extraordinary manoeuvre reverberated throughout unionism for weeks, and Jeffrey

Donaldson was forced to contemplate, for the first time, something that had never even entered his thinking all his life, up until that point.

It was the possibility of life beyond the Ulster Unionist Party.

35
FAILED DEALS

Jeffrey Donaldson had little time to come to terms with the significance of his suspension from the party before the media were clamouring for his reaction.

Within three hours of the Disciplinary Committee announcement, the Lagan Valley MP was live on BBC Radio Ulster in an interview that pitched him head-to-head with the Party Chairman, James Cooper. When invited to give his initial response to his suspension, Jeffrey immediately branded it as 'politically unlawful,' given that the rules of the Ulster Unionist Council stipulated that a full hearing of the case against any member must take place before he or she could be either suspended or expelled. He argued that this ill-advised move by the Disciplinary Committee would only serve to create further discord within the party. James Cooper, on the other hand, drawing on his experience as a solicitor, contended that the Committee was within its rights to suspend the three MPs.

It was an animated interview with the Party Chairman and one of its Vice-Presidents putting forward totally opposite views on the legality of the action taken by the Disciplinary Committee. Only one of them, though, could be right.

That evening Jeffrey consulted with his solicitor, John Mc Burney, of Mc Burney & Co. in Banbridge, and he shared the suspended MP's contention that the party had acted unlawfully. They decided that the best way forward would be to apply to the High Court for a judicial review of the Disciplinary Committee's decision to suspend three of its most senior members without affording them the opportunity to present their case at the required hearing. Jeffrey undertook to contact his two colleagues, Rev. Martin Smyth and David Burnside, the following morning, and secure their consent to apply for a judicial review.

As Jeffrey talked to many party members, from those in senior positions to lifelong grass-roots supporters, over the weekend, he discovered that a sizeable percentage of them had been left stunned by the hastily convened Disciplinary Committee's overhasty announcement.

Jeffrey believed that David Trimble's followers were misjudging the reaction of ordinary unionists to the increasing vindictiveness being displayed towards the three 'dissident' MPs by the party leadership. Some weeks earlier his main opponents in the Lagan Valley Unionist Association had tabled a vote of no confidence in him as their Member of Parliament because of his opposition to David Trimble. This action proved to be singularly shortsighted because there remained a substantial majority within the Association who were loyal supporters of Jeffrey, and the motion had to be withdrawn. Those same supporters, and others from many constituencies, including South Belfast and South Antrim, vowed to back the suspended trio as they pursued the matter through The High Court.

An application was lodged, and the date of the hearing was set for Thursday, July 3, with the case to be heard by Mr. Justice Girvan.

On the day of the hearing Jeffrey was present in court to hear barristers from both sides put the legal arguments before the judge. He was delighted with the manner in which his legal team so ably represented his case, and that of his colleagues. As the cases were submitted he was convinced that the arguments being advanced by his team were incontrovertible, but he tried not to allow himself to become overly confident. The courts had often proved reluctant to become involved in party political disputes in the past, and the result was therefore far from predictable.

As the proceedings drew to a close Mr. Justice Girvan informed the legal representatives that he hoped to deliver his judgement on Monday, July 7.

There followed a second weekend in which Jeffrey was contacted by many of his friends who assured him that 'things would go his way on Monday.' It was encouraging to be surrounded by such a groundswell of support, but all the Lagan Valley MP could do was thank such well-wishers for their call and say that 'although he hoped they were right, all anyone could do was wait and see.'

It appeared that others had also spent the weekend 'waiting to see.' The media were already gathered outside The High Court on Monday morning as Jeffrey Donaldson arrived to hear what the judge had decided.

Those permitted in the courtroom sat silently, listening to and weighing every word, as Mr. Justice Girvan outlined the background to the case before delivering his ruling. He described the disciplinary action against the three MPs as 'a draconian and previously unheard of form of suspension,' before going on to present a summary of his judgement as follows:-

'In the result I shall grant the following relief:

(1)   A declaration that the officers of the UUC have failed to properly constitute a Disciplinary Committee of the UUC for the purposes of investigating and determining charges against the

plaintiff as referred to the Disciplinary Committee by the officers.

(2)   A declaration that the purported suspension of the plaintiffs from the membership of the UUC and the purported suspension of the first and second plaintiffs from office in the UUC by members of the improperly constituted Disciplinary Committee communicated to the plaintiffs by letter dated 27 June 2003 is unlawful, invalid and of no force or effect.'

This ruling was decisive and the three MPs were immediately reinstated into membership of the Ulster Unionist Party after it was delivered. Jeffrey Donaldson, Rev. Martin Smyth and David Burnside, the plaintiffs, felt gratified and vindicated by the outcome of the hearing, which turned out to be a humiliating experience for the UUP leadership who had initiated the disciplinary action.

With Parliament once again in recess for the summer there was time for reflection, within the Ulster Unionist Party, on the damaging events of the last week in June and the first week in July. The winds circulating around the 'Low' of that fateful fortnight had whipped ripples of dissent into waves of discontent. It was becoming clear that there was growing disenchantment amongst some senior pro-Agreement members about the direction the party was taking under David Trimble's leadership.

On July 31 Jeffrey was contacted by his colleague Danny Kennedy, by then an MLA for Newry and Armagh. Danny wanted to share with him, in confidence, a discussion paper on the future of the Ulster Unionist Party. This paper had been prepared by a group of senior party members who had previously supported David Trimble but now felt that the time had come to consider a change of leader.

Jeffrey had become aware of the existence of this group, for he had already met Danny and Jim Nicholson, the party's MEP, at the Ulster Unionist office, in The Mall, Armagh, on August 22, 2002, almost a year before. It was at that meeting when Jeffrey first heard the idea of a change of party leader mooted, with Danny Kennedy and Jim Nicholson advocating that they urge Sir Reg Empey, whom they thought could bring some measure of unity to the hopelessly divided party, to challenge for the leadership. Jeffrey had rejected the idea then, arguing that a change in party policy was just as important as a change of party leader, at that particular time.

Danny Kennedy assured Jeffrey that things had changed over the previous eleven months, for the Empey-for-leader undercover campaigners had taken account of his comments and had developed a set of proposals that would include a reassessment of the party's policy position on the Agreement.

When Jeffrey was presented with the discussion paper he was interested to note that it addressed many of the issues that had given rise to the deep divisions within the party under David Trimble's leadership. In a section proposing the removal of Mr. Trimble, the paper stated, 'It would be most preferable that any change in the leadership should be managed without excessive rancour, and conducted in a proper and civilised manner, without any degree of triumphalism.'

It went on to say that 'the new agreed leadership approach would tackle all our existing political, policing, social etc. problems in a more rigorous manner, and certainly most of our early efforts would be directed against the Joint Declaration.'

The paper concluded that 'this draft is intended only as a

starting point, leading hopefully to a meaningful and productive debate.'

That debate was slow to materialise as many of the prime movers were on holiday, but during the course of the following three weeks Jeffrey shared the contents of the paper with his closest associates, including Rev. Martin Smyth, David Burnside, Lord Molyneaux and Arlene Foster. They were all agreed that whilst there were still key differences in policy terms between their anti-Agreement stance and that of the instigators of the change-of-leadership initiative, it would be worth exploring, with them, whether there was a basis on which they could work together to reunite the party under a different leadership structure.

When the chief conspirators returned from holiday Jeffrey and his colleagues arranged to meet with them to discuss their proposals. This meeting was held mid-morning on Tuesday, August 26, in David Burnside's constituency office in the town of Antrim. Sitting alongside Jeffrey were David Burnside, Arlene Foster and Councillor Adrian Watson from Antrim. Across the table from them there sat Reg Empey, Fred Cobain and Danny Kennedy, all MLAs, and Councillor Tom Elliott from Fermanagh.

It was clear from the discussions that took place that both sides recognised the party was irreconcilably split under David Trimble and that his removal was an essential prerequisite to the healing of that festering wound.

However, it was equally apparent that fundamental policy differences still existed between the two groupings. They all agreed that further work was needed to explore the potential for a common policy platform which would constitute the basis for a new party leadership. There was also a lack of consensus as to who should replace David Trimble as leader for Jeffrey and his team were far from convinced that Reg Empey was the person to revitalise the party's flagging fortunes in the country. As the meeting broke up Reg Empey undertook to prepare a further paper which would seek to address all of the issues to be resolved.

Three days later Jeffrey received a phone call to his home from Sir Reg Empey who advised him that he had compiled the first draft of his discussion document and he would fax it through immediately. The seventeen page paper, when it arrived within minutes, was indeed a comprehensive appraisal of the difficulties confronting the Ulster Unionist Party at that time.

On the party leadership Sir Reg concluded, 'Clearly the officers are, like the rest of the party, dysfunctional.'

Referring to the operation and control of Unionist Party Headquarters at Cunningham House he observed that 'there is widespread disgust at the 'shambles' that is Party H.Q.'

He described the overall party organisation in similar vein, observing that 'our membership is ageing; women are not progressing through to be public representatives and our youth wing is small and ineffective.'

It was Sir Reg's comments on the need for a more representative UUP negotiating team, though, that gave Jeffrey the clearest indication of his growing disaffection with the existing leadership. In the paper Sir Reg stated bluntly, 'Trust within the party is simply not there.' In a clear indictment of David Trimble's standing as leader of the party he commented, 'Neither republicans nor Her Majesty's Government will make the necessary moves unless they believe they are negotiating with a group of unionists who really can deliver.'

There were further exchanges between Jeffrey and Sir Reg over the following days as they attempted to bridge the gap in formulating an agreed strategy. With only a couple of issues remaining to be resolved, a further meeting of the two groups was convened in David Burnside's office on the afternoon of Thursday, September 4, 2003.

The outcome of this meeting could prove crucial as the Ulster Unionist Council was scheduled to meet two days later, on Saturday, September 6, to debate a motion on the withdrawal of the disciplinary charges against the three MPs who had resigned the Whip.

Whilst there was undoubtedly now a greater level of consensus on the need to replace David Trimble as leader, it was less clear what form a reconstituted leadership would take, and specifically who would be the new party leader.

Those present at the Antrim meeting that Thursday afternoon believed that Sir Reg Empey regarded himself as the obvious choice, but Jeffrey and his colleagues remained unconvinced. They were suspicious that Sir Reg intended to use them to initiate the downfall of David Trimble, whereupon he could step forward with clean hands and present himself as 'the knight in shining armour' to rescue the party from the brink of ruin. In addition, they felt that Sir Reg's electoral record was far from outstanding and he seemed to lack the essential attributes of a strong and charismatic leader.

The meeting broke up with the vital issue of an agreed candidate to challenge for the party leadership unresolved. Perhaps a clear contender would emerge at, or after, Saturday's UUC meeting.

Belfast's Ulster Hall provided a more traditional setting for this latest meeting of the Ulster Unionist Council, but the change of venue did not effect a change of heart amongst the delegates on either side of the great divide. As the by-now well rehearsed arguments were bitterly debated David Trimble and his supporters made it quite clear that they had no intention of withdrawing the disciplinary charges against Jeffrey Donaldson and his colleagues.

This did not come as any surprise to them, but what they saw as of greater concern was the untypical silence of Sir Reg Empey, throughout the course of the debate. Sir Reg, who had spoken at all the previous UUC meetings, sat motionless and mute. He had nothing at all to say that day. Jeffrey and his supporters took his silence to indicate a reluctance to 'stand up and be counted,' when it really mattered. He had proved incapable of expressing in public to the UUC in Belfast the worthy sentiments he had appeared to have no problem expressing in private to a select few in Antrim, just two days before.

Jeffrey, and the team who had accompanied him to the meetings over the previous two weeks, were well aware that an intervention by Sir Reg in support of their position could potentially swing the meeting against the party leader. In the absence of any such intervention the two sides voted, and the result was similar to that of all the previous unpleasant encounters, a narrow victory for David Trimble.

Critically, though, with Assembly elections looming, this limited success for David Trimble was sufficient to head off any leadership challenge. Any ambitions Sir Reg Empey had harboured were dashed to pieces on the rocks of his own vacillation.

The way was now open for David Trimble to refocus on his negotiations with the Government and Sinn Fein in an effort to broker a deal that would enable the political institutions, including the Assembly, to be reinstated following the election, promised for the autumn. Once again the Prime Minister was at the centre of this latest initiative as he endeavoured to persuade the Ulster Unionist Party and Sinn Fein to compromise with each other to break the stalemate. As the talks continued the Secretary of State and others expressed optimism about the prospects of a breakthrough.

Meanwhile, away from all the top level shuttling to and fro, the Ulster Unionist Party continued its preparation for the election, although no date for this had as yet been announced, and Jeffrey was kept busy organising his campaign within the Lagan Valley constituency.

A poorly attended party conference held in Armagh city on Saturday, October 18, was the precursor to one of the most significant weeks in the leadership of David Trimble. Behind the scenes negotiations had culminated in a tentative agreement on a carefully orchestrated series of statements and activity by the British and Irish Governments, Sinn Fein and the UUP. This would involve an act of decommissioning by the IRA and a statement by Gerry Adams that their terrorist campaign was at an end. The plan was that these statements, accompanied by decisive movement from the IRA, would form the basis of a comprehensive deal to rejuvenate the faltering 'Good Friday' Agreement.

The elaborate choreography began at 7.00 a.m. on Tuesday, October 21, with an announcement by the British Government that the Assembly elections would be held on Wednesday, November 26. By mid-morning it was Sinn Fein's turn to take centre stage, with its president, Gerry Adams issuing a statement in which he reiterated his support for the Agreement 'with its vision of a fair and just society operating exclusively democratically and peacefully.' The British and Irish Prime Ministers arrived at Hillsborough in the early afternoon to await the performance of their next star actor, General John de Chastelain. He was expected to play a leading part in the daylong drama by announcing a further act of decommissioning by the IRA.

Both Prime Ministers recognised, as did David Trimble, that General de Chastelain's assessment of the IRA's actions would be crucial in convincing unionists that they should back the deal.

They were all to be bitterly disappointed.

Their key player forgot that a play has a plot, and that it was important for him to say exactly the right lines, at the right time, for the drama to reach its intended climax.

When the General gave a statement to the assembled media at Hillsborough it soon became evident that the IRA had once again imposed severe restrictions on the amount of detail he was allowed to divulge about the act of decommissioning. The General was unable to confirm the amount of weaponry that had been 'put beyond use' or the exact nature of that weaponry.

Watching the live press conference on Sky News in his office at Westminster, Jeffrey realised immediately that these vague comments from General de Chastelain would do nothing to instil confidence within the unionist community about the IRA's intentions. He knew instinctively that the secrecy surrounding the IRA's supposed act of decommissioning would only increase the scepticism felt by many.

Back at Unionist Headquarters in Belfast David Trimble was watching the same scene unfold, with some of his closest associates, and for once his reaction would be identical to that of his erstwhile opponent, Jeffrey Donaldson.

The final act in the choreography was to involve the Unionist

Party leader stepping up to the footlights and announcing that he welcomed and endorsed the earlier events and statements of the day before giving his consent to the reinstatement of the power-sharing institutions.

Now he was faced with a dilemma.

The media circus had moved to camp in a nearby room in Ulster Unionist Headquarters to await his pronouncement, but what could he say? An earlier actor had gone and torn up the script! David Trimble found himself in a 'no-win' situation. His position as party leader was too precarious to allow him to take any further risks and so he announced that he could not conclude the sequence and complete the deal.

Totally amazed and mildly amused at such an unexpected turn of events, Jeffrey wondered what effect this failed deal would have on the future of the Ulster Unionist Party.

And even more immediately, and importantly, how would it affect the party's performance in the Assembly elections, due to take place in just five weeks time?

36
TOE THE LINE OR QUIT THE PARTY

November could never be reckoned as an ideal month in which to hold an election.

The days are short and becoming shorter, and the weather is often inclement. Both of these considerations, plus the fact that people are not particularly inclined to stand on their doorsteps and chat on damp, foggy evenings, made the planning of a comprehensive canvass of a constituency the size of Lagan Valley rather difficult. Nevertheless, Jeffrey and his campaign team were in good spirits as they embarked upon this enterprise, and the chill of the winter air was often forgotten as they knocked many doors to be accorded an extremely warm reception.

Jeffrey worked closely with two of his fellow-Ulster Unionist Party candidates, Jim Kirkpatrick and his secretary, Norah Beare, whom he was delighted to see progress to more active political involvement.

Their election agent was Mrs. Elvira Tulip, a party stalwart, and secretary of the Lagan Valley Constituency Association. With characteristic enthusiasm and efficiency she organised the party supporters into canvass teams to cover the entire constituency. It was a mammoth task but Jeffrey and Elvira both recognised the importance of making personal contact with as many constituents as possible. With Jeffrey and Norah out every available minute on the campaign trail, the work of the Lagan Valley constituency office was ably conducted by two recently appointed members of staff, David Nichol and Gillian McAllister.

Meanwhile the canvass teams were beginning to encounter a difficulty on the doorsteps. Although most of the constituents at whose homes they had called were very welcoming when they realised that the canvassers were representing Jeffrey Donaldson, they also took the opportunity to express a strong and adverse reaction to the unsuccessful policies of David Trimble.

Many were anxious to know where exactly Jeffrey and his colleagues stood in relation to these. Did they, for instance, support all the actions and statements of the party leader?

It was difficult to predict what effect this rumbling unrest, and the party's current unpopularity, would have on polling day. Jeffrey and his fellow-anti-Agreement Ulster Unionist candidates quickly recognised that it would be imperative to distance themselves from their leader and highlight their own distinct policy platform. They did this in the form of a mini-manifesto, which was based on the Stormont Principles and declared that the candidates endorsing it would seek to negotiate a better deal for Northern Ireland.

The division within the UUP reflected a wider division within unionism, and the DUP were fighting a very vigorous campaign aimed at increasing their representation in the Assembly at the expense of other unionists. They, too, were promising to deliver an agreement more acceptable to the majority of the unionist population.

A few days before the election, David Trimble was invited to take part in a one-hour live 'Talkback' programme on BBC Radio Ulster, and he was constantly being asked about the widening rift in the UUP. In response to a number of callers, the party leader asserted that all of the Ulster Unionist Party candidates, including Jeffrey Donaldson, supported his policy.

The Lagan Valley MP was listening to the interview in his constituency office in Lisburn, and was dismayed by Mr. Trimble's misrepresentation of his position. He rang the producer, requesting that a short statement of clarification be carried at the end of the programme to inform the listeners that Jeffrey Donaldson did not, in fact, endorse the 'failed policies of the party leader.'

With the programme drawing to an end the producer rang Jeffrey to offer him the opportunity to express his own reservations, in person, on air.

When Jeffrey was put on, David Dunseith, the programme presenter, introduced him by remarking to Mr. Trimble, "You will probably recognise the next caller."

The tension between the two senior party officials was apparent as each of them stated his perspective, briefly but firmly. Their encounter was not in any sense heated, but its impact on the course of the election was to prove decisive, for it afforded Jeffrey an opportunity to clarify his 'consistent stance' for the benefit of confused prospective UUP voters.

On Wednesday, November 26, polling day, more that sixty per cent of the Lagan Valley electorate turned out to register their vote in spite of the unpleasant weather. The count for the constituency commenced at 9.00 a.m. the following morning in Dromore Leisure Centre, a building with which Jeffrey had already become very familiar at previous counts. This was also the venue for the South Down count, and with Jeffrey's father, Jim, standing as an Ulster Unionist candidate for that constituency, there was intense family interest in the outcome of both counts.

The early indications in Lagan Valley appeared promising as the ballot boxes were emptied. Jeffrey seemed to have polled well across the constituency. By the time all of the ballot papers had been sorted into bundles for each candidate it had become obvious that the pile for Jeffrey Donaldson was by far the biggest. It looked as though Jeffrey would be the only candidate to be elected at the first count, and this was confirmed when the Returning Officer stood up to make her first announcement of the long counting process under the proportional representation system.

What was surprising, though, was the strength of the poll. Even Jeffrey was pleasantly taken aback by the overwhelming level of support which he had been accorded by the people of his constituency. With 14104 first preference votes he had just secured the largest personal mandate of any candidate standing in the election in Northern Ireland.

Jim Donaldson, Jeffrey's father, was delighted at his son's result although disappointed himself at not having secured a seat in South Down. As the counting progressed the distribution of Jeffrey's huge surplus vote helped to ensure the election of two other UUP candidates, Norah Beare and Billy Bell, as well as the seat won by Edwin Poots of the Democratic Unionist Party. This result saw the Ulster Unionist Party increase its representation in Lagan Valley from two to three seats, making it the only constituency in Northern Ireland to return three UUP candidates.

Next morning, when Jeffrey had studied the size and spread of first preference votes across the province, he recognised that his own outstanding personal result had not been attained by his own efforts, but took it as a demonstration of God's continuing approval of his active involvement in the realm of politics.

It was even more than that, however.

Jeffrey reflected on some of the verses from the Bible which had meant so much to him at a crisis point in his life a number of years earlier. It was so reassuring to look back on the fulfilled promise of Psalm 37. *'Commit your way to the Lord, trust also in Him, and He shall bring it to pass.'* He was happy to thank God for this unexpected margin of success. Considering the opposition that he had encountered, it was undoubtedly God who had 'brought it to pass.' His divine power was far superior to that of any earthly antagonist.

As he continued to meditate on these things Jeffrey suddenly remembered a Bible verse he had heard a minister quote during the course of a church service, some months before. The words *"Not by might, nor by power, but by My Spirit,' says the Lord of hosts,'* flashed back into his mind, out of the blue. He was to find, as he searched for it in the Bible he had beside him, that this was a quotation from Zechariah chapter four.

Jeffrey was pleased to have discovered this verse for it summarised, both accurately and eloquently, his approach, not only to his own life as a Christian but also to the state of affairs in Northern Ireland. It was so true that the situation could not be, and would never be, resolved by the might of guns or bombs. A lasting peace could only be achieved in the province when the Spirit of God began to work in changing the lives of its population.

He soon found himself flitting in thought between Tullyhappy Orange Hall and Westminster Hall once more. That other scripture quotation to which he had first been introduced in the heart of County Armagh, and which he had heard quoted so powerfully by Anne Graham Lotz in the centre of London, also still applied. A humbling amongst the people and a return to God was the only answer for Northern Ireland.

By Friday afternoon, when all the votes in the election had been finally counted and all the seats declared, two parties, one from each side of the political divide, emerged as the ultimate victors. Within unionism the Democratic Unionist Party's representation increased by fifty per cent, from twenty seats in 1998, to thirty in 2003, and on the nationalist side Sinn Fein became the larger of the two parties, with twenty-four seats. By contrast, both the UUP and the SDLP suffered a discomfiting loss of seats in the Assembly.

Jeffrey had no doubt that this further embarrassing reversal in the fortunes of the Ulster Unionist Party could be attributed to the increasingly unpopular policies of the party leader, and in the aftermath of the election he stated his opinion that it was time for David Trimble to step down. With two-thirds of all unionists having voted for anti-Agreement candidates he argued that David Trimble's position had become untenable. He contended that the unionist electorate had registered an overwhelming demand for change, and this would require the adoption of a new policy by the UUP and a change of attitude towards the Belfast Agreement.

At a meeting of Unionist Party officers held on Friday, December 5, an examination of the election result was top of the agenda. As different speakers presented their own analysis of the situation it soon became obvious from the discussion that David Trimble had no intention of either resigning or altering his policy position. The leader resolutely refused to accept that the party's dismal showing in the election represented a withering verdict by the unionist electorate on either his leadership or the Agreement.

Mr. Trimble dismissed the DUP electoral success as of no consequence. He informed the officers that he intended to speak privately to the Prime Minister in an attempt to minimise the scope of the forthcoming Review of the Agreement so that the DUP would be unable to deliver the changes they had promised. Jeffrey was horrified at this. He saw it as a betrayal of the people whom he represented, and indeed the entire unionist community. Instead of seeking to accommodate their wishes, expressed so clearly at the ballot box, the party leader was scheming unashamedly to ensure they were thwarted.

All of these matters were scheduled to be the focus of further debate at the Party Executive meeting to be held a week later, on Friday, December 12.

With the initial formalities of that meeting out of the way, the Party Chairman, James Cooper, informed the Executive that he had received a total of seventy-eight letters from party members all across the province, calling upon the leadership to expel the Lagan Valley MP. As the list of those who had sent the letters was read out Jeffrey recognised some very familiar names, including his arch-opponents from Lagan Valley, who, although a minority, were unrelenting in their attempt to undermine their MP.

It was apparent to Jeffrey, as he listened to a representative sample of these letters being read, that this had been a carefully orchestrated scheme by David Trimble's supporters to deflect the blame for the party's disastrous electoral performance on to his chief critic. Many of the letters were mere duplicates.

In his letter, Councillor Jim Dillon from Lisburn described 'Mr. Donaldson's behaviour' as being 'responsible for our current situation.' He went on to demand, 'He must resign and should he not do so disciplinary action is essential.'

Writing in similar terms another Lisburn Councillor, Sam Johnston, stated, '...the time has come for him to go. I request that he should be required to resign...'

Jeffrey felt particularly sickened at the letters from these local councillors. He recalled that just two weeks earlier they had been canvassing on the streets of the city for Ivan Davis, who had stood as an independent candidate against the Ulster Unionist Party, and had failed to win a seat. Not only had they broken the party rules, but their candidate had also suffered the ignominy of being totally rejected by the Lagan Valley electorate. How ironic, he mused, that they should accuse the candidate who had topped the poll in Northern Ireland of being responsible for the party's electoral demise.

A stormy debate followed the reading of that collection of hastily organised and mobilised sheaf of letters, which, although coming from cities, towns and villages all over the province, carried exactly the same message. Jeffrey Donaldson should resign at once. In the most vitriolic exchanges that Jeffrey had ever witnessed as a member of the Ulster Unionist Party, some senior and respected figures rose to his defence, but their contributions were completely ignored by those choosing to hurl criticism and abuse at the Lagan Valley MP.

During the course of the meeting an e-mail from Lord Maginnis, who chose to express his opinion in rather colourful terms, was read out. 'I expect no concessions to our MP/MLA,' he began. 'He can't set the house on fire; sabotage the fire engine, and then be given any role in the Fire Brigade. 'Let's say, "Goodbye Jeffrey."'

When a final motion was put to the meeting it seemed that Lord Maginnis, and all the others who had been so stridently demanding the resignation or dismissal of Jeffrey Donaldson, might just get their way. The motion demanded that Jeffrey give an unequivocal undertaking to fully support the party leader and his pro-Agreement policy or face expulsion. He would be required to comply with this ultimatum within weeks or the Party Executive would initiate disciplinary proceedings to expel him. When the motion was put to a vote the Executive voted, by a majority of 50 to 33 to support the ultimatum.

Jeffrey left that meeting like someone shell-shocked. He was stunned, disappointed and deeply hurt. The proceedings of the afternoon had come as a total surprise to him. He had walked into the meeting as normal only to be hit with a bang by a barrage of bitterness. And possibly even harder to stomach than the overt bitterness that had characterised it all had been the covert deceitfulness that seemed to have planned it all. On the way out he spoke to the waiting media and advised them that he would 'now be taking some time to consider his future.'

When back home he shared his feelings with Eleanor as he recounted the events that had unfolded during what was undoubtedly his most traumatic political meeting ever. His wife was mystified at the attitude displayed towards her husband, who a mere two weeks before had achieved the highest personal vote of any candidate in Northern Ireland, and in doing so had helped the Ulster Unionist Party secure an additional seat in Lagan Valley. She assured Jeffrey of her support whatever decision he took in relation to his future.

As he retired to bed that evening Jeffrey still felt cheated and deflated. From the mountaintop of electoral success he had been plunged abruptly and mercilessly into the valley of decision and despair. In that situation he turned to God again. This time, though, it was not with a thankful, but with a burdened heart.

He had not even dared to ask, Why? His big concern was for guidance. And his burning question was, Please Lord, what now?

The banner headline in the *Belfast News Letter* the following morning reminded the Lagan Valley MP of the stark alternatives he faced. It summarised the ultimatum presented to him by the

Party Executive as, 'TOE THE LINE OR QUIT THE PARTY.'

As he pondered and prayed over that agonised weekend Jeffrey realised that he was confronted with one of the most crucial choices of his political career. The newspaper headline had identified his only options.

Some of his closest political colleagues in the Ulster Unionist Party urged him to stay 'and fight his ground.' He had given over twenty years of loyal service to the party and the recent election results showed that he still commanded immense respect. Was he prepared to walk away from the party simply because of the threat of expulsion?

On the other hand, he could not possibly abandon his principles to support a policy which he believed to be out of step with the wishes of the majority of unionists. Nor could he ignore the commitment he had made to his constituents in Lagan Valley, to seek a better agreement. How could he fulfil his mandate by continuing to engage in the increasingly bitter and damaging 'civil war' within the Ulster Unionist Party? What honour would there be in allowing those who had been rejected by the electorate the pleasure of having him expelled from the party he had so faithfully served?

Early the following week Jeffrey received a letter from a well-wisher quoting a question from 1 Kings chapter eighteen and verse twenty-one in the Authorised Version of the Bible. It was, *'How long halt ye between two opinions?'*

That was just the spur he needed. There could be no more delay.

Jeffrey made the vital decision which he knew he would have to make sooner or later. Once certain that he was happy with it, he was careful to inform his mentor and friend, Lord Molyneaux, and the Party President, Rev. Martin Smyth, of what he had decided to do, before making any public statement.

He then chose to announce his decision to the people of Northern Ireland, many of whom had contacted him over the previous few days with the assurance of their unswerving support, at 6.00 p.m. on Thursday, December 18.

Ulster Television's news presenter Mike Nesbitt commenced the evening bulletin with the dramatic opening headline, "The Lagan Valley MP Jeffrey Donaldson has just announced his resignation from the Ulster Unionist Party." The newsreader then went on to report that Arlene Foster and Norah Beare, Jeffrey's two fellow-Assembly members who had earlier pledged to support his political stance, had taken an equally-principled decision.

This announcement caused shock waves throughout the party and across the country. It also left Jeffrey with another momentous and critical decision to make.

He had resigned from one political party.

Should he join another one?

Or would it be better, as some had suggested to him, to operate as an independent MP at Westminster and MLA at Stormont?

37

WELCOMED AT THE PARSONAGE AND INTO THE PARTY

In the years following the 'Good Friday' Agreement Jeffrey had developed a cordial relationship with many of the senior members of the Democratic Unionist Party. Latterly, during the period in which he had been without the UUP Whip at Westminster, that relationship had grown stronger. He had chatted occasionally to Dr. Ian Paisley, the party leader, in the tearoom at the House of Commons, as they discussed the political issues of the day and their shared Christian faith. Peter Robinson, the deputy leader of the DUP, and his wife Iris had become good friends with him, as had the other two DUP MPs, Nigel Dodds and Gregory Campbell. Jeffrey had long recognised that he felt more comfortable with their political position than that of the pro-Agreement lobby of the UUP, and so the bond between them continued to strengthen.

These MPs had often raised with Jeffrey in a casual way, and without any attempt at coercion, the possibility of developing a more effective political liaison between them all.

It came as no surprise then when Peter Robinson phoned him after he had been issued with his ultimatum from the UUP on that fateful Friday. Peter had called to offer him the opportunity to meet Nigel Dodds and himself to discuss his plans for the future, if he so desired. After he had announced his resignation from the Ulster Unionist Party Jeffrey decided to take them up on their invitation and they met in Peter Robinson's home in East Belfast shortly before Christmas.

This was to be the first of a number of meetings at which the two senior DUP figures assured Jeffrey that he, Arlene Foster and Norah Beare would be given a warm welcome should they decide to join the DUP. They were anxious to make it clear, however, that they were not seeking to shunt the three former UUP members into their party. It was simply a case of assuring them that the door was ajar. All they had to do was push it.

The indication that senior figures in the DUP appreciated the fact that he was an experienced negotiator, and that they would certainly find a place for him on their negotiating team in further top-level discussions, was of particular importance to Jeffrey. Crucially, there would also be key roles for Arlene and Norah as part of the DUP Assembly group. With the Democratic Unionists now the largest party in the Assembly, Jeffrey realised that gaining a place on their negotiating team would enable him to fulfil the mandate he had been given by the electorate in Lagan Valley. He would then be in a position to help secure a more acceptable agreement.

While he was maintaining contact with the DUP leadership but keeping his options open, there were still those who continued to urge him to remain as an independent, both at Westminster and in the Assembly.

Jeffrey considered this suggestion carefully but recognised that there were two major disadvantages to adopting that position. Firstly, as an independent he would have no role to play in any future dialogue and therefore could not properly requite the wishes of his constituents who had supported him so faithfully. The other reason was more to do with party numbers than personal conscience. If Jeffrey were to remain as an independent member at Stormont the unionist representation on any future Northern Ireland Executive would be reduced. Alternatively, if he and his two colleagues were to join the DUP, then his new party, and unionism, would gain an extra ministry under the complex formula that operated in the Assembly.

Following his meetings with the senior members of the Democratic Unionist Party, and having rejected the idea of remaining as an independent MP and MLA, Jeffrey was much clearer in his mind as to what would be his best, and most politically productive, course of action.

On Sunday, December 21, Jeffrey, Eleanor and the girls had just arrived home from the morning service in their church in Dromore when Jeffrey said to his wife, "Eleanor, I have made the final decision about my future, and I want to tell you about it first, before I let anybody else know. I have now no doubt whatsoever that my only honourable and sensible choice is to join the Democratic Unionist Party."

Before formalising his position with the DUP leadership Jeffrey consulted Arlene and Norah, both of whom agreed with him that this was the only reasonable option open to all three of them. Jeffrey called Peter Robinson and told him of his decision and the deputy leader of the party sounded thrilled to have 'him aboard.'

Over the Christmas holiday period a few more contacts were made and Jeffrey Donaldson, Arlene Foster and Norah Beare officially joined the Democratic Unionist Party. They agreed with the party leadership that it would be best to postpone any public declaration of their position until early in the New Year.

On Saturday, January 3, 2004, Jeffrey was invited to meet Dr. Paisley at his home in east Belfast. As he approached the door of 'The Parsonage' that morning Jeffrey was delighted to have the founder and leader of his new party come out to greet him in person.

Sitting in the comfortable lounge later on, with Dr. Paisley and Maurice Morrow, the Party Chairman, enjoying the tea and scones provided by Mrs. Paisley, and discussing the party's plans for the future in relaxed fashion, Jeffrey knew immediately that he had made the right decision. He already felt welcome in his new party. What a contrast there was between that cosy drawing-room scene and some of the acrimonious encounters he had experienced at recent UUP events.

As they continued to chat away amicably, Jeffrey recalled the Sunday evenings when he, as a teenager, used to stop outside the Martyrs Memorial Free Presbyterian Church on his way down the Ravenhill Road in Belfast. All he had wanted to do in those days was catch a glimpse of 'The Big Man,' outside the church at the end of a service.

Little did he think then, that one day he would be welcomed, as a senior colleague, to whole-hearted hospitality in 'The Parsonage.'

Two days later, on Monday, January 5, at 10.00 a.m. the scene was set at Stormont for the public announcement by Jeffrey, Arlene and Norah. A press conference was convened in the Great Hall and the three new recruits were joined by Dr. Paisley, his deputy Peter Robinson and the Party Secretary, Nigel Dodds The party leader made a few opening remarks before introducing the first speaker, Jeffrey Donaldson, now of the Democratic Unionist Party.

In the course of his speech, which was soon to be broadcast across the province by the waiting media, Jeffrey repeated one of his main reasons for joining the DUP. He said,

'I have consistently advocated a greater unity amongst unionists. During the elections, Arlene, Norah and I, along with some other UUP candidates, published what became known as a 'mini-manifesto' in which we stated clearly that we would 'promote greater co-operation between unionists to more effectively represent the unionist case in the negotiations that will follow the election.' Consequently, our decision to join the DUP is entirely consistent with our electoral mandate. It affords us the opportunity to work with unionists of like mind to build a stronger unionist movement that will prevent Sinn Fein/IRA from dominating Ulster politics. That is where the real battle lies, not in some futile unionist civil war.'

Arlene Foster and Norah Beare also spoke passionately about their decision to become part of the Democratic Unionist team at Stormont, and Dr. Paisley formally responded on behalf of his party, saying that they were delighted to receive these new members, who were highly respected within traditional unionism. He described that moment as 'a watershed for unionism' before going on to observe that it was 'indicative of the growing support for the principled stand of the DUP.'

Following a further round of media interviews Jeffrey was on his way back to Lisburn in the afternoon when he received a call on his mobile phone. His former parliamentary colleague, John Taylor, now Lord Kilclooney, was on the line.

"I have just heard your interview, Jeffrey," the former UUP deputy leader began, "and I am ringing to wish you all the best for the future. Although I will be sorry to lose you from the Ulster Unionist Party, I believe you have made the right decision. There is no future for independents in Ulster politics."

Jeffrey was not only pleasantly surprised to hear from Lord

Kilclooney but also genuinely encouraged by his call. It was reassuring to know that there was at least one senior party member, who, although a supporter of David Trimble, had been able to rise above all the recent acrimony to understand the dilemma which the Lagan Valley MP had faced.

That evening, Jeffrey, Arlene and Norah travelled to Fivemiletown in County Tyrone to attend the annual dinner of the local DUP Constituency Association, but the party faithful, already assembled in the Valley Hotel, were blissfully unaware of the arrival of their three new public representatives.

When they were led into the dining room by a Scottish piper closely followed by Maurice Morrow, people quickly sprang to their feet and clapped and cheered. Jeffrey had never been given such a spontaneous and positive welcome anywhere before in his life!

When Parliament resumed at Westminster after the Christmas recess, on Wednesday January 7, Jeffrey Donaldson changed his seat in the House of Commons. He began the new parliamentary session on the green benches, at Prime Minister's Question Time, as the Democratic Unionist Party MP for Lagan Valley.

Later that day David Trimble attacked his former colleague's decision to resign from the Ulster Unionist Party, suggesting that Jeffrey's action should give rise to a by-election in Lagan Valley.

Jeffrey, in response, pointed out that the mandate he had received to negotiate a better agreement had been upheld in his decision, and that it was the party leader's action in seeking to force his resignation that was dishonourable. He observed that David Trimble had challenged Rev. Martin Smyth, David Burnside and himself to resign from the party in June 2003, declaring then that 'resignation would be the principled course of action.' On the by-election issue Jeffrey reminded Mr. Trimble that Sir Winston

Churchill, who had just been voted 'the greatest Briton of all time,' had changed parties twice without a by-election ever having been called.

On January 21 the DUP in Lagan Valley organised a rally in Lisburn Orange Hall to welcome Jeffrey, and the many former members of the UUP in the constituency, who had by then joined the party.

The hall was packed to overflowing and many of those who came were attending their first political meeting of any kind. It soon became evident that in addition to those who were already actively involved in politics, whether as former members of the Ulster Unionist Party or life-long patrons of the Democratic Unionist Party, there were many others who had come along simply to register their allegiance to their MP by following his lead and joining the DUP.

This gave Jeffrey a tremendous sense of satisfaction. It was the first clear sign that there was strong support in the constituency for the bold step he had taken.

The rapid growth of the party in Lagan Valley created an imminent need to find larger accommodation for the constituency headquarters and offices. The three local MLAs discussed the matter and it was decided that Jeffrey and his colleague Edwin Poots would establish their offices in Lisburn, with Norah based in the south of the constituency in Dromore.

The historic Old Town Hall was identified as the most suitable Lisburn location and Jeffrey's staff set about the task of moving to their new premises. His election to the Assembly had entitled the Lagan Valley MLA to recruit some much needed additional staff members. This led to the employment of Barbara Wilson and Paul Stewart in the constituency office and Robin Ramsey as a research assistant at Stormont.

With an expanded headquarters established in Lisburn and a network of advice centres across the constituency Jeffrey Donaldson was even more suitably equipped to fulfil his main political purpose.

That was to represent all his constituents in Lagan Valley as considerately, diligently and efficiently as possible.

38

IN THE HANDS OF A
HIGHER POWER

Shortly after his move to the Democratic Unionists, Jeffrey was appointed by the Party Executive as one of the Party Officers who have day-to-day responsibility for the management of party affairs. This meant that he then held the same level of seniority within his new party as he had once done with the Ulster Unionists.

With the results of the Assembly elections, and the emergence of the DUP as the largest political party in Northern Ireland, the Government recognised that changes would be required and finally arranged a Review of the Agreement. Thus Jeffrey was soon to become involved, as a member of the party's senior negotiating team, in a fresh round of talks with the British Government and other Northern Ireland political parties. He felt pleased to be back at the negotiating table where he hoped to work with his DUP colleagues to achieve the objectives which they had set for themselves in their respective manifestos.

Whilst most of these talks had taken place at Stormont it had become traditional for representatives from the Northern Ireland political parties and the British and Irish Governments to decamp to Washington D.C. for the annual St. Patrick's Day celebrations on March 17. Jeffrey had been before with the Ulster Unionist Party and when invited to be part of the DUP delegation in 2004 relished the chance to renew some old acquaintances on Capitol

Hill. He joined Peter Robinson, Nigel Dodds, Jim Allister and Richard Bullick, head of the DUP policy unit, on the trans-Atlantic trip.

There were a number of high-level meetings with Senators, Congressmen and officials from the US Administration, but undoubtedly the highlight of the visit for Jeffrey was an unforeseen opportunity to hold a brief but cordial personal conversation with President George W. Bush.

Having already met the President at the White House early on St. Patrick's Day, Jeffrey then attended the annual luncheon, hosted by the Speaker of the House of Representatives, on Capitol Hill.

The DUP delegate was frustrated to be delayed by the security team as he entered the Capitol building, but he had arrived at exactly the same time as the President and everything was held up until he was seated. This meant that Jeffrey was kept back for a few minutes and by the time he entered the dining room all the principal guests had taken their seats. As he made his way over to his designated table Jeffrey caught the eye of the Irish Prime Minister, Bertie Ahern, who was sitting next to the President at the top table.

Mr. Ahern beckoned him across.

Jeffrey immediately changed direction and crossed to the top table where Mr. Ahern introduced him to the President as, 'Jeffrey Donaldson, MP for Lagan Valley in Northern Ireland.'

Realising the dinner was soon about to begin, and that the time for any conversation would of necessity be brief, Jeffrey acknowledged the Irish Prime Minister's introduction before crouching down between the two leaders and addressing the President of the United States.

"I would just like to convey to you the best wishes of the people of Northern Ireland, Mr. President," he said. "We appreciate the lead you are giving to the world in the fight against international terrorism and we wish you every success in the Presidential elections in November. We trust that you will be given a further term in office."

"Thank you very much, that is very kind," the President replied. "I believe, though, that these matters are not entirely in our hands. Our destiny is in the hands of a Higher Power."

Seizing on what he understood to be a reference to Mr. Bush's ultimate dependence on God, Jeffrey went on to remark, "We good Presbyterians would call that predestination, Mr. President."

George Bush laughed heartily before pointing playfully across at the Irish Prime Minister and quipping, "Yes. You're right. But this good Catholic here wouldn't understand all of that!"

It was a memorable moment for Jeffrey, when three men, from different countries, and with vastly different levels of political responsibility within those countries, met each other, laughed together, and eventually went their separate ways.

On returning from Washington, Jeffrey continued to have a high media profile as a spokesman for the Democratic Unionist Party. On one such occasion in late April he was invited to participate in the popular Radio 4 programme, 'Any Questions?' chaired by Jonathan Dimbleby. This particular Northern Ireland edition of the programme was to be broadcast from the Elmwood Hall at Queen's University.

When Jeffrey entered the building he noticed his former party leader, who had also been invited to take part, standing alone at the end of the corridor. The Lagan Valley MP had not spoken personally to Mr. Trimble since resigning from the Ulster Unionist

Party, and this was clearly going to be an awkward moment. However, Jeffrey decided to 'break the ice' and went across to speak to him.

They had only time for a short conversation before being called on stage, as the programme was about to begin.

When the show got under way, someone asked the panellists, in one of the questions from the floor, if they regretted any of the decisions they had made in their respective careers. The chairman directed the question to Jeffrey, reminding him that he was seated next to his 'arch-rival from the UUP, Mr. Trimble.'

Well aware that this question had been passed to him for a purpose Jeffrey was quite happy to announce that he had no regrets about any of the major decisions he had made in his political career in recent days.

The presenter then turned his attention to David Trimble and began, "Well, Mr. Trimble, you have just heard that in spite of all the headaches he has caused you, this man has no regrets, what do you..." At this point David Trimble reached for a small bottle of still water which was sitting on the table in front of him, and when he had lifted it, pretended to crack it over the Lagan Valley MP's head. The audience immediately exploded into fits of laughter and Jonathan Dimbley was left with the task of explaining to the listeners what had just occurred on stage.

'The ice' was well and truly broken!

On Saturday, May 8, Jeffrey paid a return visit to the Ramada Hotel in south Belfast, but this time it was to attend his first Democratic Unionist Party Conference. This was to be a day of both jubilation and anticipation. In addition to celebrating the party's success in the Assembly election and increasing acceptance in the country, the delegates were looking forward to the forthcoming European poll with their candidate Jim Allister carrying the DUP standard following Dr. Paisley's decision to stand down from Strasbourg.

The following day, Sunday May 9, Jeffrey flew to London to participate in a special event organised jointly by the Israeli Embassy and the Prayer for the Nations group. He had been involved in the organisation of this afternoon of 'Prayer for Jerusalem,' in Westminster Central Hall.

Lady Sainsbury welcomed the audience to this gathering of concerned Jews and Christians and read the words from Psalm 122 to which Rabbi Michael Melchior had already drawn attention at the National Prayer Breakfast, more than a year before. *'Pray for the peace of Jerusalem. May they prosper who love you. Peace be within your walls, prosperity within your palaces...'*

A message was delivered on behalf of the Israeli Government by the then acting ambassador, Zvi Ravner, and this was followed by Rabbi Aaron Goldstein who brought a message on behalf of the Jewish community.

Jeffrey was then invited, in his role as a member of the Parliamentary Christian Fellowship, to lead the meeting in prayer. On rising to do so, he prayed not only for the people of Israel and the peace of Jerusalem, but also for the peace of his native Northern Ireland. Jeffrey had always been interested in the nation of Israel, and his work with the Holocaust Educational Trust and his visit to Auschwitz had strengthened that interest into a desire to become more deeply involved.

It was clearly evident that the love he had for his home province was mirrored in the love he displayed for Israel, as he prayed earnestly that God would replace 'the violence of terrorism in both of these trouble-torn countries with His peace, 'which passes all understanding."

Back in Northern Ireland political progress was being made, and on June 25 the British and Irish Prime Ministers convened a summit of the two Governments and the Northern Ireland parties. They aimed to evaluate recent developments and determine the best way in which to take matters forward.

The conference was held in Lancaster House in central London, a location which had been the scene of many international and inter-governmental gatherings in the past. The DUP negotiating team, including Jeffrey Donaldson, was present for all the discussions, including a constructive meeting with the two Governments.

At the end of the talks the British and Irish Governments issued a highly significant joint statement in which they recognised for the first time that change was required if a new agreement was ever to be reached. The DUP team was pleased with the agenda that had been drawn up for the further negotiations that were scheduled to take place in the autumn.

These included issues such as 'a definitive and conclusive end to all paramilitary activity; the decommissioning of all paramilitary weapons, to an early timescale and on a convincing basis; and support for policing from all sides of the community...' These were all matters which they had included in their manifesto and on the basis of which they had expressed themselves willing to negotiate a better agreement for Northern Ireland.

Speaking to the media outside Lancaster House Dr. Paisley summarised the DUP reaction to the summit by saying that 'it was now possible to detect the faint outline of a new deal.'

Jeffrey saw this as another step forward towards the fulfilling of his personal political objective, which was an agreement acceptable to all the people of Northern Ireland.

Away from the political scene, there was cause for concern at home. Claire's condition had flared up again and she was admitted to hospital at the beginning of the summer holidays for a further intensive course of treatment. It was a worrying time, but as the treatment was administered the family were relieved to witness a gradual improvement in Claire's condition. Again they were most grateful for the prayer and support of their many caring Christian friends.

Although not travelling far from home during the summer, Jeffrey made a political journey, which was to attract the attention of the Northern Ireland media and catch the imagination of the nationalist community.

On Wednesday, August 4, having accepted an invitation from the organisers of the West Belfast Festival, Jeffrey attended a panel discussion entitled, 'West Belfast Talks Back,' in St. Louise's Comprehensive School on the Falls Road.

This was like an expedition into uncharted waters for him, and as he was driven across the city to keep this appointment he was glad of two things. These were the support of his team from the Close Protection Unit and the assurance of the presence of God. Jim, Bill, Hugh and Bob of the CPU had accompanied the Lagan Valley MP to all sorts of events, but Jeffrey, who was always appreciative of their company, and impressed by their cool professionalism, was never happier to have some of them beside him than he was that evening. He was also glad to have the company of DUP Press Officer, Timothy Johnston.

As they drove up the Falls Road Jeffrey prayed for help and guidance. God had promised to be with him, wherever he was, so that must include his current position as a unionist politician in a nationalist area of west Belfast.

When Jeffrey arrived at St. Louise's the assembly hall was already filled to capacity, with almost a thousand people crammed into it, and there were still long queues of people outside unable to gain entry.

Inside, he was pleased to be given a courteous welcome by the audience, as the debate got under way. The other panellists contributed to the discussion when required, but it was significant that the majority of the questions seemed to be directed towards the Lagan Valley MP. These included a challenge from a former IRA activist on the thorny issue of decommissioning, and the audience warmed to the frank exchange of views. They appeared to respect the transparent honesty with which Jeffrey presented the unionist position.

There was also a touch of humour when the subject of the Irish Government's 'no-smoking ban' was raised by a member of the audience. Jeffrey spoke of his support for the introduction of a similar ban in public places in Northern Ireland, and this view was shared by a high percentage of the audience.

The chairman of the panel, BBC Northern Ireland newsreader, Noel Thompson, remarked, "That must be tomorrow morning's headline. 'Jeffrey Donaldson reaches agreement with the residents of West Belfast.'"

Jeffrey responded immediately with, "I thought you were going to say, Noel, tomorrow morning's headline will be, 'Jeffrey Donaldson agrees with the Irish Government!'"

The evening, which had begun with a calculated courtesy, was beginning to take on an air of cordiality, as the audience broke out into laughter.

Next day, and for a number of days after that excursion into west Belfast, Jeffrey was to receive a succession of phone calls and e-mails from unionists and nationalists alike, appreciating his 'courage,' and complimenting him on his 'performance in the lions' den.'

Perhaps the most gratifying, but also most humbling, comment came from a group of residents he saw interviewed on TV News the next morning. They were each asked why they had attended the 'West Belfast Talks Back,' event in St. Louise's Comprehensive School and in each case the reply was the same.

"To hear Jeffrey Donaldson," the first replied.

"To hear Jeffrey Donaldson, of course," the second confessed.

"To hear Jeffrey Donaldson. Why else?" a third responded.

As Jeffrey watched the interview he was moved.

'Why else?' the woman had asked the interviewer with an air of incredulity.

'Why me?' he wondered.

Why had all those people packed into a school hall in unfamiliar territory to hear what he had to say?

Jeffrey knew that the answer lay not with him, but with God.

The situation had presented him with a unique opportunity to share his conviction that it was *'not by might'* that the problems of Northern Ireland would be resolved.

And what of the future?

What does Jeffrey feel about the years that lie ahead?

Does he have any particular plans?

Not really, but he is sure God has.

He often recalls the verse from Jeremiah that a member of the Youth Fellowship in Kilkeel sent to him when he was embarking upon his political career.

It was, *'For I know the plans I have for you, declares the Lord, plans to prosper you and not to harm you, plans to give you hope and a future…'* (NIV)

Or as George W. Bush put it so succinctly, 'My destiny is in the hands of a Higher Power.'

And if that assurance is good enough for the President of the United States it will certainly be good enough for the Member of Parliament for Lagan Valley.

Jeffrey Donaldson is quite content to leave it there.

'…supplications, prayers, intercessions…for all who are in authority;'

1 Tim. 2 : 1-2

Would you like to pray more effectively for Parliament and the nation?

To receive our monthly prayer bulletins e- mail

jeffrey@prayerforparliament.com

or write to

Jeffrey Donaldson MP, Prayer for Parliament, PO Box 15027,

LONDON SE5 0YS